AF334752

# ADVANCES IN LIBRARY AUTOMATION AND NETWORKING

*Volume 5* • 1994

# ADVANCES IN LIBRARY AUTOMATION AND NETWORKING

*Editors:*   **JOE A. HEWITT**
*Associate Provost for University Libraries*
*The University of North Carolina at Chapel Hill*

**CHARLES W. BAILEY, JR.**
*Assistant Director for Systems*
*University of Houston*

---

## VOLUME 5 • 1994

**JAI PRESS INC.**

*Greenwich, Connecticut*                    *London, England*

*Copyright © 1994 JAI Press Inc.*
*55 Old Post Road No. 2*
*Greenwich, Connecticut 06836*

*JAI PRESS LTD.*
*The Courtyard*
*28 High Street*
*Hampton Hill*
*Middlesex TW12 1PD*
*England*

*All rights reserved. No part of this publication may be reproduced, stored on a retrieval system, or transmitted in any form or by any means, electronic, mechanical, photocopying, filming, recording, or otherwise, without prior permission in writing from the publisher.*

*ISBN: 1-55938-510-3*

*Manufactured in the United States of America*

# CONTENTS

# INTRODUCTION

A decade ago it was common to characterize the previous decade as the era of online bibliographic networks. It was during the 1970s and early 1980s that OCLC extended its reach to libraries throughout the nation and served as a catalyst for widespread and profound change in the way libraries operated. This characterization of an earlier period of library automation was frequently coupled with the prediction that the predominant trend of the next decade—the one just past—would be the local implementation of online public access catalogs (OPACs). Such has indeed been the case. But while OPACs have been almost universally adopted over the past decade and have greatly improved the techniques by which access to library collections is provided to users, in many respects OPACs remain embryonic; they have a long way to go before they fulfill their ultimate potential as information systems.

In her paper on next generation OPACs, Carolyn Frost provides what might well be viewed as a developmental agenda for realizing the full potential of the OPAC. She describes in some detail both the basic research and the systems development work currently in progress that could lead to substantial extensions of the range and depth of OPAC coverage and to new paradigms for access and retrieval. The ultimate outcome of Frost's model is an OPAC that more effectively meets the traditional objectives of the library catalog as formulated by Charles Ami Cutter, while at the same time vastly expanding the original purposes of the catalog.

One avenue for expanding the domain of the OPAC that is noted by Frost is to provide access to full-text databases. Carol Tenopir, who for more than a decade has written a monthly column for *Library Journal* on online databases, provides an advanced introduction to full-text databases and retrieval systems. Tenopir's chapter describes the various categories of full-text databases, surveys available full-text databases, including online and CD-ROM options, briefly discusses the methods for creating full-text databases, and describes search and display requirements for full text in some depth. Tenopir's contribution touches on almost all of the major aspects of a development in information retrieval that holds enormous implications for library services. Her treatment of this subject should be extremely useful to librarians and library administrators who need to develop an informed orientation to this important topic.

In recent years, the professional literature related to networking has focused increasingly on the Internet and the National Research and Education Network (NREN), which represent transforming infrastructure developments. If the NREN is to realize its potential for improving and expanding library services, libraries must work to insure that traditional library goals and principles such as universal and affordable access are incorporated into network planning, policy development, and management. Mark Kibbey and Geri Bunker contribute a chapter that provides background, context, and structure for the discussion of planning and policy issues related to the development of the NREN. The underlying theme of this paper is that librarians must take a more proactive approach to developing goals, strategies, and plans for taking advantage of the NREN if it is to serve the needs of library users to its fullest possible extent.

One use of the NREN that holds profound implications for library services is electronic document delivery. John Ulmschneider and Tracy Casorso provide an overview of electronic document delivery and describe a development and demonstration project aimed at bringing digitized document delivery to a large-scale community of researchers in the agricultural sciences. The project investigated administrative, procedural, technical, and user issues related to providing electronic document delivery services in a real environment. Ulmschneider and Casorso's contribution furthers our understanding of the issues involved in deploying integrated electronic document delivery systems in libraries and also serves as an article of record for a significant project demonstrating digitized document transmission in the delivery of research support services.

Library-based information represents but one part of a constellation of information resources required by students and faculty in academic institutions. Campus-Wide Information Systems (CWIS) have been developed to provide access to information of general interest such as event calendars, job announcements, class schedules, grant and funding opportunities, campus directory information, and so on—the scope and variety of information available on these systems seems boundless. CWISs are self-evidently useful and are not technically difficult, but their development and ongoing operation do present an array of demanding policy and procedural issues. Judy Hallman, an early advocate of the CWIS concept, provides a definition and history of the CWIS, a state-of-the-art review of systems, and an exploration of a number of issues related to the deployment of CWISs and their ongoing operation, including the roles of libraries in the provision of CWIS services.

In spite of the widespread deployment of OPACs in the field, some libraries are just acquiring systems for the first time, while many others are acquiring their second and even third systems. The procurement of library systems from commercial vendors, including writing RFPs, evaluating responses and systems features, and negotiating contracts remains an important technical and administrative activity in libraries. Dissatisfaction with the pattern of the typical procurement scenario has been voiced by vendors and librarians alike. Few decisions in a library have the breadth of implications as the choice of an OPAC, yet it is a decision frequently made in a narrow framework imposed by the constraints of a procurement process. In a paper entitled *Use of a General Concept Paper as RFP for Library Systems: A New Model for Library System Procurement*, a group of librarians from the Triangle Research Libraries Network (TRLN) describe an attempt to move away from the traditional procurement model in favor of one that emphasizes selection of a library system as a strategic decision. In this model, the relationship between the library and the systems vendor and the compatibility of their visions of future library systems are more critical elements in the procurement decision than currently available functionality and performance factors.

The Mercury Electronic Library Project at Carnegie Mellon University is a well known model of library innovation, representing an early conceptualization of the virtual library. As such, developers of the Mercury Project have faced many of the problems of design and implementation that others pursuing the vision of the virtual library will face in the future. Denise A. Troll, a research scientist associated with the Mercury Project, provides a functional and technical description and analysis of the Mercury Project. More importantly, however, Troll reports on research with users through techniques such as focus groups by which organized input was provided to the development team. By these means users' evaluations of systems features were influential in the ongoing modification and enhancement to various Mercury Project systems. This paper is valuable both for its reporting of findings of this research and their possible implications for other virtual library development settings, and also as a model of an iterative information systems development process. A continuing criticism of many information technology development programs is that they represent the technologist's unexamined assumptions about what users need. These assumptions, it is said, tend to be derived from an expert but narrow perspective. Troll's paper demonstrates how an active systematic research program can help orient a development project to the needs of real users in actual settings.

I am joined as editor of this volume of ALAN by Charles W. Bailey, Jr., Assistant Director for Systems at the University of Houston Libraries. Mr. Bailey is widely known in the library systems community as founder of *Public-Access Computer Systems Forum* (PACS-L) and founder and Editor-in-Chief of *Public-Access Computer Systems Review*. Mr. Bailey is an innovative thinker and talented editor whose broad perspective on library automation and networking is an excellent match for the goals of this series.

I must point out that the papers that make up this volume were written in 1992. Various circumstances caused a delay in publication for which I take full responsibility. Although some of the information in the papers is dated, it was the judgement of the editors that these treatments of the issues are still timely and relevant. Several of the papers represent the most thorough and systematic publications on the topics available and others present valuable perspectives on fundamental issues in library automation and networking.

Joe A. Hewitt

# NEXT-GENERATION ONLINE PUBLIC ACCESS CATALOGS:

## REDEFINING TERRITORY AND ROLES

Carolyn O. Frost

## INTRODUCTION

The past decade has witnessed both the debut of the online public access catalog (OPAC) and the evolution of a technology that first matched and now surpasses the card catalog's capabilities. The OPAC is now well on its way to realizing its full technological potential, going far beyond the replication of its manual predecessor towards a dramatically expanded capability. We are now at the stage where OPAC development signals new roles for public-access information retrieval systems.

This paper suggests a model for OPACs of the future through a focus on developments that reflect a redefinition of the roles previously served by the traditional catalog. The model will serve as a contextual framework for examining new developments and harbingers of the future.

**Advances in Library Automation and Networking, Volume 5, pages 1-41.**
**Copyright © 1994 by JAI Press Inc.**
**All rights of reproduction in any form reserved.**
**ISBN: 1-55938-510-3**

The defining characteristics of the model will first be presented in an overview, which will reflect the sequence of topics comprising the body of the paper.

## Extended Range of Coverage

Next-generation catalogs are taking fuller advantage of the expansive, flexible capabilities of online systems. We will consider the ways in which the catalog's domain extends beyond the intitution in which it is physically located to resources "owned" by other sites. The catalog acts as a gateway to provide access to external databases, including the catalogs of other libraries and commercial abstracting and indexing databases.

## Extended Depth and Variety of Coverage

We will consider the extended depth and variety of coverage found in emerging models of the catalog. Previously, access was provided to bibliographic units representing a book or journal as a whole. Now, there are increased opportunities for catalog users to identify individual works within monograph collections and to specific articles within journals.

Whereas conventional catalogs limited the content of their records to the standard MARC (Machine-Readable Cataloging) formats for bibliographic data, emerging models include records for non-traditional data. Some catalogs provide records or linkages to tables of contents, abstracts, subject pathfinders, and book reviews that assist the user in judging the relevance of retrieved items.

While present catalogs provide access only to citations (or document surrogates), next-generation catalogs will allow access to the sources themselves, in the form of full text, graphic images, audio, and video.

While conventional catalogs offer one catalog for all users, some next-generation catalogs go beyond a single level of coverage to a customized catalog for group or individual information management.

## New Paradigms for Access and Retrieval

Advances in access and retrieval capabilities of next-generation OPACs have been strongly influenced by research in information retrieval. These developments characterize a model that imposes less stringent requirements on the user in formulating a search statement and provides more assistance in refining and navigating the search process.

## Search Aids

A variety of search aids can assist the user in formulating a query. In conventional catalogs, entry terms come from a controlled vocabulary (usually the *Library of Congress Subject Headings–LCSH*) and/or words in a book's title. By contrast, some next-generation models expand the catalog's index vocabulary to increase the chances of a match. Access terms can be taken from abstracts, from tables of contents and indexes found in books, and from content terms used in classification schemes such as the Dewey Decimal Classification.

Conventional models require an exact match of the user's and the catalog's index terms; thus, materials relevant to a user's need or topic must be represented by index terms from a controlled vocabulary or title keywords. Next-generation models allow natural language query, and they manipulate the user's entry terms to match the catalog's index terminology. Systems can allow a retrieval on a close match rather than limiting the user to an exact match. Some catalogs link terms from a free-text search (e.g., title words) to the corresponding subject headings or class numbers representing a broader range of related materials.

## Refining the Search Process

The catalog can improve the search process by providing mechanisms to enable the user to refine an initial query. Conventional catalogs require users to initiate a request for help when a search fails and to identify and execute appropriate alternative strategies. Newer catalog models assist the user by automatically suggesting alternatives or executing alternative search methods.

Users of conventional catalogs are often frustrated when large sets of retrieved items are presented as unranked citations. Newer systems can help by ranking retrieval output in decreasing order of probable relevance or "closeness" to the user's search criteria. Systems can also invite feedback in evaluation of retrieved citations, and they can interact with the user to refine the search.

*Browsing Aids*

Conventional systems assume focused information seeking behavior, and they require that users begin a catalog search with known information needs/topics. We will look at evidence of increased attention given to the role of browsing in a user's search and consider systems that assist browsing by allowing the user to recognize, rather than formulate, a search statement.

Users of conventional catalogs are required to approach the catalog in a structured, linear way. Next-generation systems facilitate flexible, exploratory searching using techniques of associative navigation and hypertext. Systems can provide links in a variety of directions from displayed records, and they can lead the user from found information to related linked information.

The browsing structure of conventional systems is limited to alphabetical or chronological listings, with topic-based organization applied only to physical materials in the stacks. Some new systems assist browsing by offering a classified subject search at the catalog and by supporting browsing in classification outlines.

No one system incorporates all of the features that characterize the "new model." Some of the features to be described in this paper are present in systems that are now available. Many of the systems that are described are prototypes and, as experimental or research undertakings under evaluation, are not commercially available. Yet, all of the prototype systems contribute, in their broader concept of access capabilities, to the visualization of the new model.[1]

Table 1 contrasts the conventional OPAC model with the next-generation OPAC model.

## EXPANDING THE CATALOG'S DOMAIN

In the new model, the catalog serves as a consolidated entry point or gateway to external electronic information resources. Now, within the catalog's domain are databases created not only by libraries but by other information providers, such as government, commercial, and independent agencies. Even the coverage within an institution is more inclusive and encompassing. For example, local collections that were frequently excluded from the primary catalog and accessible only through auxiliary finding tools are now available in

### *Table 1.* Comparison of Conventional and Next-Generation OPACs

| | *Conventional Model* | *Next-Generation Model* |
|---|---|---|
| Range of Coverage | Limited to institutions. | Gateway to external databases, other libraries' catalogs, and commercial databases. |
| | Access only to title of book or journal. | Indexes individual works: article-level for journals and chapter level for books. |
| | Standard MARC records. | Non-traditional records; e.g., abstracts, book reviews, tables of contents, and pathfinders. |
| | Access to item surrogates. | Access to full text, visual images, and audio. |
| | One catalog for all users. | Catalog customized to individual and group information management. |
| Search Aids | Entry terms from controlled vocabulary and words in title. | Expands index vocabulary to terms from tables of contents, indexes, classification, vocabulary, abstracts, and subject-rich terms from bibliographic records. |
| | Requires exact match on catalog's index terms. | Allows natural language query; manipulates entry terms to match catalog terminology. |
| | | Links free-text terms to subject headings or class numbers. |
| | | Allows closest, best-match retrieval. |
| Refining the Search Process | Requires users to initiate help. | Suggests or executes alternative strategy. |
| | No interaction with user. | Uses clues and feedback from user to refine search. |
| | Displays unranked items. | Ranks items in decreasing order of relevance. |
| Browsing Aids | Assumes focused search. | Facilitates browsing. |

(*continued*)

*Table 1*   Continued

| Conventional Model | Next-Generation |
| --- | --- |
| Requires structured, linear search. | Flexible, multidirectional search behavior, Associative navigation and hypertext. |
| Browsing structure limited to alphabetical or chronological listings. | Supports browsing in classification outlines. |

the catalog. Access to institutional information resources outside the library is also possible through links with campus information systems.

The new model is characterized not only by its wider breadth of coverage, but also by its greater depth of coverage. While the coverage of conventional catalogs is primarily at the level of title of an entire volume for books and journals, the new model provides access to individual titles of articles within a journal and individual chapters within books. Such depth of coverage, while unusual for today's catalogs, has precedents in some nineteenth century catalogs. For example, the preface of the 1883-1892 book catalog of the Peabody Institute of the City of Baltimore states:

> This catalogue is constructed on the idea that the best possible catalogue is that which best makes known to the average reader the entire contents of a library. It is intended to answer the three most important questions: Is a given book in the library? Are the works of a given author there? What books, articles, and information does a library contain on a given subject? A perfect catalogue would furnish complete answers to all these questions.[2]

## EXTENDED RANGE OF COVERAGE

### Access to the Whole of a Library's Resources

Catalogs have traditionally excluded from their listings a wide range of library resources for which bibliographic information is not readily accessible. The new model of catalog extends its breadth of coverage to achieve a more inclusive representation of the library's holdings. Now, listings for local holdings, such as newspaper collections, dissertations, community resource files, and local history collections, are included in some catalogs. Examples of OPAC access to specialized collections include Georgia Tech's index to television scripts and Arizona State's listing of its solar energy collection.[3] The desire for this type of expansion was reflected in a 1982 nationwide survey of OPAC use sponsored by the Council on Library Resources.[4]

## Access to Other Libraries' Collections

Increasingly, the OPAC is being viewed not only as a source for information about resources at the user's home institution, but as an electronic gateway to collections on a national and international scale.

A number of library systems and vendors offer the capability to search external catalogs. The CARL network (Colorado Alliance of Research Libraries) provides access to the catalogs of any of its member libraries. Similar access is provided by the LCS network in Illinois and MELVYL in California.[5] A user of CARL's OPAC at one site can search another database or catalog in the network by executing a simple command that automatically re-initiates the search in the desired database.[6]

NOTIS' PACLink permits a user at one NOTIS site to enter and search another NOTIS OPAC at a remote site without the necessity of learning the command language of the remote-site catalog.[7]

Data Research's software facilitates database access to external libraries via the Internet. After selecting an external database from a menu, the user can re-execute a previous search and see the data displayed with the essential elements of the local system.[8]

National and international standards will be central to the realization of broad-scale searching of databases across institutional boundaries. The goal of the NISO Z39.50 standard (*Information Retrieval Service Definition and Protocol Specification for Library Applications*) is to achieve a single user interface among systems, regardless of the hardware, software, or operating system in use by each system. This would facilitate the exchange of data between like systems as well as between two entirely different systems. It would also eliminate the need for the user to learn different command languages, menu choices, and displays for every system's database that was connected on a network. Efforts are now underway to implement Z39.50. In one such example, a development partnership of Data Research, Digital Equipment Corporation, and the UC Davis library has been formed to engage in a Z39.50 testing program under the auspices of the Coalition for Networked Information.[9]

## EXTENDED DEPTH OF COVERAGE

### Article-Level Access for Journals

While conventional catalogs have largely restricted their access to the level of an entire work and excluded access to the individual chapters of a book or articles within a journal, newer OPAC models are providing more in-depth access to libraries' collections.

*Loading A&I Indexes onto OPACs*

Catalog access to the titles of individual journal articles restores a function already recognized by late nineteenth century catalogs. It was not uncommon for catalogs of this era to include references to periodical articles. For example, catalog-size cards available from Readers' Guide were integrated into library records of title-level holdings. While this service became less feasible with the growth of periodical publications and was replaced with printed indexes that had to be searched separately, the demise of article-level access within the catalog can be attributed more to the limits of the existing technology (i.e., the card catalog and its impact on cataloging practice) than to a diminishment of the functionality of this service from the user's standpoint. Indeed, when users' opinions were surveyed in the 1982 CLR study of online catalogs, OPAC users placed high priority for article-level access on their "wish list" of OPAC features.

An increasingly common strategy for providing article-level access is the mounting of external abstracting and indexing (A&I) databases onto local OPACs. Libraries have loaded onto their OPACs files such as the set of databases available from IAC (the Information Access Company), MEDLINE, AGRICOLA, the H.W. Wilson indexes, ABI/INFORM, Sci Search, and INSPEC. While in most instances the user must execute separate searches to retrieve items in the main and the external databases, some systems (e.g., Bibliofile) enable the user to retrieve all the items relating to a given author or subject without regard to whether they are books or journal articles.

The merging of abstracting and indexing databases with the library's own bibliographic database results in separate, unrelated searching vocabularies. Machine-assisted mapping between vocabularies is one strategy for assisting users in searching controlled vocabularies in multiple databases. Machine-assisted mapping systematically links terms from one indexing vocabulary with equivalent terms from a second vocabulary. An example of an alternative approach is the Vocabulary Switching System developed by the Battelle Columbus Laboratories. This approach does not attempt to achieve complete conversion between different vocabulary systems. Instead, the source vocabularies are manipulated to create a switching language for interrelating vocabularies, through a wide variety of computerized techniques (e.g., word and phrase stemming), to locate all related terms. The system then matches the user's query terms with the augmented terms of each vocabulary.[10]

*Table of Contents Data*

Another option for article-level access in OPACs is provided through the CARL and OCLC networks. The CARL system's Uncover database is made up of the tables of contents of journals received by its member libraries. Introduced in 1988, the service includes articles from more than 12,000 unique journal titles. Articles can be retrieved through key words in titles, abstracts, or summaries. Users can also retrieve citations by name of author. A display representing the table of contents page for each journal issue is another retrieval option. Complementing the system is an article delivery service, which provides delivery by facsimile transmission for every article cited in the database.[11]

OCLC, in partnership with Faxon, offers a similar service of table of contents for journals. Two databases, Article Finder and Contents Finder, are available on OCLC's EPIC service and FirstSearch Catalog. While Contents Finder recreates the table of contents, displaying all the articles of a given issue, Article Finder provides access to a particular subject or author. These databases allow patron access to the tables of contents and articles of more than 11,000 journal titles. Users are able to place orders for articles to be sent via facsimile transmission.

Records for the two OCLC/Faxon databases are provided through Faxon Research Services, Inc., with OCLC adding subject and holdings information to the table of contents and citation records. The databases include articles published since January 1990, and they are updated weekly. In addition to articles, the types of journal content that are indexed include news stories, editorials, technical communications, proceedings, reviews, and letters to the editor. In searching, users are able to narrow searches by type of item.[12]

## Chapter-Level Access for Monographs

Efforts to provide access to chapters within monographs have been largely initiated by individual libraries, with data input on a manual basis. Some libraries have worked within the existing MARC format to add chapter-level data in the contents note, using this field to provide author and title listings for individual items within collections of essays or short stories. If contents notes are indexed, a library's OPAC can then provide access to discrete units within monographs.[13]

The Engineering Library at Purdue has provided chapter-level access in its OPAC by adding data from the edited tables of contents for the majority of monographs in its collection. Items within the file can be searched by key words. The process involves considerable human effort, including scanning, editing, and manually inputting tables of contents; however, the costs in time and expense have been considered justified because of the additional terms available for searching as well as the benefits derived from displaying a book's table of contents when attempting to judge the utility of a retrieved item.[14]

A related project was undertaken at Carnegie Mellon University (CMU), which has added table of contents data to selected categories of new monographs. The impetus for the program came from the needs of drama students to find plays contained within collections.[15]

The costs incurred in editing and manually inputting table of contents data make this process of doubtful value to most libraries, and it bears noting that initiatives to provide table of contents data for monographs have typically been applied to specialized collections of relatively small size.

An experimental project to circumvent the obstacles of manual conversion of table of contents data was undertaken by the

Bibliographic Services Division of the British Library. In this project, tables of contents were read, edited, and formatted by a digital page scanning system to produce a machine-readable file. The file could then be merged with the matching MARC records.[16]

## Non-Traditional Data Elements

While summary notes providing descriptions of the contents of a document have been an accepted—although not widespread—part of bibliographic practice, data providing evaluations of content have generally been considered inappropriate. Yet, it could be argued that, in some instances, readers seek judgments from others in making a choice. While Koenig's vision of a catalog supplemented by users' evaluations is still just an idea,[17] at least one vendor is offering access, albeit indirect access, to book reviews. Data Research offers a capability for users of a library's OPAC to request display of a book review for a given bibliographic item retrieved in the online catalog. Reviews available from *Choice* and *Library Journal* for a given work can be linked to the corresponding bibliographic record.[18]

Another type of "nonstandard" method of providing "reader's assistance" for library patrons is the provision of *pathfinder* records in the catalog. Pathfinders in printed form are commonly used in bibliographic instruction to guide the user to introductory materials and key citations in the literature of a specific subject. Jarvis and Dow describe an experiment in incorporating this type of data into an OPAC, utilizing a pseudo-bibliographic MARC record.[19]

## Access to Full Text

The provision of full text dramatically alters the character of a library's catalog from a tool that directs users to surrogates of documents to a tool that displays the documents themselves. The distinction between ownership and access emerges, with accompanying collection management issues.

While the rendering of documents in electronic format is now widespread, the major obstacles of copyright, telecommunications, storage costs, and a common format standard such as the emerging SGML (Standard Generalized Markup Language), among other issues, leave the full realization of electronic publishing in question for the present. Still, some efforts are already underway that suggest the eventual power and potential of this expansion of the catalog's domain and role.

Some libraries have mounted ready reference databases onto their online catalogs. Online access to the full text of reference tools, such as dictionaries and encyclopedias, can serve dual roles in the catalog. First, they help the user in the intermediary stages of formulating and navigating a search. Second, they act as information sources in their own right. CARL has provided its member libraries with the capability of including a number of ready reference works in machine-readable form such as Grolier's *Academic American Encyclopedia*, the *American Heritage Dictionary, Roget's Thesaurus*, and the *World Almanac*.

The loading of machine-readable journals onto online catalogs is another aspect of full text. *Commerce Business Daily* has been mounted onto Georgia Tech's Online Information System and is updated daily.[20] Carnegie Mellon University, whose Project Mercury has launched several efforts with the goal of building a large-scale electronic library, has negotiated agreements with publishers, and it is acquiring machine-readable journals and technical reports in the field of computer science.[21]

The University of Michigan's UMLIBTEXT is a system for network-based access to software and texts needed for textual analysis. It provides access to 300 titles (via Internet and campus networks) by title, author, date, or characteristics of text.[22] While these and other academic initiatives provide scholars with access tools to support detailed linguistic and textual analysis, a different and more sophisticated kind of access will have to be provided for users who read texts in a more conventional manner. In developing tools for browsing a book online, system designers will need to take into account the ways that readers skim a text to ascertain its coverage. In addition to sequential perusal of a text, users will need to have access to such guides as chapter headings and indexes, and they will need to move among different sections of the book in other than a strictly linear fashion. OCLC's prototype Graph-Text software supports this kind of structural browsing.[23]

Buckland summarizes some of the ways in which full text access in OPACs may lead to a redefinition of the catalog:

> Historically, a library catalog was a guide to local *holdings*. Yet what matters to a library user is convenient *access* to texts. With documents on paper, what

is locally owned is conveniently accessible. ... Databases (which are copied, not borrowed) at a distance are likely to be more reliably accessible than paper documents owned by one's local library. What is needed, then, is a bibliography of what is conveniently accessible rather than the much narrower concept of a catalog of what happens to be locally owned.... To the extent that texts are available in electronic form, the whole view of library collections changes: location and ownership of copies of texts becomes a technical detail for librarians irrelevant to the reader. What counts is what is conveniently accessible.[24]

## Access to Multimedia

Access to "full-text" multimedia information through the online catalog is another area in which prototypes and experimentation are evident, but which has yet to see widespread implementation. The challenge to provide online delivery of images, which requires the use of high-speed networks and massive storage capabilities, will be daunting.

One experimental program designed to offer catalog records and finding aids, plus original texts in electronic form, is the Library of Congress American Memory Project, inaugurated in 1989 for a six-year pilot stage. The project hopes to deliver electronic copies of parts of LC's collections of photographs, graphic art, motion pictures, recorded sound, and music as well as print materials. While presently utilizing videodisc and compact disc technology, the project plans call for eventual delivery of materials to libraries online.[25]

The Avery Architectural and Fine Arts Library at Columbia University has undertaken to enter its collection of 6,500 bibliographic records and 45,000 architectural drawings into the RLIN network as well as to store the images on videodisc. Topic and genre access is provided through the *Art and Architecture Thesaurus* subject terms. A user at Columbia can search for an item using a variety of textual indexes and see the image on video, or, alternatively, browse through collections of images and then retrieve the corresponding MARC bibliographic records.[26]

An experiment at MIT offers delivery to workstations of 7,000 images stored on videodisc. The project covers a collection of slides used in the teaching of architecture. The system allows the user to search a catalog using one window and to retrieve an image for display in a separate window.[27]

The limitations of analog optical disc technology have not allowed present prototypes to provide network access to graphic images. As telecommunication capabilities are strengthened and extended, the development of digital image technologies can come closer to reaching their potential.

## System Navigation for Campus-Wide Information

The catalog now acts as a gateway to a variety of external information resources that have been created independently. Since these resources lack a common interface, the catalog can facilitate access by assisting the user in navigating the array of available information. Such assistance can be twofold: to facilitate access on a mechanical level by removing the need for the user to learn a separate protocol for each system, and, on a conceptual level, to help the user identify and select the source appropriate to a given information need.

Ohio State University has developed a prototype for a networked instructional user interface called Gateway. Gateway is linked to the OSU OPAC and to other computer files. It offers a common front-end to electronic indexes, and thus makes accessible the text of relevant encyclopedia articles and journal indexes on CD-ROM. Designed initially for undergraduates, Gateway assists users in finding, evaluating, and selecting a variety of information retrieval tools, including the OPAC, CD-ROM databases, and other files both within and outside the campus. The system's step-by-step search strategy process begins with a broad information source, such as an encyclopedia, to help users in narrowing the scope of their topic, and it suggests options such as periodical indexes and books. By identifying which materials will best meet a user's specific information need, informing the user where these materials are located, and telling the user how they are best used, Gateway assumes a role familiar to bibliographic instruction librarians.[28]

At the University of Houston, librarians developed an expert system, Index Expert, to assist users in selecting appropriate indexes and abstracts in both print and CD-ROM formats. The system was designed to capture for the user some of the guidance normally provided by a reference librarian, and it was the first step of a larger plan to develop reference expert systems. In the next phase of the project, the system planners developed a second expert system, Reference Expert, to help users select a variety of reference materials (e.g., dictionaries, encyclopedias, and handbooks).[29] A related example can be found at Northwestern, where librarians developed software for a program to inform users of available CD-ROM database options.[30]

By developing programs that integrate the library's reference resources, alert users to the choice of databases available on an OPAC or other locations, and assist users in their utilization, libraries are taking over a responsibility that cannot be assumed by vendors of commercial databases. While this type of guidance has been and will continue to be provided by bibliographic instruction librarians, the catalog is now beginning to take on some of these instructional roles. This may be seen as reflecting a larger trend in which libraries are increasingly serving as a gateway to remote information sources, providing users with better information to make their own informed choices for information resources, and facilitating access to remote source materials.

Now, OPACs increasingly provide access to more than library material. In a typical model of a university information system, data generated by agencies outside the library, such as academic departments, is accessible through the library's online system. In the Dartmouth College Information System (DCIS), to select one of many, the library system is viewed as one component of a campus-wide network comprised of a variety of information resources. DCIS's plans include a capability to allow a user to search any of the host sources using a common protocol; the search results will be displayed in a uniform format. The user's workstation provides access to the library's catalog along with, for example, a file of scholarly reference sources maintained by an academic department or a list of student employment opportunities.[31]

## Customized Databases for Information Management

While the catalog's domain has been expanded to include a variety of information resources, there is a complementary vision of the catalog as a personalized information management tool, containing information relevant to the needs of individuals or groups with common research interests. Some experimental ventures have been attempted, although these efforts are not yet beyond the design stage.

Researchers at Lund University created a system design called HYPERcat that would allow users to create their own levels of online catalogs, either for an individual or for a group or team. For example, a catalog for a university research department might contain a core of information whose boundaries are defined by the department. Such a departmental collection could include reports, books, and conference proceedings; a specialized thesaurus; heavily used bibliographies; and information about conferences and workshops. In a collection at the group or team level, members could integrate their own finished papers and papers in progress.[32]

At the University of Michigan, Belew and Holland developed a prototype microcomputer-based system to enable scholars with mutual research interests to share materials from individual personal bibliographic collections.[33] Another experimental project at Michigan is being designed to offer an integrated campus-wide information system on research interests and opportunities that will be used by the University's research community. The system would allow users to search a variety of files simultaneously, using a single search language.

## SEARCH AIDS

### Table of Contents and Index as Sources of Entry Terms

In searching by subject in a conventional OPAC, users are limited to terms from controlled vocabularies and keywords derived from title terms in the bibliographic record. A number of initiatives have been underway to expand the entry vocabulary through the addition of terms from sources such as summary notes in the bibliographic record, tables of contents, and indexes as well as content-bearing terms from classification schedules.

One of the most formidable barriers faced by users of present OPACs is matching their search terms with the terminology of the catalog's controlled vocabulary. By expanding the entry vocabulary to include access points from additional sources, the catalog can increase a user's chances of matching the catalog's indexing terminology and of retrieving desired citations.

Atherton's landmark Subject Access Project (SAP) at Syracuse University in the late 1970s augmented access points in MARC records by adding approximately thirty entries per book from the table of contents or index. Since these books do not always provide significant subject content or useful vocabulary for retrieval, the project's methodology included the establishment of criteria for selecting appropriate terms.

Atherton performed controlled tests to compare the results of online searches in the database without enhancements with searches in the augmented database. She found that the searches in the augmented database resulted in greater access to books with relevant information, provided greater precision, proved less costly because less online search time was required, and answered some queries that were impossible to answer without the enhanced information.[34]

Atherton's study served as the model for many subsequent projects to enhance bibliographic records with additional subject content. At Lund University in Sweden, the SAP method was tested in an online database of Swedish government reports. The database contained records enhanced with subject terms from tables of contents, indexes, figures, and table captions. Another project at Lund applied the SAP method of subject enhancement to a database of 400 records in the field of environmental protection and ecology. The researcher found that the system demonstrated not only increased subject retrieval power, but also greater cost-effectiveness.[35]

The best-known examples of table of contents enhancements to monograph records in library catalogs are found at the Engineering Library at Purdue University, Carnegie Mellon University, and the Australian Defense Force Academy. All three examples involve the manual editing and input of data to catalogs of relatively small collections.

The system at Purdue's Engineering Library uses subject terms from edited tables of contents to enhance records for over 20,000 monographs in the library's collection. The file can be searched by keywords. The system was judged to be superior to conventional *LCSH* access in its provision of additional search terms and its ability to deal with conference proceedings and other monograph collections.[36]

Carnegie Mellon has developed a selection process for adding table of contents information to monograph records. Criteria for inclusion require that the additional terms provide valuable information not found in the book's title or subject headings. Terms in any content field of the records are retrievable. Only a small percentage (7.85%) of the books cataloged since the start of the experiment have been given enhanced records. At present, CMU is not making its enhanced records available for use by other libraries in the OCLC system because of the apparent lack of support from other OCLC users for this kind of enhancement.[37]

In a project conducted at the Australian Defense Force Academy Library, an average of 20 to 25 keywords from chapter-level headings were added to the MARC records of a group of 6,000 books. When needed, index information was included. Keyword access was provided to the terms. A preliminary evaluation of the study revealed that retrieval increased by 300%. Byrne and Micco found that the project affirmed the viability and cost-effectiveness of this technique. Nevertheless, while the number of subject access points was substantially increased without a serious increase in false drops, the authors concluded that "the number of records retrieved even in this small database of 160,000 titles is unmanageable" and strategies were needed to assist users in narrowing their searches.[38]

At Indiana University of Pennsylvania, Micco is using the enhanced records from the Australian Defence Force Academy Library in an experimental OPAC that links keywords from a book's title and table of contents to related *LCSH* headings.[39]

A key question emerging from a review of these experiments is whether the addition of access points increases the catalog's retrieval capabilities. Researchers at OCLC have conducted studies to assess the effectiveness of adding abstracts and tables of contents to bibliographic records in library catalogs. The findings indicate that the addition of content-bearing information in bibliographic records will improve the overall retrieval effectiveness; however, the increase in recall is accompanied by a decrease in precision.[40]

Lancaster's research on the retrieval effectiveness of terms derived from tables of contents and indexes led him to conclude that:

> even if [the addition of table of contents and index data] were economically feasible, it would make little practical difference to the retrieval capabilities of a large catalog because the resulting lack of precision would be completely intolerable. It is safe to say that many searches on such extended records would retrieve thousands of items rather than the hundreds retrieved in many of the searches on existing records alone. Only in the case of an atypically specific search involving a rare word or a name might the enhanced record improve search results. In other cases, any improvement in recall would be accompanied by a disastrous decline in precision.[41]

Diodato collected information about tables of contents and index terms in books borrowed by patrons in order to determine which of these terms were the same as the words used by patrons to describe the books. He concluded that additional terms would increase the likelihood that the catalog would link an appropriate book with a term that matches a reader's search term.[42]

Even if libraries can be convinced of the effectiveness of subject term enhancement, the time and effort needed for manual editing and input will likely serve as a powerful deterrent, especially for those libraries with large catalog files. Systems that offer a computerized means of subject term enhancement offer the most promise, such as the aforementioned project at the British Library to develop an experimental system for automated addition of tables of contents data to MARC records.[43]

## Entry Terms From Classification Schedules

Markey's Dewey Decimal Online Project demonstrated the potential to enrich catalog records with subject content using the text from a library classification scheme. The machine-readable Dewey Decimal Classification was used as a source for computerized assignment of subject terms to a bibliographic record. Subject content from the classification system was assigned to a record when the classification number of the record matched the number associated with a schedule caption or index entry in the text of the classification. While the process was largely automatic in nature, some editing decisions were necessary in order to ensure that the subject enrichment would be of value in the retrieval process.[44]

Liu and Svenonius' experimental DORS system, designed as an interface to an OPAC, enhances searching vocabulary by providing keyword access to significant terms from the Dewey Decimal Classification schedule captions and relative index.[45]

Two recent prototypes have employed content terms from the Library of Congress Classification (LCC) to enrich subject access. Experimental OPACs developed separately by Larson[46] and Hildreth[47] draw from LCC as a source of expanded lead-in vocabulary.

## Natural Language Query Processing

Hildreth argues that conventional information retrieval systems adopt an "all or nothing approach," in which users retrieve materials only if there is an exact match between the catalog's and the user's search terms. The burden of determining the exact term is placed entirely on the user. This model of information retrieval activity assumes that the user's information need is not only known, but can be expressed in a precise query. It also assumes that there are index terms in the catalog that represent materials relevant to the user's information need.[48] Even casual users of the catalog will recognize that this conceptual model does not accurately reflect information seeking behavior.

Many of the features of information retrieval systems designed for search specialists (e.g., keyword and Boolean searching) lose their retrieval effectiveness when incorporated into OPACs designed primarily for end-users who are largely inexperienced in the use of sophisticated retrieval strategies.[49]

Increasingly, attention is being given to ways of relieving the burden imposed upon the user. The application of natural language processing techniques to OPACs is a recent phenomenon. It recognizes the premise that users should be able to enter queries without altering the structure of their search statements or second-guessing the vocabulary of the indexing system.

To achieve searching in a "free-form" expression, natural language processing relies on a variety of strategies that maximize the chances of a successful match of user and system vocabulary. Developers of some new system models have adopted a variety of mechanisms that allow users to express queries in "natural language" statements rather than in statements formulated to meet the requirements of the system. The user's entry vocabulary can be manipulated through techniques such as changing the word order (e.g., from direct to inverted), correcting the spelling, changing or disregarding the suffix, and searching for words with similar meaning. A number of experimental ·OPACs use these techniques.

*OKAPI*

At the Polytechnic of Central London, researchers have developed a prototype OPAC with a number of capabilities for natural language processing. In subject searches, OKAPI asks users to describe their subjects using words or a short phrase. The system draws from an index containing words from fields in the bibliographic record that may have subject content (e.g., titles, subtitles, subject headings, and content notes) to attempt a match with terms entered by the user. If at least two words are found in the index, the system combines these words using an implicit Boolean AND. Records retrieved using this strategy are then shown to the user.[50]

OKAPI is constantly evolving, and its effectiveness is evaluated through transaction log analysis and interviews with users. The system has given researchers the opportunity to test a variety of linguistic computing techniques that assist in natural language processing, such as automatic stemming algorithms, automatic cross referencing, and semi-automatic spelling correction. When researchers found that about 10% of OKAPI users' searches contained miskeyed or misspelled words, a subsequent version of the system was designed to respond to users' mistakes by automatically invoking a spelling correction procedure. The correction is then suggested to the user. Stem-matching is also attempted, and if this fails to yield a result, words are matched against the system's special dictionaries and indexes. If this too proves to be unsuccessful, the recalcitrant word is bypassed and the system attempts a match on any remaining search words.

The automatic cross referencing feature attempts synonym control through the use of a table containing entries such as abbreviations and their full expressions, words with alternative spellings, and pairs of terms (e.g., *Great Britain* and *U.K.*). The list was compiled largely from search terms that had appeared in logs of searches input by the library's users.

A test of the system found that the spelling correction algorithm corrected about half of the spelling/miskeying errors. The stemming procedure was successful in increasing recall in most searches without sacrificing precision. A similar measure of success was achieved by the automatic cross referencing procedure. About 25% of the searches studied contained a word or phrase that matched one in the cross references list. In almost all of the cases of an automatic reference switch, recall was increased without a decrease in precision.[51]

## CITE

CITE was an experimental OPAC used by patrons of the National Library of Medicine in the mid-1980s. The system's clientele included a broad spectrum of users, most of whom were infrequent visitors to NLM. CITE offered natural language searching as part of its overall goal of placing "prime emphasis on end-user access." Patrons entered their subject queries in free-form language, such as lists, phrases, sentences, and paragraphs. The system broke up the query into component keywords, and it filtered keywords against an extensive stopword list. Unlike some systems, CITE did not attempt to translate the query into a Boolean expression.[52] Terms from users underwent a stemming procedure, and matches were sought in both free-text indexes and the *MeSH* thesaurus. For example, a search on the term *treatment* would be extended to include stem variants of *treat* and *treating*. These terms were also mapped into the controlled vocabulary of *MeSH*, to automatically link the authorized term *therapy* with its synonym *treatment*. CITE's stemming procedure was able to take advantage of special characteristics of medical terminology, such as words ending in *itis* denoting inflammation. CITE employed a variety of other retrieval techniques including automatic term weighting, closest-match search strategy, feedback for search refinement, query expansion, and ranked display of retrieved records.[53]

*SPRILIB*

SPRILIB, an OPAC in use at the Scott Polar Research Institute Library at Cambridge University, allows search entries in natural language, and it provides relevance feedback and ranked output. The system allows the combination of Boolean and probabilistic retrieval. Thus, terms in a Boolean result set can be weighted, and individual citations can be displayed in order of decreasing relevance.[54]

*ERLI*

In France, a natural language database access software called ERLI has been adopted as the retrieval software for access to RAMEAU, an online subject authorities file maintained by the Bibliotheque Nationale and available as a public file to libraries. The software, designed for bibliographic retrieval in large thesaurus-controlled databases, utilizes a variety of artificial-intelligence-based linguistic processing methods to support natural language query processing and to transform natural language requests into descriptors in the thesaurus. Its techniques include: stemming; spelling correction; structural analysis of compound terms; use of a thesaurus to identify related, broader, or narrower terms; and the automatic formulation of a Boolean query.[55]

Automatic language processing techniques have been a frequent focus of information retrieval research. In addition to research conducted on operational OPAC prototypes, experimental studies have evaluated specific natural language query techniques. Lester's doctoral research tested a variety of methods to improve subject retrieval. Drawing from transaction logs of actual searches in Northwestern's NOTIS system, Lester extracted users' subject terms that did not achieve exact matches on *LCSH*, and she subjected these terms to a variety of subject retrieval improvements. The strategies included: (1) the correction of user input (e.g., spelling correction); (2) the processing of user input (e.g., right truncation, string searching with adjacency, and keyword-and-Boolean searching); (3) augmentation of the database with subject authorities, full text of bibliographic records, and name authorities; and (4) processing of the augmented database with right truncation and other techniques. Right truncation, string searching, and keyword searching were found to be particularly effective.[56]

Lancaster's evaluation of methods for subject access improvements resulted in rather gloomy conclusions. His stringent criteria for success went beyond a mere match of the user's and the system's subject terms. Instead, he judged a search successful only if it resulted in locating material identified by acknowledged experts as "the best." He concluded that retrieval techniques such as truncation, word-fragment searching, expanded thesauri, semantic networks, and entry vocabularies can have only "a marginal effect" when applied to conventional bibliographic records.[57]

## REFINING THE SEARCH PROCESS

### Suggesting and Executing Alternative Search Strategies

As part of the overall goal of relaxing the requirements made of catalog users, some new systems relieve users of the burden of deciding which search strategy is best for a given situation. There are presently a number of examples of OPACs that suggest alternative formulations or strategies if a search is unsuccessful. Going a step farther, some systems automatically select and execute the appropriate alternative search strategies. In effect, the system is acting as a surrogate expert and advocate for the user, and it is making judgments and executions that might be expected of experienced search intermediaries. As seen in some of the examples of natural language query processing, the system may execute an automatic stemming routine to broaden a search, to help locate synonyms, or to apply Boolean operators. This approach helps to free the user from the burden of mastering the technical intricacies of the search.

At the University of Illinois at Urbana, searchers' terminals are equipped with specially designed user interface software. If a user's subject heading phrase search results in no matches, the system automatically reprocesses it as a title keyword search, and it targets the search to a different database. The user is informed of the change and is presented with resulting citations for relevance assessment. A search using uncontrolled title words can be directed to subject headings assigned to works in which the title words appear.[58]

The PaperChase software program, developed for searching medical literature, monitors a user's search and suggests alternative strategies. For example, the system may suggest that a user employ a *MeSH* search term rather than a title word. The system makes the link between the title word and the related *MeSH* terms, and it offers the user the choice of both title word and *MeSH* strategies.[59]

In BiblioFile's "Intelligent Catalog," users can enter their search terms in a natural language statement. When a user's compound statement fails to achieve a match in the indexes, the system automatically reformulates the statement as a Boolean AND query.[60]

In its most advanced version, CARL offers the automatic processing of name and word queries as keyword, Boolean AND searches. Dartmouth College's and PALS' OPACs also perform an automatic Boolean query on a user's search terms.[61]

Drabenstott (Markey) and Vizine-Goetz point out that although some conventional OPACs offer more than one subject searching approach, they provide the user with little guidance as to which approach is most appropriate for a given search situation. The authors maintain that OPAC systems can be designed to assist the user in the search process by automatically determining the most appropriate approach. Their conclusions were reached after a study of OPAC logs at three libraries. Users' subject queries were analyzed to determine whether search terms could be manipulated (e.g., by disregarding capitalization, punctuation, qualifiers, and stopwords) in order to effect a form matching the system's index terms.[62]

The premise suggested by this research is being tested by Drabenstott in a follow-up study. She is developing and evaluating an experimental subject access design in which search trees control system responses and determine appropriate subject searching approaches to user queries. The selection of the system's approach is based on the extent to which users' queries match the catalog's controlled vocabulary. The search trees are formulated as a result of Drabenstott and Vizine-Goetz's empirical study of the subject terms that users enter into online catalogs.[63]

## Increasing Precision Through Output Ranking and Relevance Feedback

Suggesting alternative strategies is one way in which the OPAC can provide feedback in refining a search. Another strategy is the involvement of users' input in negotiating and refining the search process. Feedback and interaction can be achieved through a number of strategies. After citations are generated in response to a user's search statement, some systems allow the user to judge which citations are most relevant, and they then act on the user's feedback to automatically expand the query.

In a third and related strategy, the system can determine which items most closely match the user's search terms, so that it can display citations in decreasing order of relevance. The use of statistical techniques to increase the number of relevant documents is a methodology derived from information retrieval research. Words in a database are examined to assign weights or values based on the frequency of their occurrence in the text. Probabilistic models can suggest the likelihood of a document's relevance to the user by comparing the frequency of the query term to terms in the retrieved documents and to documents in the database as a whole. This approach can be contrasted with the matching of query terms against controlled headings such as *LCSH* assigned by indexers and catalogers. Both approaches have their limitations, but they can complement each other to provide different dimensions of access.

CITE responded to a user's natural language query with a display of suggested search terms including free text terms, *MeSH* headings, and topical subheadings. The user could select and rank terms according to their order of importance for a continuation of the search. The citations displayed first were those that were the "closest-match" (i.e., have all or most of the search terms specified by the user). By identifying relevant citations, the user could direct the system to find similar items, as determined by a frequency analysis of the subject headings and classification numbers. The user could continue to add new terms and modify the ranking order to further the search.[64]

SPRILIB at Cambridge University also provides relevance feedback and ranked output. Citations are presented in order of decreasing probability of relevance. The system prompts the user to provide feedback by posing the question *Relevant?* after each displayed citation. The user indicates a response using function keys. This feedback serves to expand the query further. In a feature similar to CITE, documents that the user has deemed to be relevant are used to automatically generate terms to expand or redefine the search.[65]

OKAPI initiates a "best match" search strategy if a user's initial natural language query proves unsuccessful. If at least three words of the query occur in the index, the system takes the user's words and assigns weights that are inversely proportional to their frequency in the file. Words that are less likely to occur in the file receive higher weights, and the sum of the weights determines the order of the output of the records.

Techniques similar to OKAPI's and CITE's "best match" search can be found in other experimental systems. The LIBERTAS integrated library system available from the British firm of SWALCAP Library Services, Ltd. also employs this technique.[66]

CHESHIRE, an experimental prototype OPAC developed by Larson at Berkeley, is designed to reduce the cognitive load on the user in selecting relevant documents. The system supports natural language search queries. Through statistical techniques, groups of records are ranked on the probability that they will contain items relevant to the user's query. The highest ranked records are displayed to the user. *LCSH* terms derived from the items selected can be used to further pursue the initial query.[67]

## BROWSING AND NAVIGATION AIDS

In a focused search, a user enters a search statement that precisely expresses the user's information need. Typically, however, catalog users do not have a clear-cut idea of their information needs at the initial point of a subject search. And even a clear view in the user's mind of the subject needed will often fail to coincide with the selection of terms that the catalog has assigned to a given subject. For these reasons, the role of browsing in a catalog subject search is receiving increased attention.

## The Classified Approach

Classification systems can assist in the browsing process by imposing a structured, classified approach to topics. By ordering topics into subject categories and by providing a hierarchical structure, classifications can assist users in broadening a search, narrowing a search, and placing a search term into context.

Classification browsing also offers the user an alternative to an alphabetical search. While classified catalogs (i.e., catalogs organized by subject classification) existed in some nineteenth century libraries and are not uncommon in today's European libraries, classified access in the catalog has been largely unfamiliar to American users. While many OPACs offer call number access, this type of retrieval acts only as a finding tool for known items rather than as a browsing aide.

In searching for books on a subject, a common strategy is to identify a book on the topic in the catalog, and then use the call number on the catalog record to browse the shelves. Recently, libraries have begun to make it possible for users to carry out this type of search at the catalog, and some OPACs have the capability to move from a relevant bibliographic record to browsing the shelves. For example, Bibliofile has a shelf-browsing feature that allows searchers to see records whose classification numbers are adjacent to the retrieved title.[68]

A number of classification-based OPACs have been developed as prototypes. Experimental systems have used the terminology and organizational structure of classification schemes to provide unique mechanisms for subject access.

### *Dewey Decimal Classification*

The Dewey Decimal Classification (DDC) lends itself very well to catalog browsing, since its hierarchical structure can assist in pointing the user to broader and narrower aspects of a given topic. Another attractive feature of DDC for online catalog use is the availability of the system in machine-readable form, thus making possible the mounting of the classification onto online systems. Although a number of earlier experimental OPAC systems had employed some form of classification searching structure, the first prototype using a large database did not occur until after DDC became available in machine-readable form in the mid-1980s.[69]

Markey's landmark DDC Online experiment compared two online catalogs: The Dewey Online Catalog (DOC), enhanced with the machine-readable DDC (19th edition) and the Subject Online Catalog, which did not incorporate the DDC feature. DOC's database included: (1) machine-readable MARC records in selected subject areas, (2) the schedules (i.e., body of the classification structure), and (3) the Relative Index, which provides essentially an alphabetical enumeration of the main headings in the classification schedules. Four distinctly different libraries—the Library of Congress, the New York State Library, the Public Library of Columbus and Franklin County, and the University of Illinois at Urbana-Champaign—participated in the project. A DOC was developed for each library that contained the library's own bibliographic records (between 8,000 and 12,000 records each) and the DDC Schedules and Relative Index in one of the four subject areas selected by the particular library. Each library conducted online retrieval tests with the assistance of their library patrons and staff. Test results showed that the online DDC improved the search performance of users searching by subject in the online catalog.

DOC users had the choice of either an alphabetical or a classification search. The alphabetical approach displayed a list of DDC Relative Index entries in alphabetical proximity to the entry term. If no match occurred on the relative index entries, users could select an option for a classification search. To initiate a classification search, the user was not required to be familiar with the classification structure or notation. Access to the classification areas was provided by users' own search terms, which were matched with words from the catalog's terminology through a keyword and implicit Boolean search that was automatically performed by the DOC system. Sources of the catalog's terms included DDC Schedule captions and notes, DDC Relative Index entries, and the first subject heading listed in bibliographic records. The system displayed a list of the general areas in which bibliographic records containing the entered keywords are classed, and it assisted the user in navigating the hierarchical arrays of headings from DDC schedules. Headings attracting the user's interest could be used to generate a display of bibliographic records appropriate to the heading.[70]

The incorporation of the DDC schedules and index into the OPACs enabled the DOC researchers to design and develop new strategies for online subject searching. In viewing a display of the hierarchical arrays of related terms surrounding a given topic in the schedules, users could see the "neighborhood" and context of a topic, allowing them to browse topics that were more specific or more general. Since many topics contain "Schedule notes" that give more detailed information on how the topic was treated in the classification schedule, a display of these notes can give a user further guidance as to the scope and definition of a topic in the schedules.

Another prototype system using the Dewey Decimal Classification is The Dewey Online Retrieval System (DORS), developed at UCLA. DORS was implemented as an interface to an online catalog, and it consists of a database comprising the DDC 700 (Arts) schedules, a database of 2,992 reduced bibliographic records, a database of *LCSH*, and a Chain Index to the DDC schedules.

The Chain Index is the distinctive feature of DORS. It was created by the automatic extraction of significant terms from the schedule captions and the DDC Relative Index. These terms were then constructed into chains based on their hierarchical relationships. The purpose of the Chain Index is to facilitate global browsing in a classified search. A search relying on the Schedules alone is restricted to topics within one of the ten broad decimal categories (e.g., the Arts). Relying on the Relative Index alone restricts the user to an essentially alphabetical approach. The advantage of the Chain Index is that it can group topics by subject even when the topics fall in different parts of the ten broad categories. DDC is like other discipline-based classifications in that topics or concepts treated from different perspectives or points of view are scattered throughout the schedules. For example, the topic of *gold* can be viewed from the perspectives or contexts of chemistry, economics, mining, arts, and so forth. Depending on how the topic of gold is viewed, it could thus appear in several of the ten decimal categories. By displaying all perspectives from which a given topic is treated in DDC, the Chain Index has the ability to contextualize search terms. As such, the Index provides a capability not found in actual shelf browsing.

If the Chain Index can be said to facilitate browsing across hierarchies, the Schedule display facilitates browsing within hierarchies. The schedule's tree display offers the more conventional "top-down" approach to browsing, with the broader class followed by its full array of subclasses.

DORS can also display a listing of titles associated with a given class. This feature can be reached from any schedule display, and the user has the option of browsing titles either under an exact class number or under a truncated class number. The first choice offers a precision advantage: a user looking for materials in only a particular class (e.g., Tie-dyeing) can browse the titles that have been assigned the exact number for that class (i.e., 746.664). The second choice offers a recall advantage: the user interested in materials in categories falling under the broader class can browse titles associated with the truncated class number (e.g., 746—Textile arts and handicrafts). In this way, the system takes advantage of DDC's hierarchical structure and "expressive" notation, which allows one to broaden a topic by dropping the rightmost digits from a DDC notation. These features of DDC are also exploited in DORS' class number search. If the user's class number query fails to match the class numbers in the schedules, DORS successively drops digits from the rightmost end of the class number until a match is achieved.[71]

In considering classification as a means of organizing subjects in the catalog, some limitations must be recognized. This information retrieval strategy rests on a tool originally developed for an entirely different purpose. Classification schedules, even more so than subject heading lists, were designed primarily for the person assigning classification notation (i.e., the cataloger/indexer), not the end user. In addition, the logic of classification hierarchies developed for a given subject area may be of scant value to a user interested in broadening or narrowing a search. Svenonious gives the example of the *abominable snow man*. In the Dewey Decimal Classification, this subject falls under the category of *mysteries*, which is in turn a subclass of *controversial knowledge*, which is part of the broad category of *knowledge*. As Svenonius observes, "It is hard to imagine a user who would want to broaden a search using a chain like this."[72]

*Universal Decimal Classification*

Terminology from the schedules of the Universal Decimal Classification (UDC) has been used in ETHICS, an operational

OPAC in Zurich. Descriptors formulated for UDC numbers have been added to the system's searchable indexes. A user's query generates a display of browsing lists containing descriptors in the alphabetical neighborhood of the user's entry term. The system will also display logical arrangements of descriptors ordered by UDC number.[73]

## Library of Congress Classification

The Library of Congress Classification (LCC) does not lend itself easily to incorporation into an online catalog for subject browsing. LCC is not yet available in machine-readable form. In addition, LCC lacks a comprehensive index for the totality of its 21 schedules, which number over 45 separate volumes. Still, a few research projects have been undertaken using experimental catalogs incorporating LCC.

CHESHIRE (California Hybrid Extended SMART for Hypertext and Information Retrieval Experimentation) was developed at Berkeley. One of the classic models of information retrieval research, Salton's SMART system, served as a partial basis for the system's design. A basic aim of this experimental OPAC is to use technologies from information retrieval research to provide a means for alleviating two common and related problems of subject access: (1) the problem of too little or no retrieval due to lack of knowledge of *LCSH* terminology, misspellings, and so forth and (2) the problem of too much retrieval, or "information overload," because the user's search has employed high-frequency terms common to many subject headings.

CHESHIRE addresses the problem of too little or no-match by expanding the lead-in vocabulary. The system provides a method for the automatic construction of a thesaurus-like index based on LCC numbers, subject headings, and title keywords derived from MARC records. In this way, the system increases the number of access points for locating a given record by pooling the items from a classification region.

The problem of information overload is addressed by reducing the number of items users must examine to locate books relevant to their needs. Statistical ranking of retrieved items is employed to assist the user in selecting relevant documents. The highest ranked clusters are displayed in response to a user's query. Feedback from the user can augment the initial query with concepts (*LCSH* terms) derived from the selected items. The user may also choose to browse through the bibliographic records associated with a class cluster in shelf list order.

While subject access points (classification numbers, subject headings, and title keywords) are usually isolated from each other in OPACs, classification clustering combines these access points. Each LCC class number in the system has a record that contains a set of the most frequently used subject headings and title terms for bibliographic records within that class.

CHESHIRE's database is comprised of 30,471 MARC records. Since the classification cluster records are maintained in a separate database file, no modifications are required for the bibliographic records or for other database files.[74]

Hildreth has also developed an experimental OPAC that uses the vocabulary from classes HB-HJ of the LCC schedules. The system provides an enriched entry vocabulary, links the LCC and *LCSH* thesauri, and provides a contextual subject browsing approach. Each record in the database of 30,000 MARC bibliographic records contains not only the LCC class number and Library of Congress subject heading, but also the captions associated with class numbers in the LCC printed schedules. These enhancements were displayed as pseudo-subject headings along with the *LCSH* headings assigned to each work.[75]

Bibliofile's Intelligent Catalog displays LCC or DDC classification outlines, and, by selecting a given classification number, the user can see a display of records falling within that category.[76]

Micco's experimental OPAC at Indiana University of Pennsylvania links *LCSH* headings to LCC classification numbers. Links are also established from controlled subject headings to natural language terms occurring in a book's title and table of contents. In response to a user's query for information on a topic, the system can generate a list of class numbers and their related subject headings from all books that contain chapters on the topic.[77]

## Navigation

The classification-based OPACs offer alternative navigation strategies for subject searching. Most of the display capabilities in conventional OPACs limit the searcher to an up/down linear form of subject browsing. The presentation of titles and bibliographic records is largely in alphabetical sequence, with some systems offering a shelf-list display of brief citations in a rudimentary subject classification display and some displays by date.[78]

This kind of sequence does not reflect users' thought processes as they watch bibliographic elements and clues scroll past on the screen. Nor does it allow for the user to give feedback to the system to generate a refinement of the search. When the browser is restricted to a backward/forward sequence, there is little opportunity to take advantage of clues that pop up in the course of display that suggest the idea for a different type of search. For example, a user might retrieve a citation and find it interesting to pursue title words, subject headings, or classification/shelf-browsing areas suggested by elements in the record. By building on clues and suggestions drawn from searching across fields, a user can refine and reformulate the search.

Alternatives to the linear model for OPAC displays can be seen in some prototypes for classification-based searching. The hypertext concept, which permits the user to navigate through a database in many different directions, offers further promise of breaking the linear mode.

A key feature of Hildreth's experimental OPAC is its provision of explicit navigation linkages between *LCSH* headings and LCC-based descriptors. This OPAC uses a database management and retrieval software that permits linkages between different fields in the bibliographic record. The linkages were employed to facilitate browsing and navigation among data fields and citations. A "rudimentary form of hypertext" is thus achieved. When a citation is displayed, users can "point" to a selected data element and retrieve other records in which the data element appears. For example, the user can select a title word from the citation display and "navigate" from that word to retrieve all works whose titles had at least one occurrence of the selected word. Likewise, subject headings from the controlled subject vocabulary assigned to the work could also serve as a navigation point. Results of Hildreth's controlled experiment (using a total of 54 participants for data analysis) revealed that navigation on subject headings or title keywords resulted in higher recall, but precision suffered significantly in title-word navigation. He concluded that "navigation did not seem to aid subject searching performance after greater familiarity with the system was achieved."[79]

Another example of a prototype OPAC in the hypertext mode is HYPERCATalog, developed by researchers at Linkoping University in Sweden. The HYPERCAT is different from most online catalogs in that its structure of information elements is dynamic rather than static. While the database is made up of some pre-defined structures and elements, a user can link any one type of information with any other information element. Users can also add to and manipulate the database as well as establish and apply subject filters for specialized interests or needs.

Comprised of both public and private levels, HYPERCAT retains a structure of pre-defined elements at the public level, while allowing customized levels for group or individual use. As such, the system resembles a personal information management system, where the bibliographic information of the library catalog can be integrated with knowledge structures defined by the user and information can be imported at the user's command.

A major premise underlying the development of the model is that most users are not able to articulate their information needs and it is easier for a user to recognize a desired item than initiate a formal information request. HYPERCAT is designed to allow the user to identify and recognize needed information rather than describing it explicitly. For example, the user can be shown examples of information structures that other users have found to be useful.[80]

Buckland envisions a catalog in which the user retrieves a catalog record, examines a book in machine-readable form, and takes advantage of the internal references within the text to navigate an information quest.

> the user could move to the table of contents by depressing a key, then go on to examine a chapter. Next, the user might want to look for specific terms or names in the index, online, thence to specific patches of text, again online. Since the text is online, one could expect a concordance providing access to all of it. The user might abandon that text, follow up a reference (from inside the text or from a citation index) to another text, go back to the catalog records to look for another book, or scan the subject headings with a view to reformulating the search. A continual change between the broad view and focus on details is possible. The system would have what Kochen has described, by analogy with a camera lens, as "zoomability."[81]

Buckland's vision is still far from realization, but some rudiments of his ideal are evident in prototypes under development.

## CONCLUSION

This paper has described a model for next-generation OPACs. The model is comprised of features in developing catalogs that reflect a redefinition of the roles previously served by the traditional catalog. The paper first examined ways in which the content of the catalog and its coverage have been expanded and redefined. The catalog can now be seen as a gateway to external databases, including the catalogs of other libraries and commercial abstracting and indexing databases.

The paper next considered the extended depth and variety of coverage found in emerging models of the catalog. Extended depth is provided through article-level access to journals and access to individual works within monographs. Access is now possible to non-traditional data, full-text, and multimedia information.

The second category of next-generation catalog developments dealt with access and retrieval capabilities. Underlying these developments was the assumption that there should be less stringent requirements placed on the user in the search process and greater assistance provided in refining and navigating the search.

A variety of search aids can assist the user in formulating a query. Some next-generation models expand the catalog's index vocabulary to increase the chances of a match. A number of prototypes allow natural language searching, and they manipulate the user's entry terms to match the catalog's index terminology. Systems can also allow a retrieval on a close match rather than an exact match.

Catalogs can interact with a user to refine a search, by suggesting alternatives or automatically executing alternative search methods as well as by ranking retrieval output in decreasing order of probable relevance.

Increased attention has been given to the role of browsing, and some systems facilitate multi-directional searching. Browsing has also been facilitated through the use of classification in subject searching.

Advances in OPAC development have been characterized by a welcome blending of theory and practice. In the fast-breaking field of OPAC development, much of the substantive progress can be credited to information retrieval research. In 1986, Borgman stressed the need for continuing research and development in OPAC systems.[82] Some significant progress has been made. Recent research efforts have been based on empirical evidence and sound theory, and they have been tested by rigorous methods of performance evaluation. They offer promise for establishing a sound basis for OPAC development.

### Future OPACs and Cutter's Catalog Functions

In their most generic sense, the original objectives of the catalog as formulated by Charles Cutter over a hundred years ago remain basically valid for today's and tomorrow's catalogs. While tomorrow's catalog will be dramatically different in coverage and retrieval ability from Cutter's nineteenth-century model, the insights of research into information seeking behavior as well as the research and development in information retrieval technology serve only to strengthen and expand the catalog's potential for achieving Cutter's objectives:

- To enable a person to find a book of which either the author, the title, or the subject is known.

- To show what the library has by a given author, on a given subject, or in a given kind of literature.

- To assist in the choice of a book, as to its edition, or as to its character.[83]

In the new model, the catalog provides access with a breadth and depth far beyond the parameters of its predecessors. Cutter's original purpose for the catalog—to enable access by author, title, and subject to the holdings of one library—is expanded to provide the same possibilities for coverage without regard to institutional or geographic boundaries. Information retrieval research has vastly strengthened the first of Cutter's objectives (i.e., the catalog's finding function). At the same time, it relaxes the requirement that a user "know" a subject in the way that exactly matches the catalog's index terms. Developments such as the expansion of numbers and types of subject entry terms and the provision of natural language searching put the user in a much stronger position to "find" a citation to a given work.

In the second objective ("to show what the library has"), the gathering, or collocating, function of the catalog is strengthened by the provision of more sophisticated browsing mechanisms. As before, the catalog brings together works on a given subject, but in more varied and interesting ways, including the use of classification outlines, hypertext, and navigation mechanisms.

In the third objective, the choosing function is strengthened by the provision of additional information to assist the user in deciding on the relevance of a given citation. Information retrieval research has also contributed weighting and ranking mechanisms to reduce instances of large retrieval sets as well as feedback devices to assist the user in the refinement of a search.

These features of the new model help support Cutter's vision of the ideal catalog: "A catalog is designed to answer certain questions about a library, and that is the best which answers the most questions with the least trouble to the asker."[84]

## ACKNOWLEDGMENTS

Robin Downes and Karen Drabenstott provided valuable comments on earlier drafts of this paper. Their assistance is greatly appreciated.

## NOTES

1.   Many of the features which describe the new model are discussed by Charles Hildreth in his article: "Advancing Toward the E3OPAC: The Imperative and the Path," in *Think Tank on the Present and Future of the Online Catalog: Proceedings* (RASD Occasional Papers, No. 9), ed. Noelle Van Pulis (Chicago: Reference and Adult Services Division, American Library Association, 1991), 17-38.

2.   *Catalogue of the Library of the Peabody Institute of the City of Baltimore* (1883-92), p. iii-iv, cited in Michael K. Buckland, "Bibliography, Library Records, and the Redefinition of the Library Catalog," *Library Resources & Technical Services* 32 (October 1988): 303.

3.   William Gray Potter, "Expanding the Online Catalog," *Information Technology and Libraries* 8 (June 1989): 100.

4.   Karen Markey, *Subject Searching in Library Catalogs: Before and After the Introduction of Online Catalogs* (Dublin, OH: OCLC, 1984), 84-87.

5.   Potter, "Expanding the Online Catalog," 101, 102.

6.   Charles R. Hildreth, *Intelligent Interfaces and Retrieval Methods for Subject Searching in Bibliographic Retrieval Systems* (Washington, DC: Cataloging Distribution Service, Library of Congress, 1989), 61.

7.   Jane Burke (Presentation at the University of Michigan, 30 October 1991).

8.   Carl Grant, "The Data Research Information Gateway," in *The Online Catalog Book*, ed. Walt Crawford (New York: G.L. Hall, 1992), 207-218.

9.   *DataLine: The Data Research Newsletter* (Winter 1992).

10.   Charles W. Bailey, Jr., "Integrated Public-Access Computer Systems: The Heart of the Electronic University," *Advances in Library Automation and Networking* 3 (1989): 25, 26.

11.   "Uncover," Carl Systems, Inc.

12.   "OCLC/Faxon Finder Databases," OCLC, Inc.

13.   Potter, "Expanding the Online Catalog," 100.

14.    Edwin D. Posey and Charlotte A. Erdmann, "An Online UNIX-based Engineering Library Catalog: Purdue University Engineering Library," *Science and Technology Libraries* 6, no. 4 (1986): 31-43.

15.    Thomas J. Michalak, "An Experiment in Enhancing Catalog Records at Carnegie Mellon University," *Library Hi Tech* 8, no. 3 (1990): 33-41.

16.    Charles R. Hildreth, "Beyond Boolean: Designing the Next Generation of Online Catalogs," *Library Trends* 35 (Spring 1987): 661, 662.

17.    Michael E. D. Koenig, "Linking Library Users: A Culture Change in Librarianship," *American Libraries* 21 (October 1990): 844-849.

18.    *DataLine: The Data Research Newsletter* (Winter 1992).

19.    William E. Jarvis and Victoria E. Dow, "Integrating Subject Pathfinders into a GEAC ILS: A MARC-Formatted Record Approach," *Information Technology and Libraries* 5 (September 1986): 213-227.

20.    Potter, "Expanding the Online Catalog," 103.

21.    William Y. Arms and Thomas J. Michalak, "Carnegie Mellon University," in *Campus Strategies for Libraries and Electronic Information*, ed. Caroline Arms (Bedford, MA: Digital Press, 1990), 243-273.

22.    John Price-Wilkins, "Text Files in Libraries: Present Foundations and Future Directions," *Library Hi Tech* 9, no. 3 (1991): 7-44.

23.    Caroline Arms, "Other Projects and Progress," in *Campus Strategies for Libraries and Electronic Information*, ed. Caroline Arms (Bedford, MA: Digital Press, 1990), 316.

24.    Buckland, "Bibliography, Library Records, and the Redefinition of the Library Catalog," 306-308.

25.    James H. Billington, "Library of Congress to Open Collections to Local Libraries in Electronic Access Plans," *American Libraries* 22 (September 1991): 706-709.

26.    Avery Architectural and Fine Arts Library, "Aviador (Avery Videodisc Index of Architectural Drawings on RLIN)," unpublished typescript, 15 April 1987.

27.    Caroline Arms, "Other Projects and Progress," 312, 313.

28.    Virginia Tiefel, "The Gateway to Information: A System Redefines How Libraries are Used," *American Libraries* 22 (October 1991): 858-860.

29.    Charles W. Bailey, Jr., Jeff Fadell, Judy E. Myers, and Thomas C. Wilson, "The Index Expert System: A Knowledge-Based System to Assist Users in Index Selection," *Reference Services Review* 17, no. 4 (1989): 19-28; and Charles W. Bailey, Jr., "The Intelligent Reference Information System Project: A Merger of CD-ROM LAN and Expert System Technologies," *Information Technology and Libraries* 11 (September 1992): 237-244.

30.    Brian Nielsen, "Roll Your Own Interface: Public Access to CD-ROMs," *Database* 12 (December 1989): 105-109.

31.    Potter, "Expanding the Online Catalog," 102, 103.

32.    L. Bjorklund, B. Olander, and L. C. Smith, "The Personal Hypercatalog," in *Proceedings of the 52nd Annual Meeting of the American Society for Information Science* (Medford, NJ: Learned Information, Inc., 1989), 118.

33.    Richard K. Belew and Maurita Peterson Holland, "BIBLIO: A Computer System Designed to Support the Near-Library User Model of Information Retrieval," *Microcomputers for Information Management* 5 (September 1988): 147-167.

34. Pauline A. Atherton, *Books Are For Use; Final Report of the Subject Access Project to the Council on Library Resources* (Syracuse: Syracuse University, School of Information Studies, 1978), 84-86.

35. Karen Markey and Karen Calhoun, "Unique Words Contributed by MARC Records with Summary and/or Content Notes," in ASIS '87, *Proceedings of the 50th ASIS Annual Meeting*, ed. Ching-chih Chen (Medford, NJ: Learned Information, 1987), 154.

36. Posey, "An Online UNIX-Based Engineering Library Catalog."

37. Michalak, "An Experiment in Enhancing Catalog Records at Carnegie Mellon University," 35, 39.

38. Alex Byrne and Mary Micco, "Improving OPAC Subject Access: The ADFA Experiment," *College and Research Libraries* 49 (September 1988): 432, 433, 440.

39. Mary Micco, "The Next Generation of Online Public Access Catalogs: A New Look at Subject Access Using Hypermedia," *Cataloging & Classification Quarterly* 13, nos. 3/4 (1991): 103-132.

40. Martin Dillon and Patrick Wenzel, "Retrieval Effectiveness of Enhanced Bibliographic Records," *Library Hi Tech* 8, no. 3 (1990): 43-46.

41. F. W. Lancaster, Tschera Harkness Connell, Nancy Bishop, and Sherry McCowan, "Identifying Barriers to Effective Subject Access in Library Catalogs," *Library Resources & Technical Services* 35 (October 1991): 387.

42. Virgil Diodato, "Tables of Contents and Book Indexes: How Well Do They Match Readers' Descriptions of Books?" *Library Resources & Technical Services* 30 (October/December 1986): 411.

43. Charles R. Hildreth, "Beyond Boolean: Designing the Next Generation of Online Catalogs," 661, 662.

44. Karen Markey Drabenstott, Anh N. Demeyer, Jeffrey Gerckens, and Daryl T. Poe, "Analysis of a Bibliographic Database Enhanced with a Library Classification," *Library Resources & Technical Services* 34 (April 1990): 196.

45. Songqiao Liu and Elaine Svenonius, "DORS: DDC Online Retrieval System," *Library Resources & Technical Services* 35 (October 1991): 359-75.

46. Ray R. Larson, "Evaluation of Advanced Retrieval Techniques in an Experimental Online Catalog," *Journal of the American Society for Information Science* 43 (January 1992): 39.

47. Charles R. Hildreth, "An Experimental Comparison of Hypertext, Related-Record Subject Searching in OPACs: Summary Notes" (Presentation at the ALISE Research Roundtable, 12 January 1992).

48. Hildreth, "Advancing Toward the E3OPAC: The Imperative and the Path," 23.

49. Hildreth, *Intelligent Interfaces and Retrieval Methods*, 39, 40.

50. Stephen Walker, "OKAPI: Evaluating and Enhancing an Experimental Online Catalog," *Library Trends* 35 (Spring 1987): 634.

51. Hildreth, *Intelligent Interfaces and Retrieval Methods*, 76-78.

52. Tamas E. Doszkocs, "CITE NLM: Natural-Language Searching in an Online Catalog," *Information Technology and Libraries* 2 (December 1983): 376.

53. Ibid, 366-369.

54. Hildreth, *Intelligent Interfaces and Retrieval Methods*, 101.

55.    Ibid, 78-83.
56.    Marilyn A. Lester, "Coincidence of User Vocabulary and Library of Congress Subject Headings: Experiments to Improve Subject Access in Academic Library Online Catalogs," (Ph.D. diss., University of Illinois, Graduate School of Library and Information Science, 1989).
57.    Lancaster et al., "Identifying Barriers to Effective Subject Access in Library Catalogs," 389.
58.    Hildreth, *Intelligent Interfaces and Retrieval Methods*, 89, 107.
59.    Gary L. Horowitz and Howard L. Bleich, "PaperChase: A Computer Program to Search the Medical Literature," *The New England Journal of Medicine* 305 (15 October 1981): 929.
60.    Hildreth, *Intelligent Interfaces and Retrieval Methods*, 55.
61.    Ibid, 61.
62.    Karen Markey Drabenstott and Diane Vizine-Goetz, "Search Trees for Subject Searching in Online Catalogs," *Library Hi Tech* 8, no. 3 (1990): 7-20.
63.    Press release, University of Michigan, January 1992.
64.    Doszkocs, "CITE NLM," 368-374.
65.    Hildreth, *Intelligent Interfaces and Retrieval Methods*, 101-104.
66.    Walker, "OKAPI," 636-7.
67.    Larson, "Evaluation of Advanced Retrieval Techniques."
68.    *The Bibliofile Public Access Catalogs Handbook* (Inwood, WV: The Library Corporation, 1991).
69.    Karen Markey, "Searching and Browsing the Dewey Decimal Classification in an Online Catalog," *Cataloging & Classification Quarterly* 7 (Spring 1987): 37-39.
70.    Drabenstott et al., "Analysis of a Bibliographic Database Enhanced with a Library Classification"; Karen Markey and Anh Demeyer, *Dewey Decimal Classification Online Project: Evaluation of a Library Schedule and Index Integrated into the Subject Searching Capabilities of an Online Catalog* (Dublin, OH: OCLC, 1986); and Karen Markey, "Searching and Browsing the Dewey Decimal Classification in an Online Catalog," 37-68.
71.    Liu and Svenonius, "DORS: DDC Online Retrieval System."
72.    Elaine Svenonius, "Use of Classification in Online Retrieval," *Library Resources & Technical Services* 27 (January/March 1983): 77.
73.    Karen M. Drabenstott, "Online Catalog User Needs and Behavior," in *Think Tank on the Present and Future of the Online Catalog: Proceedings* (RASD Occasional Papers, No. 9), ed. Noelle Van Pulis (Chicago: Reference and Adult Services Division, American Library Association, 1991), 71.
74.    Ray R. Larson, "Managing Information Overload in Online Catalog Subject Searching," in *Proceedings of the 52nd Annual Meeting of the American Society for Information Science* (Medford, NJ: Learned Information, Inc., 1989), 129-135; and Ray R. Larson, "Evaluation of Advanced Retrieval Techniques in an Experimental Online Catalog," *Journal of the American Society for Information Science* 43 (January 1992): 34-53.
75.    Hildreth, "An Experimental Comparison of Hypertext, Related-Record Subject Searching in OPACs."
76.    *The Bibliofile Public Access Catalogs Handbook.*

77.   Micco, "The Next Generation of Online Public Access Catalogs," 109-10.

78.   Hildreth, *Intelligent Interfaces and Retrieval Methods*, 10.

79.   Hildreth, "An Experimental Comparison of Hypertext, Related-Record Subject Searching in OPACs."

80.   L. Bjorklund, B. Olander, and L. C. Smith, "The Personal Hypercatalog."

81.   Buckland, "Bibliography, Library Records, and the Redefinition of the Library Catalog," 306.

82.   Christine L. Borgman, "Why are Online Catalogs Hard to Use: Lessons Learned from Information-Retrieval Studies," *Journal of the American Society for Information Science* 37 (November 1986): 387-400.

83.   Charles A. Cutter, *Rules for a Printed Dictionary Catalogue* (Washington, DC: Government Printing Office, 1876), 10.

84.   Charles A. Cutter, *Library Catalogs* (Washington, DC: U.S. Bureau of Education, 1876), 526.

# FULL-TEXT RETRIEVAL:
## SYSTEMS AND FILES

Carol Tenopir

---

## INTRODUCTION

Much of the development in the first 30 years of library automation has been in solving the problem of identifying relevant sources. Automation of the library's card catalog provides a finding tool for the library's collections. The books, journals, films, and other materials located through the catalog still mostly reside in their original form, with no direct connection to the automated finding tool.

Most of the early development in electronic publishing was also aimed solely at identifying information sources. Secondary publishers, notably publishers of indexing/abstracting serials, were the first to provide their resources in electronic form. Throughout the 1970s and much of the 1980s, indexing/abstracting (bibliographic) databases were predominant in the online database world. The first CD-ROM databases for libraries were many of these same bibliographic files. Traditionally (and still) bibliographic databases are the most widely used type of electronic resource in libraries.

Advances in Library Automation and Networking, Volume 5, pages 43-71.
Copyright © 1994 by JAI Press Inc.
All rights of reproduction in any form reserved.
ISBN: 1-55938-510-3

Starting in the mid-1980s, due to great increases in disk storage capacities and better document conversion techniques, full texts of certain types of documents became more widely available. In the 1990s, full-text databases (files) are the most rapidly growing type of commercially available database. Better text-retrieval software is leading to more locally created full-text databases as well. Perhaps in this decade we will at last electronically solve the document delivery problem as well as the document location problem.

## TYPES OF COMMERCIALLY AVAILABLE FULL-TEXT DATABASES

Libraries have access to a variety of full texts on a pay-per-use basis via commercial online information systems or at a one-time purchase rate or fixed fee subscription rate on CD-ROM. A few published texts are available on diskette or magnetic tape as well. Just as with printed publications, electronic full-text publications are not all the same, so it is helpful to define them and to categorize them by document type.

A commonly accepted definition for full text is given in the *Directory of Online Databases*: "Full Text [databases] contain records of the complete text of an item, for example, a newspaper article, a specification, a court decision, or a newsletter."[1] They are categorized as a subset of "Source Databases. Those that contain original source data, the full text of original source information, or materials prepared specifically for electronic distribution."[2]

A further elaboration is given in a user's guide to the *Directory of Online Databases*:

> This classification is assigned to databases that contain the complete text of published works (e.g., journal articles, specifications, court decisions, newspaper items)—regardless of whether charts, footnotes, illustrations, or other such enhancements in the original work are included. In most cases, the Full Text database corresponds, in whole or significant part, to a publication. However, Full Text also covers databases of "items" that have been prepared expressly for online distribution and that have no corresponding printed publication.[3]

Still, although it is changing, the vast majority of current full texts are just electronic counterparts of printed publications.

All of these definitions of full text exclude complete texts of directories, which are categorized as directory or referral databases, but include a variety of other types of documents. Full-text databases can be categorized into 10 general types.[4] These categories are not always mutually exclusive, nor does every text neatly fit into a category, but they help to differentiate the complexity of a general term such as *full text*.

1. *Statutes, Court Decisions, and Other Primary Legal Documents.* The intended audience is most often legal experts. Materials included here are decisions from U.S. federal and tax courts, laws and legislation from each U.S. state, and various legal materials from many other countries. Length and characteristics of the documents vary widely, but certain key elements are particularly important for searching. These include such things as name of the judge, names of the defendants, the case name and number, cases cited as precedent, date, court, location, and other particulars.

The major online systems in the United States that provide these materials are LEXIS and WESTLAW. CD-ROM regional subsets are offered by a growing number of companies. For example, Michie Company provides New Mexico Law on CD-ROM, and Info-One International and Diskrom Australia offer a variety of Australian case law online and on CD-ROM.

2. *Other Government Documents, Patents, Regulations, and Other Official Publications.* The intended audience varies; patents are often accessed by experienced patent searchers. Each publication has its own characteristics, varying from the short requests for proposals in *Commerce Business Daily* to detailed regulations in *Code of Federal Regulations.* Some cover many different topics; others are more narrowly focused. Important information elements include issuing agency, date, patent or contract numbers, type of document, and subject. LEXIS has patents; NEXIS offers many U.S. documents, such as the *Code of Federal Regulations* and the *Federal Register.* DIALOG has *Commerce Business Daily.* West provides a government contracts file on CD-ROM.

3. *News Releases and Other Unpublished Information Intended for Subject Experts, Other Business People, or Journalists.* Most cover one narrow topic, and the length is rarely more than two pages. Press releases are issued by a government agency or company to announce new products or give new information. They usually

include name and phone number of a contact person. Unpublished reports may also be summaries of new developments or information about an organization. Important access points include date, issuing company, contact person, and subjects. These are most often part of another database and are available primarily online on systems such as DIALOG, NEXIS, and CompuServe.

4. *Newspaper Articles.* Intended audiences include people of all ages who are interested in current events. Frequent users include news professionals and reference librarians. Newspaper databases include articles, columns, and other selected features on a variety of topics. Length varies from several paragraphs to long feature stories. Often articles are written with important information in the first paragraph. Most newspaper databases do not include everything found in the printed equivalent; typical exclusions include such things as advertisements, classified listings, weather forecasts, sports scores, syndicated columns, and stories taken from wire services. Major national and international papers, such as *Wall Street Journal, Pravda,* and *The Times,* are available, as are local dailies or weeklies, such as the *Fresno Bee, Allentown Morning Call,* and others, in whole or in part. Major suppliers of newspaper databases online are NEXIS, VU/TEXT, DIALOG, Dow Jones News/Retrieval, and InfoGlobe search service. On CD-ROM, major suppliers include NewsBank, UMI/Data Courier, and DIALOG.

5. *Newswire Services.* Intended audiences are the same as those of newspapers. Newswire stories vary in length, but are often concise summaries of major news events. Timeliness is critical and they are often updated frequently. Slightly different versions of the same story may therefore occur several times in the same database. Backfiles may not be kept online for long on some systems. Many major newswires from all over the world are available online, including Associated Press, Reuters, Tass, and Kyodo English Language News. Major online systems for newswires include DIALOG, NEXIS, NEWSNET, Dow Jones News/Retrieval, and CompuServe.

6. *Newsletters.* Intended audiences are subject experts or information professionals, usually within a corporate or research environment. Each newsletter has its own style and language, and a database may consist of a single newsletter or many. They are subject specific and often highly technical or of interest only within the target industry. Information may be very time sensitive.

Important access points include date, newsletter title, and subject. Hundreds of newsletters are available online, from many different industries. The two major online systems for newsletters are NEXIS and NEWSNET.

7. *Reference Books.*   Intended audiences range from school children to researchers, depending on the book. There is much variety in terms of style, length, audience level, graphics included, and useful access points. Many are used primarily for fact retrieval and most are highly structured into short, fairly consistent sections. Encyclopedias are the most widely available type of reference book; the CD-ROM versions of encyclopedias may include graphics, motion, and sound as well as text. Footnotes and cross references are important access points in encyclopedias in addition to subjects. Other reference book databases range from highly technical standard works, such as *Kirk-Othmer Encyclopedia of Chemical Technology* and the *Merck Index*, to Internal Revenue Service tax information, to the Bible, to Quanta's About Cows reference CD-ROM. Online systems with reference books include BRS, DIALOG, NEXIS, STN International, Data-Star, and Dow Jones News/Retrieval. CD-ROM books are often available directly from the book publisher, such as Britannica Software, National Geographic Society, or WorldBook. Others are sold by third parties such as CMC ReSearch, SilverPlatter, and so forth.

8. *Other Books.*   A growing number of novels, collections of short stories, and other books are being converted into electronic form. Unlike reference books, these books are intended for reading, with fact retrieval playing a minor role; however, they may be used for text analysis. CD-ROM is the publishing medium of choice for electronic books. Several titles are available from CMC ReSearch Inc., including Shakespeare on Disc. OCLC and G.K. Hall produce an American Authors disc.

9. *Scholarly or Technical Journal Articles.*   The primary audience is subject specialists, usually researchers. Most articles are lengthy with many footnotes. Sentences and paragraphs may be long, and language is technical. Printed versions include many tables, figures, and equations that may or may not be in the database version. Abstracts may precede the article. Usually, only the major articles are included in the online version: letters to the editor, book reviews, news stories, and columns from the printed versions may not be in the online version. Subject access is most important, but journal

name, authors, cited authors, and dates are useful as well. Many of the journals from the American Chemical Society are online, as are major medical journals such as the *New England Journal of Medicine, Lancet*, and the *British Medical Journal*. STN International, BRS, and DIALOG are major online systems that provide journals. The ADONIS CD-ROM project provides journal articles from over 400 scientific and biomedical publications. CD-ROM journals may be ASCII text like online versions or image files that look just like the print versions.

10. *Nonspecialist or General Interest Magazine Articles.* Most of these are for the general reader. They are especially useful for students or laypeople for personal or school-related information. The writing style, subjects, and length of articles varies greatly, but most do not include technical language, footnotes, or abstracts. The printed versions contain many photographs, charts, sidebars, and other graphics, most of which are not included online, although captions may be. By far the most important access point is subject, but magazine title and date are useful as well. Several hundred magazines are available, either as stand-alone titles or within a multi-title database such as Magazine ASAP. Online systems that provide access to magazines include BRS, DIALOG, and NEXIS. Information Access Company's Magazine Rack is a popular, inexpensive CD-ROM full text for home users, while a CD-ROM version of their Magazine ASAP is marketed to libraries. UMI/DataCourier and Ebsco also have magazines on CD-ROM.

## NUMBERS OF FULL-TEXT DATABASES

According to industry leader Martha Williams, there are now over 2,040 full-text databases, available either online, on CD-ROM, on magnetic tape, on diskette, or on a combination of electronic options.[5] Full text now make up 44% of the total number of *word-oriented* databases.[6] Figure 1 shows how full text has grown in the last decade in both numbers and percent of total databases.

A more meaningful figure may be the number of electronic full-text sources available, whether they are mixed with other sources into one database or available alone as a separate file. It is difficult to tell just how many magazines, journals, newspapers, and so forth are represented in a figure like 2,040. Some titles are available as stand-

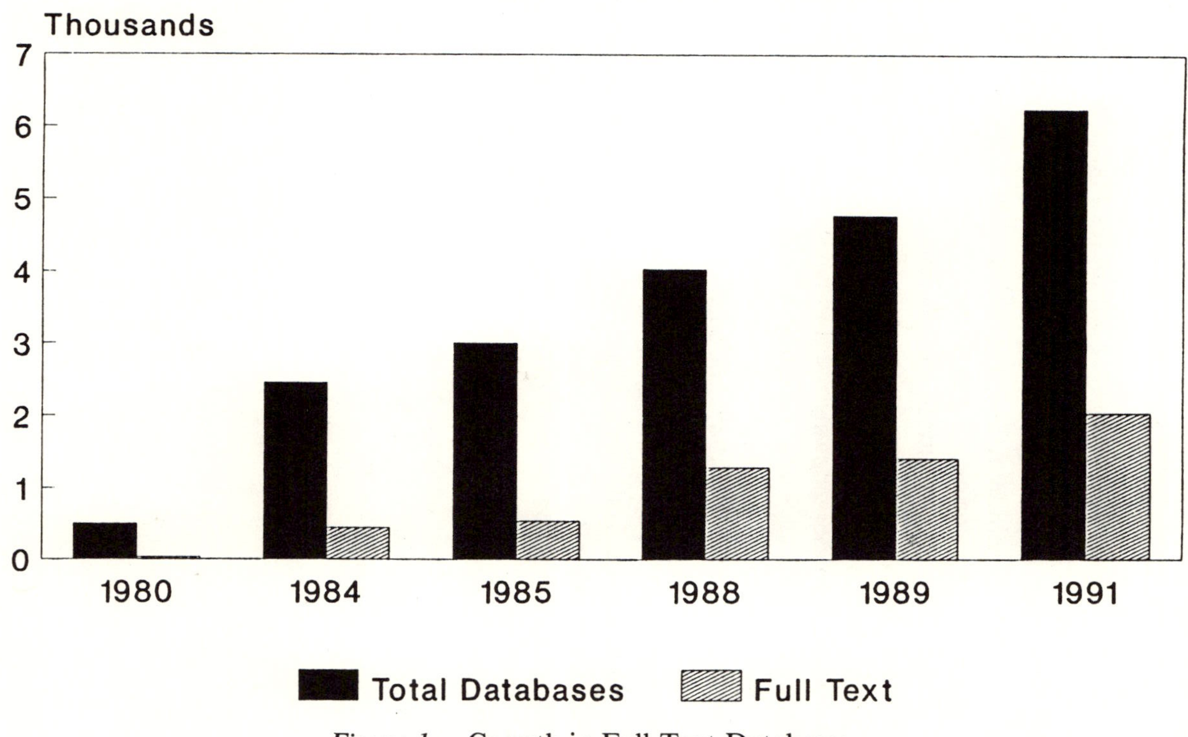


*Figure 1.*   Growth in Full-Text Databases

alone databases (for example, *Harvard Business Review, Los Angeles Times*, and Compton's MultiMedia Encyclopedia); others are part of one large mega-database (for example, Magazine ASAP and Trade & Industry ASAP, ACS Journals Online, and Newsbank) that may combine hundreds of periodical titles. A current trend is to create *hybrid* databases that mix full text with some bibliographic records in one database (for example, ABI/INFORM and PTS PROMPT).[7] Other CD-ROM databases, such as PComm, combine full-text articles and news with directory information and computer programs.

The total number of titles available in full text is thus difficult to estimate, but, thanks to the efforts of a small publishing company, it can be estimated for online versions of serials such as magazines, journals, newspapers, newswires, and newsletters. BiblioData's 1992 edition of *Fulltext Sources Online* includes listings for over 3,000 serial titles available via nineteen online systems.[8] (This is up from 1,700 titles listed in the 1989 edition.)

Each source title is listed separately in the directory, even if on some systems it is part of a single multi-title database. Thus, the listing for *Financial World* shows it as part of the multi-title database Trade & Industry ASAP on BRS and DIALOG, part of the Business Library on Dow Jones, part of the Dow Jones file on DataTimes, but available separately on NEXIS (FINWLD) and Reuters (FINWO). Each entry also gives coverage of the title on each system, because there may be great variation. *Financial World* is included from January 1983 to present on BRS, DIALOG, and Mead (NEXIS); from January 1985 to present on Dow Jones; from September 1986 to present on Reuters; and from January 1987 to present on DataTimes.

Just because a title is listed in *Fulltext Sources Online* doesn't mean that everything in the print equivalent will be found online. According to the editor, "Fulltext means that complete articles are found online. It does not mean that a periodical is found cover-to-cover in the database. Database producers often choose to include only the most meaningful articles."[9] The editor also indicates that although:

> one would like to think that a journal or newspaper described as being available online in fulltext is available cover-to-cover ... [t]his is rarely the case. Coverage policies differ widely from one periodical to another and from one database vendor to another.

In no case do online periodicals reproduce advertisements that appear in the original. None, to our knowledge, reproduces long tabular material such as pages of stock quotations. Because of copyright restrictions, most newspapers exclude wire service stories and syndicated columns online, limiting themselves to items written by in-house staff. In addition, many newspapers omit letters to the editor, editorials, obituaries and filler material. Magazines often omit announcements, index to advertisers, book reviews, notices, corrections, information for authors, classified ads and meetings calendars.[10]

Even when an article from a print issue is included, rarely is the entire article online. Orenstein explains:

The notion of a complete article has its pitfalls. Given the current state of technology, few articles are provided online with their tables, charts, graphs, illustrations or photographs intact. These things are sometimes noted or described, and published if short. In general, the term *"fulltext"* means that the entire *text* of an article is available online.[11]

A random sample of entries in the 1989 *Directory of Online Databases* showed that approximately 68% of the full text listings were for periodicals, with 5% for monographs and 27% for all other categories.[12] A source such as *Fulltext Sources Online* thus describes a majority of online full-text resources, but it is safe to estimate that there are at least 1,500 additional full-text titles.

BiblioData's newer *Newspapers Online* is an alphabetical directory of North American daily newspapers available online or on CD-ROM.[13] The first edition (1992) includes detailed information on electronic availability of 138 papers. Only general-focus papers that are published at least five times a week are included. Online or CD-ROM versions must contain "substantially all articles of the newspapers ... ; that is, the contents of the newspapers are available electronically virtually 'cover-to-cover.' Newspapers in which only a few articles are selected for inclusion in a file (such as the Business Dateline collection) are not [included in the directory]."[14]

## ONLINE SYSTEMS FOR FULL TEXT

*Fulltext Sources Online* covers the serial titles available on nineteen online systems that include large amounts of full text. All of the online systems also offer other types of information in addition to full text, including bibliographic citations, abstracts, directories, statistics, financial information, or stock prices.

The online systems are available worldwide, although they are headquartered in several different countries, as can be seen in Table 1.[15]

*Newspapers Online* also includes papers online via CompuServe (Columbus, Ohio).

In the library/information center market, use is dominated by just two systems—DIALOG and Mead Data Central, as can be seen in Figure 2.[16] A total of just five of the full-text systems (DIALOG, Mead, BRS, STN, and Westlaw), along with two bibliographic systems (NLM and Orbit) account for almost all online searching in libraries and information centers.

*Table 1.*   Online Systems with Full-Text Databases

---

UNITED STATES

BRS Information Technologies (A division of Maxwell Online, headquartered in McLean Virginia)
Burrelle's Broadcast Database (Livingston, NJ)
DataTimes (headquartered in Oklahoma City)
DIALOG Information Services Inc. (located in Palo Alto, California, and owned by Knight-Ridder)
Dow Jones News/Retrieval (Princeton, NJ)
Mead Data Central (LEXIS/NEXIS) (Dayton, Ohio)
NewsNet (Bryn Mawr, PA)
Nikkei Telecom (Nihonkeizai Shimbun America) (New York)
STN International (A joint venture of the U.S. Chemical Abstracts
Service [Columbus, Ohio], German FIZ Karlsruhe, and Japan Information Center of Science and Technology)
VU/TEXT (located in Philadelphia, owned by Knight-Ridder)
WESTLAW (West Publishing Company, St. Paul, MN)

CANADA

Info Globe (Toronto, Ontario)
Infomart Online (Don Mills, Ontario)
QL Systems Ltd. (Kingston, Ontario)

EUROPE

Data-Star (Switzerland, with offices in U.S. and U.K.)
G.CAM/EDD (France)
Genios Wirschaftsdatenbanken (Germany)
Reuters Ltd. (United Kingdom)
FT PROFILE (United Kingdom)

---

# Williams, Information Market Indicators

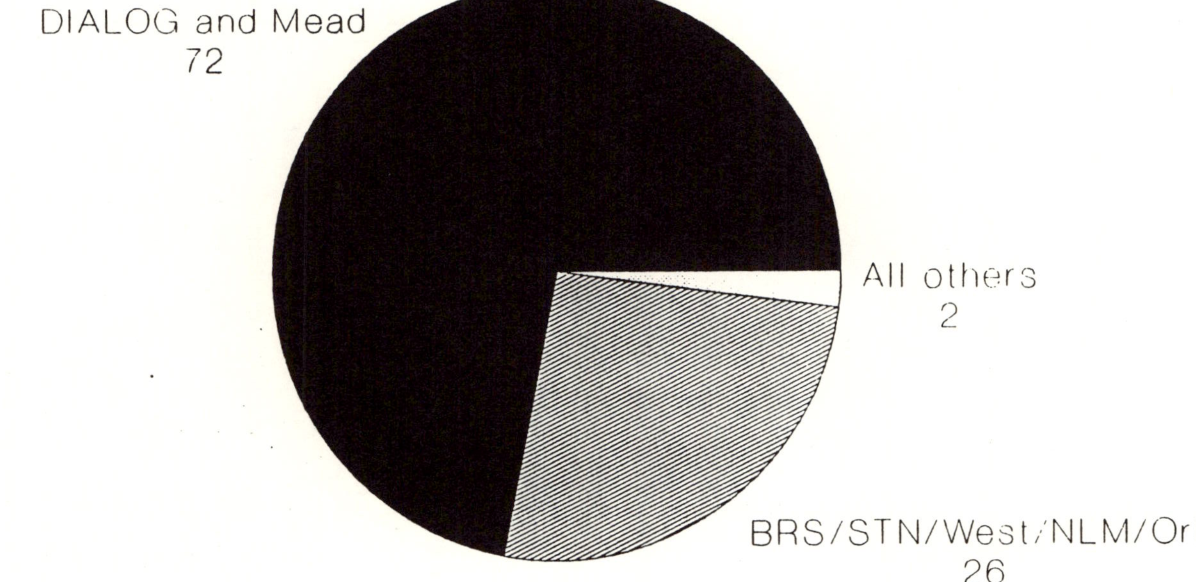


*Figure 2.*   Online Use in Libraries and Information Centers

Many of these online systems originally were developed for bibliographic databases. The search and display features were designed for shorter indexing/abstracting records. When full text was added, they found it necessary to add other search and display features to enhance full-text searching.

## CD-ROM SYSTEMS FOR FULL TEXT

The arrangements for creating and marketing commercially available CD-ROM databases are not so clear-cut as the established online model. CD-ROM databases can be sold under a vendor-database producer arrangement just like online systems, but often a database producer arranges for a CD-ROM software company to provide just the software, maintaining marketing and distribution rights. Or, producers may develop proprietary software and do all of the development, marketing, and maintenance themselves.

CD-ROM full-text databases developed and sold under the vendor model are available from such vendors as DIALOG, SilverPlatter, Microsoft, and OCLC. Database producers who have developed their own proprietary software include UMI (ProQuest), Newsbank, Oxford University Press, Information Access Company (InfoTrac), and many others. Database producers who have used other companies for CD-ROM development or CD-ROM software include Grolier (Online Computer Systems), Ebsco (Fulcrum), Bowker Electronic Publishing (Online Computer Systems), and CMC ReSearch (DiscPassage).[17]

With full-text databases, the arrangements may be complex. For example, the H.W. Wilson Company has its own CD-ROM software, WILSONDISC, which it uses for bibliographic files. Wilson contracts with UMI to provide a full-text database on ProQuest, which is a companion file to Wilson's Social Science Index. Other such cooperative arrangements are likely to be forthcoming.

*The Directory of Portable Databases* (October 1991 edition) lists 934 total CD-ROM databases, 319 (34%) of which are full text, in whole or in part.[18] These are of all types. Much of the innovation in multimedia is taking place with CD-ROM full-text databases because the development costs are lower and, unlike online files, they do not have the limitations of transmitting over the telephone lines. After examining four CD-ROM directories, Nicholls reported 341 multimedia CD-ROM titles (17% of the total) as of June 1991, up from only 40 titles in 1989.[19]

There may be great variation in the appearance and the search features available in CD-ROM full-text files. They may be machine-readable ASCII text like their online counterparts, where every word of the text is a potential search term and texts or portions of text can be downloaded and transferred into word processing or database programs. Ebsco's full text version of Magazine Articles Summaries, Information Access Company's full-text InfoTrac files, and Ziff-Davis's Computer Select are ASCII searchable text.

Or, CD-ROM versions may be combination files that include graphics with ASCII text. In these cases, the text is usually fully searchable, while the graphics can be displayed with relevant text portions. Grolier's Encyclopedia is of this type. The American Chemical Society/OCLC Chemical Online Retrieval Experiment (CORE) project of full-text chemical journals combines ASCII text plus graphics on magnetic media with page images on an optical jukebox.[20]

Finally, CD-ROM versions may just be page-image files. Scanned image files do not support full-text searching, but are usually meant to be used in conjunction with a bibliographic database for document delivery. Once an article is located through the bibliographic database, the CD-ROM scanned image articles can be located and retrieved using a control number. UMI ProQuest texts are of this type: Business Periodicals Ondisc carries page images of journals that correspond to the ABI/INFORM bibliographic CD-ROM file, and General Periodicals Ondisc corresponds to Periodical Abstracts.

## FULL TEXT ON DISKETTE OR TAPE

Some full-text databases in ASCII form are now available for lease or purchase on magnetic media. Floppy diskette or magnetic tape are popular options for distributing bibliographic data for use in libraries. The library must then load the data from the diskette or tape onto the hard drive of their local micro- or mainframe computer. In the case of diskette distribution, microcomputer search and retrieval software may come with the text subscription or purchase. Databases on magnetic tape are normally sold without retrieval software; it is up to the subscribing library to load the tapes using compatible and appropriate search software. With bibliographic databases, this is often the same software that is used for the library's online public access catalog.

Diskette distribution is reserved for small files or those that require frequent updates. It is usually a low-cost alternative, with many full-text files costing under $100. Of 545 diskette databases listed in *The Directory of Portable Databases*, 154 (28%) are classified as full text, in whole or in part. They are of all types, ranging from the *U.S. Code of Federal Regulations*, to the Bible, to selected works of Benjamin Franklin.

Magnetic tape databases, to be loaded on a library's large computer, are as yet mostly bibliographic, directory, or numeric. *The Directory of Portable Databases* lists 45 full-text databases out of 430 tape titles (10.5%). This small number is probably because full-text databases take up so much computer space and require extensive computer resources for loading, maintaining, and searching. A library may not be able to support large full-text databases on the same system that runs their OPAC, bibliographic files, and other library operations. Many government publications are available on tape, including documents from the Internal Revenue Service, Securities and Exchange Commission, Department of Defense, and others.

A growing number of specialized machine-readable texts are available in the humanities for text analysis research. They are outside the scope of this chapter. For more information on this topic, see a recent article by Price-Wilkin.[21]

## FULL-TEXT BOOK LIBRARIES

Undoubtedly, the number of full-text sources available through commercially available online systems and on CD-ROM and other distribution media will continue to grow. Some of the most exciting developments are happening at the network level, where much of the experimentation and innovation in large online textual database creation is taking place.

Several notable projects are converting large numbers of books and other texts into electronic books for access over Internet or other online networks. Project Gutenberg strives to convert and provide access to 10,000 important out-of-copyright books by the year 2000.

Public Access Xanadu is Theodor Nelson's vision of a hypertext network of online documents.[22] The U.S. Marine Corps' Online Books project provides an online hypertext library of the complete Marine Corps University's warfare collection.[23]

Library involvement in such projects will provide new levels of access to all types of materials. Libraries can take a leading role in other cooperative ventures to make electronic publications more widely available.

## TRUE ELECTRONIC JOURNALS

Electronic journals that are not derived from print journals have existed—at least experimentally—for quite some time and hold much promise for the future. At least 15 refereed electronic journals are currently available on BITNET and other networks.[24]

In 1991, the American Association for the Advancement of Science and OCLC launched *The Online Journal of Current Clinical Trials*, an online refereed research journal. The journal publishes peer-reviewed research articles that include charts, tables, and graphs; it has videotext-quality typeface. Articles can be searched and downloaded, and the system offers hypertext links to Medline abstracts. If successful, this journal could lead to a new standard for original online full texts.

Non-refereed full texts are also becoming an important part of the research process. This text-based invisible college is accessible through list servers and similar systems on networks such as BITNET and Internet, and it can be a part of a library's text-based services. However, these informal full texts are outside the scope of this chapter.

## CREATION OF FULL-TEXT DATABASES

Most full texts commercially available today are still byproducts of printed publications. Few are available only in electronic form. These texts are converted into machine-readable form in several main ways, including keyboarding, scanning with OCR conversion, and direct purchase. Some online system databases receive direct feeds from wire services.

## Keyboarding

Keyboarding means hiring data entry clerks to key the text directly into the computer. For in-house databases, it is the most common method when the documents going into a database are generated locally. Surprisingly, until quite recently this was also the most common method used by commercial database publishers to convert printed publications into full-text databases. Such rekeying can be labor intensive, but, with verification, accuracy rates can be high and costs low. Throughout the 1980s it remained less expensive to pay overseas data input operators to rekey the text portions of magazines, journals, and books directly from the printed source than to pursue more automated options. Keyboarding is still used by commercial database producers to convert texts that are printed on thin newsprint, that include many special characters, or that use unusual typefaces. Keyboarded databases usually include text only.[25]

## Scanning

In the 1990s, the most common method for creating textual databases from printed publications has changed to scanning. Scanning is used to create image files from many different types of original texts. Scanned image files reproduce the document in page image, but do not produce fully searchable text. Images are compressed, but, even so, have large storage requirements if the resolution is to be acceptable.

For example, OCLC estimates the page image storage requirements for one year of a full-text database that contains 10,000 journals (5,390,000 pages) to be approximately 540 more gigabytes than would be required for ASCII text, graphics, and indexing.[26] On viewing, software must decompress an image file, and response time may suffer.

To create ASCII text from a scanned text involves first scanning the printed document, then converting the characters with optical character recognition (OCR) software.[27] The newest generation of OCR software and scanning equipment, including the latest Calera and Kurzweil machines, produce high accuracy rates at about the same costs as offshore keying and lower costs than in-house keying. Combination image/ASCII files retain graphical material in compressed image files that are linked to appropriate sections of the ASCII text.[28]

## Direct Purchase

Another textual database building option is to purchase typesetting tapes directly from the print publisher. Almost all publishers create their printed publications with computer typesetting programs that dictate page layout, arrangements, and typefaces. Since the text is in machine-readable form, such typesetting files can be converted to a format compatible with the database system software. This option is not used as often as the other two simply because publishers use a wide variety of typesetting software and markup conventions. Conversion programs are required for each different package, and, if a publisher changes the format, programs must be rewritten by the database producer. Although a markup standard exists (SGML—Standard Generalized Markup Language), it is not yet in widespread use.[29]

## Wire Service Feeds

Some wire services provide a direct online feed to the online systems that load their information. Wire service feeds may come in 24 hours a day, just as they do to major newspapers, and they are used for online databases that are updated frequently. Online system conversion software is created to allow the feeds to be immediately loaded into the online system files.

## Storage Considerations

Full-text databases, especially if they include images, have massive storage requirements. The OCLC Office of Research estimates just *one page* of mixed text and graphics for an ACS chemistry journal can take between 8.5 to 100 kilobytes of storage. SGML-coded ASCII text takes the least (8.5 KB); SGML text plus extracted graphics takes 10 KB; text, graphics, and indexing take 25 KB; and page images take 100 KB.[30]

Careful design of software for machine indexing and compression is needed, especially for CD-ROM full-text databases, to ensure acceptable response times when searching this inherently slow medium. Design of software for CD-ROM full texts is discussed in Witten, Bell, and Nevill.[31]

## SEARCH AND DISPLAY REQUIREMENTS FOR FULL TEXT

Many of the commercial online systems developed their software with bibliographic databases in mind. Almost all were developed 10 or more years ago, with a continuing patchwork of revisions as full-text databases got larger and more plentiful. A user of commercial online systems may not have much to say about desired features for full-text databases—the user must accept what is offered by the system. Still, several of the systems have a number of features that enhance full-text searching; these features have been identified through a combination of research and experience. Almost all of these features have been tested at one time or another.[32]

There may be more variation and more innovation in CD-ROM software. CD-ROM software is not constrained by the bandwidth limitations imposed by online systems' communications lines. In addition, CD-ROM developers can often provide search or display features geared to one specific text, such as the National Geographic Mammals Encyclopedia or the Compton's MultiMedia Encyclopedia. The tyranny of tradition that inhibits online development may not hold true in the CD-ROM world, although neither may the common sense that comes with years of experience. Jacso discusses in detail criteria and methods for evaluating CD-ROM software.[33]

Software for databases created from texts distributed on diskette or magnetic tape or from in-house texts have even more variation. The purchaser has more choices of search and display features, but also must carefully evaluate each package. Criteria and methods for evaluation are detailed in Tenopir and Lundeen.[34]

Software features for full-text databases can be separated into three levels: (1) minimal for all textual databases—all of these features should be present; (2) important for full-text databases—most of these features should be present; and (3) useful for better text retrieval—some of these features may be present to enhance search and retrieval.

### Level One Software Features

Level one features have become de facto standards for textual files, whether they are bibliographic or full text. They are accepted features on all of the major online search systems and almost all of the CD-ROM systems. They are available on many software packages for in-house databases, although they may not be present in software created for library automation rather than for information retrieval.

Level one features are possible because of how the information is structured in most text-retrieval systems. All of the major online system software and most of the CD-ROM software and software for in-house databases rely on the inverted index file structure. Inverted index systems generate a separate dictionary index (or indexes) of all searchable words in each record in a database. Searches are made in the inverted files and postings are reported to the searcher. The system goes to the actual full records from pointers in the index only when a user wants to view a record. Inverted indexes facilitate certain basic search features, including inverted index display, truncation, set building, Boolean logic, proximity operations, and field searching.

The ability to view words in the indexes helps a user to develop a search strategy and to check the consistency of form of entry. Only the words or phrases in the index are available for searching; if, for example, pages and volume information are not put into the index, they cannot be searched even though they may be present in the records. Each system has its own rules for inverted index creation, including how it treats punctuation, but the ability to view the index makes these rules evident to the user.

There may be one inverted index that includes all of the searchable words or phrases from anywhere in the records, or there may be many separate indexes specified by fields. For example, a system may place words from all subject-related fields, such as title, descriptors, and full text, into one index (Basic Index on DIALOG), but create separate indexes for all other fields. For full-text searching, either method is acceptable as long as a user may specify a given field as needed. For example, the searcher should be able to restrict a search to just the date field or just the title field.

Truncation (word stemming) helps resolve some of the problems that arise from inconsistent word forms and entry. Truncation is especially important with full-text files, since much variation can be expected to occur in texts. Minimally, truncation should be user-specified right-hand stemming so that users can retrieve singulars, plurals, and other ending variations (such as *-ed, -ing*, and *-tion*).

Boolean logic is still the common foundation of working retrieval systems and is useful in certain cases for full-text files. At a minimum, systems should offer the three basic Boolean operators: OR, AND,

and NOT. Boolean OR operations are crucial with full texts, especially those that do not also have controlled vocabulary indexing. Different authors may use different words for the same concept; the searcher must be able to specify *Native Americans OR American Indians*. Boolean AND operations are best to link text words with other fields such as publication year, author's name, or journal name. The Boolean NOT operator is useful to eliminate known irrelevant items such as articles by a certain author, specific document types such as fiction, or phrases such as *IBM AND NOT IBM-PC*. Searchers should be able to specify the order of execution of Boolean operators using nesting (parentheses).

With full-text searching, proximity operations are crucial and are recommended instead of the Boolean AND operator to link concepts within texts. Word adjacency is a minimal capability. It may be taken care of automatically when a user enters two or more words separated by blanks, or it may require a special operator such as ADJ. Also desirable are: (1) the ability to specify within a certain number of words (*gone* within 2 words of *wind*), and (2) the ability to specify word order (*gone* must precede *wind*).

Finally, set building is necessary for a search to be truly interactive. Set building allows searches to be modified, narrowed, or broadened. Full-text searches often retrieve many records, so modification is essential. Different systems handle set building in different ways, from creating a set for every term entered (DIALOG), to creating a set just for the product of an entire line of input (Mead and BRS). Regardless of how it is handled, full-text searchers should be able to refer back to previously created sets to modify, narrow, or broaden a search.

Minimum display features for full text require flexibility in the amount of information viewed or printed. Users should be able to view just titles or a small part of a text, selected portions of a text, or the complete textual records.

## Level Two Software Features

The second group of software features may or may not be present in software designed for bibliographic databases, but are important features for full-text files. Many are extensions of the basic level one features.

In addition to user-specified right-hand truncation, a full-text system should do a certain amount of right-hand word normalization automatically. Regular forms of plurals and possessives should be automatically retrieved when singular forms are entered and vice versa. Ideally, a user should be able to turn this off, however. For example, the user may want to retrieve *electronic journals*, but not *electronics journals*.

To achieve better precision, a user should be able to specify how many characters should appear after a right-hand stem. For example, if a user wants only *compute, computes, computer*, or *computers*, but not *computerization*, the user should be able to specify two characters only following the stem *compute*. If all variations are wanted, an unlimited stemming capability should be present.

Left-hand truncation is important only for certain types of documents. A chemistry collection is better searched, for example, if left-hand truncation can retrieve all phenol compounds, such as nitrophenol, dichlorophenol, and so forth, in one statement. Because of the way inverted indexes are created and searched, left-hand truncation is more difficult to achieve, and it is not available on most large commercial online systems. In-house software may offer left-hand truncation by sequential scanning or by creating a separate inverted index with the words spelled backwards.

The last truncation variation useful for full texts is the ability to do internal truncation. One variation on this capability is *wild card* replacement, which requires a one-to-one relationship of characters. For example, $M*N$ will retrieve man or men, but not every word that starts with $M$ and ends with $N$. True internal truncation allows any number of characters to appear between the specified letters. This is especially useful for retrieving spelling variations (for example, *colour* or *color*). Ideally, the user should have the choice of either wild card or internal truncation.

Many common spelling variations should be handled automatically by the full-text system, rather than requiring the user to search for all possible variations. Simple things such as differences between British and American spelling are easily identified in dictionaries and should be automatically searched by a full-text system that includes American and British Commonwealth documents.

In addition, standard abbreviations should be automatically matched to the spelled out versions. Months, days, years, and numbers can be normalized to allow automatic retrieval of *January 1988* if a user inputs *1/88*. More complex equivalencies such as automatic matching of abbreviations to spelled out versions of government agencies and organizations (for example, *F.B.I.* equals *Federal Bureau of Investigation*) are offered by Mead. Software for in-house full-text databases should allow the creator to specify equivalencies and build term-synonym dictionaries.

As mentioned earlier, proximity operations that allow a searcher to specify the relationships between words are crucial in full-text searching. In addition to the minimum capabilities of word adjacency and searching within a specified number of words, software for full text should recognize some of the grammatical structure of texts.

Searching for words within the same grammatical paragraph or the same sentence allows a searcher to take advantage of the inherent structure of texts. Presumably an author will put words that represent intersecting concepts within a sentence or paragraph. Consequently, searching within those units will allow more precision. Ideally, a user should be able to search for words within a specified number of paragraphs or sentences, although this feature is not so commonly available in online or CD-ROM systems.

Some full texts, such as research reports or newswire stories, have inherent structure and writing style. For these types of documents, there are other useful proximity operators, such as the ability to specify which portion of a document (e.g., both words within the lead paragraph or within the conclusions). For books, specifying within a chapter is useful.

With this range of proximity operations, full set building (i.e., the ability to modify previously created sets to narrow or broaden a search) provides the most interactivity. For example, a searcher who retrieves too little from linking words within the same sentence should be able to easily respecify within the same paragraph. If too many false drops arise from words within the same paragraph, a user should be able to limit the search to words occurring only in the conclusion or introduction paragraphs. Marchionini found with school students that, to be most successful, full-text searching should allow maximum flexibility and interactivity.[35]

Displaying lengthy full texts requires a wider range of display features than displaying bibliographic information or short texts. Most important is the ability to display only the portions of the texts that contain the search terms. Such KWIC (Key-Word-in-Context) features are common in full-text software, with variations on how much text is displayed surrounding the search terms. Most systems display a 25 to 50 word text window; ideally, users should be able to enlarge the window as they view any document. Search terms should be highlighted.

To facilitate browsing and reading of electronic texts, users must be able to move around fully in retrieved documents. This means paging back and forward, enlarging KWIC windows at will, viewing next paragraphs or sentences, and skipping to specified sections or pages of documents. This is more common with CD-ROM and in-house software than with online systems.

## Level Three Software Features

All of the software features mentioned so far are widely available in online, CD-ROM, and in-house systems. Although not every variation mentioned is available on every system, most features are widely available on systems that cater to full-text retrieval. Level three features, on the other hand, are less common. They provide a shopping list of special features that enhance full-text search and retrieval, but that are rarely all available on any one system.

Hypertext links are being widely implemented on CD-ROM full texts, especially encyclopedias and similar reference books. Hypertext provides an alternative to traditional indexing by building links between related concepts, documents, parts of documents, or files. In a hypertext encyclopedia, for example, a user may be able to view related articles that contain further information about a topic discussed in the current article, or the user may be able to view related pictures. Hypertext is popular in the Macintosh environment with the HyperCard program and, on a larger scale, is an important part of the ACS/OCLC CORE Superbook project.[36]

Relevance feedback involves using a user's judgment of a document's relevance to find additional similar documents. A user may mark useful documents, and the relevance feedback system will use some algorithm to find other documents that are "like" those. One simple relevance feedback method is to use word frequency of the relevant documents to locate documents that contain a certain percentage of the same words with similar occurrence rates.[37]

Many of these extended features provide ways to increase precision of searches. Word occurrence information with ranked output allows the most potentially relevant documents to be displayed first. The most basic version of this feature is to have the software calculate how often the search terms occur within each document. The documents with the most occurrences will be displayed first. More complex algorithms for ranking output exist, but research has indicated that all algorithms seem to work equally well for full-text retrieval.[38]

Other modified Boolean search methods serve to increase recall using a variety of partial-match techniques. One simple method is to allow partial membership in a set; documents will be retrieved even if all concepts linked by ANDs are not present. Those with all concepts may be displayed first, followed by documents in descending order by how much of the search query they contain. Sound-alike searching allows items to be retrieved that contain words similar to input search terms that are not exact matches. For example, if a user searches on the name *Brown*, a sound-alike system may also retrieve *Browne* and *Braun*.

Other partial-match methods, although not yet widely available in commercial systems or software, are being added to some software for the creation of in-house databases. These include fuzzy sets, probabilistic retrieval, and vector space retrieval.[39] Belkin and Croft discuss all of these search methods and more.[40]

Display with full text is still at its infancy. Due to the limits of standard phone lines, online full-text files are almost completely ASCII text only. They are unaesthetic, without the typefaces, spacing, and page layout that make printed texts so attractive. (*The Online Journal of Clinical Trials* is a noteworthy exception.) Without graphics, sidebars, photographs, or special characters they include only part of what makes many texts valuable.

CD-ROM and in-house systems do not have the limitations of online systems and should offer many more attractive display features. At setup, the librarian should be able to specify type styles, size, and colors for full-text display. Texts should be displayed with sections and subsections set apart through appropriate headers and spacing. Users should be able to move between sections.

Finally, images are becoming a part of many CD-ROM texts and are supported by some in-house software packages. Hypertext links between text and images create a hypermedia database that makes the most efficient use of the power of ASCII text and linked image files. Due to more efficient compression algorithms, multimedia products can now also include moving images as well as still images. An extended discussion of compression for CD-ROM full texts is beyond the scope of this chapter.[41]

All search, retrieval, and display features must, of course, be balanced with ease of use and appropriateness for the users. Sometimes there is a trade-off between power and ease of use in any software package. Features that are confusing or of no use to the users of a system hinder rather than help the retrieval process.

## SOFTWARE FOR IN-HOUSE DATABASES

There are a growing number of powerful and friendly software packages that allow libraries to create their own full-text databases with texts generated internally or from texts leased or purchased from publishers. Table 2 shows a partial list of these. Even more so than online or CD-ROM full-text systems, software for creating in-house databases has great variety. Not all packages are useful for all types of texts, so it is useful to categorize them according to their general characteristics.[42]

*Structured Text-Retrieval Packages* require fields and field characteristics to be specified before records are added to the file. Usually there is a configuration module that is used for this initial setup. Field structure allows for faster and more precise searching,

*Table 2.*   Selected Software for In-House Textual Databases

---

askSAM (for micros)
Basisplus (for minis and mainframes)
BRS/Search (for micros, minis, and mainframes)
CAIRS-TMS Information Retrieval Package (for micros and minis)
Concept Finder (for micros and minis)
Concordance (for micros)
Excalibur (for micros and minis)
FolioViews (for micros)
Fulcrum (for micros)
GOfer (for micros)
Hypercard (for the Macintosh)
IBM/STAIRS (for mainframes)
Inquire/TEXT (for mainframes)
Lotus Magellan (for micros)
Personal Librarian (for micros and minis)
Sonar Professional (for the Macintosh)
Topic (for micros, minis, and mainframes)
ZyINDEX (for micros)

---

and it provides more control over formatting of output. Structured text-retrieval packages are traditionally used for bibliographic data and are the most common type in use in libraries. Commercial online systems are structured, so they are familiar to online searchers. Of the packages listed in Table 2, Personal Librarian is of the structured type.

*Unstructured Text-Retrieval Packages* are less common in a library setting. They require no initial setup and accept incoming text files without any field structure. These packages often recognize inherent structures of text, such as sentences and paragraphs, but they do not recognize fields. This means they lack the capabilities to search, sort, or customize output based on field criteria, but they are good for free-text searching of texts. Unstructured text-retrieval packages are especially suited to managing existing unfielded word processing files or files downloaded from a variety of incompatibly fielded databases. If texts already exist in machine-readable form, they can be used to create a full-text retrieval system very quickly. Unstructured text-retrieval packages include ZyINDEX and Lotus Magellan.

*Combination Text-Retrieval Software* are becoming the most common option and offer the advantages of each of the other two categories. They support defined field structure in addition to unstructured text. Thus, standard bibliographic information, such as author, title, date, and source, can be put into specified fields that can then be searched, sorted, or output. Textual portions of documents can be treated as unstructured text to be searched with more powerful search features. Combination packages include Concept Finder, Concordance, and Topic.

Libraries can use these packages to manage their locally generated texts, such as pathfinders, bibliographies, reports, manuals, and curricular materials. Optionally, within the provisions of copyright regulations, they can download full texts from online or CD-ROM systems or lease machine-readable versions of full texts directly from publishers for loading on an in-house system.

## CONCLUSION

Whether they are accessed through a commercial online search service, leased or purchased on CD-ROM, magnetic tape, or diskette, or created locally, full-text systems and files are becoming an important part of library services. A bibliographic database without full text support solves only half of the retrieval problem. Paper-based collections take up space and are getting too expensive; paper-based document delivery systems waste natural resources and provide documents that cannot be manipulated. Full-text files and systems will increasingly help solve the information retrieval problem.[43]

## NOTES

1. *Directory of Online Databases*, vol. 12, nos. 3 and 4 (Detroit: Cuadra/Gale, 1991), viii.

2. *Directory of Online Databases*, vii.

3. *Online Database Selection: A User's Guide to the Directory of Online Databases* (New York: Cuadra/Elsevier, May 1989), 18.

4. Carol Tenopir and Jung Soon Ro, *Full Text Databases* (New York: Greenwood Press, 1990); and Carol Tenopir, "Users and Uses of Full Text Databases," in *Proceedings of the International Online Meeting, London, December 1988* (Oxford: Learned Information, Ltd., 1988), 263-270.

5. Martha E. Williams, "The State of Databases Today: 1992," in *Computer-Readable Databases: A Directory and Data Sourcebook*, 8th ed. (Detroit: Gale Research Inc., 1992), xi-xxi.

6. Williams separates databases into "word-oriented, number-oriented, image, audio, electronic services, and software." Word-oriented, which make up 72% of the databases listed in the directory (4,661), include "bibliographic, Patent/Trademark, Full Text, Directory, Dictionary, and other."

7. Carol Tenopir, "Hybrid Databases," *Library Journal* 117 (1 February 1992): 64-66.

8. Ruth M. Orenstein, ed., *Fulltext Sources Online: For Periodicals, Newspapers, Newsletters & Newswires* (Needham Heights, MA: BiblioData, 1992).

9. *Fulltext Sources Online*, iii.

10. *Fulltext Sources Online*, v.

11. Ibid.

12. Tenopir and Ro, *Full Text Databases*, 16.

13. Susan Bjorner, comp. and ed., *Newspapers Online* (Needham Heights, MA: BiblioData, 1992).

14. Bjorner, *Newspapers Online*, 1. Inclusion criteria is given in detail in the front matter.

15. Ruth M. Orenstein, *Fulltext Sources Online*.

16. Information given to me by Martha E. Williams and available in her quarterly report: *Information Market Indicators* (Monticello, IL: IMI).

17. For more examples, see: Paul T. Nicholls, CD-ROM *Collection Builder's Toolkit: 1992 Edition* (Weston, CT: Eight Bit Books, 1991).

18. *Directory of Portable Databases* (Detroit: Cuadra/Gale, October 1991).

19.   Nicholls, *CD-ROM Collection Builder's Toolkit.*

20.   Lorrin Garson et al., "CORE: The Chemical Online Retrieval Experiment," in *Annual Review of OCLC Research: July 1990-June 1991* (Dublin, OH: OCLC, 1991), 32-33.

21.   John Price-Wilken, "Text Files in Libraries: Present Foundations and Future Directions," *Library Hi Tech* 9, no. 3 (1991): 7-44.

22.   For more information on several projects and an excellent overview of electronic books, see: Reva Basch, "Books Online: Visions, Plans, and Perspectives for Electronic Text," *Online* 15 (July 1991): 13-23.

23.   Bruce Flanders, "On-Line Books: An Advanced Technology Electronic Library System," *Computers in Libraries* 12 (January 1992): 44-47.

24.   Michael Strangelove and Diane Kovacs, *Directory of Electronic Journals, Newsletters and Academic Discussion Lists,* 2nd ed. (Washington, DC: Office of Scientific and Academic Publishing, Association of Research Libraries, 1992).

25.   Ernest Perez, "Low-Budget, Cost-Effective OCR: Optical Character Recognition for MS-DOS Micros," *Library Software Review* 9 (July-August 1990): 209-217.

26.   Stuart Weibel, "The CORE Project: Converting a Large Document Collection for an Electronic Library Project." (Presentation at the American Society for Information Science Annual Meeting, 30 October 1991).

27.   Lori Grunin, "OCR Software Moves Into the Mainstream," *PC Magazine,* 30 October 1990, 299-356.

28.   Clyde W. Grotophorst, "Keyless Entry: Building a Text Database Using OCR Technology," *Library Hi Tech* 7, no 1 (1989): 7-15.

29.   Betsy N. Kiser, "Standard Generalized Markup Language: Why Reference Librarians Should Care," *Reference Services Review* 18 (Fall 1990): 37-40, 52.

30.   Weibel, "The CORE Project."

31.   Ian H. Witten, Timothy C. Bell, and Craig G. Nevill, "Indexing and Compressing Full-Text Databases for CD-ROM," *Journal of Information Science* 17, no. 5 (1991): 265-271.

32.   Carol Tenopir, "Full-Text Databases," *Annual Review of Information Science and Technology* 19 (1984): 215-246; and Tenopir and Ro, *Full Text Databases.*

33.   Peter Jacso, *CD-ROM Software, Dataware, and Hardware: Evaluation, Selection, and Installation* (Englewood, CO: Libraries Unlimited, 1992).

34.   Carol Tenopir and Gerald W. Lundeen, *Managing Your Information: How to Design and Create a Textual Database on Your Microcomputer* (NY: Neal-Schuman, 1988).

35.   Gary Marchionini, "Information-Seeking Strategies of Novices Using a Full-Text Electronic Encyclopedia," *Journal of the American Society for Information Science* 40, no. 1 (1989): 54-66.

36.   Dennis E. Egan et al., "Hypertext for the Electronic Library? CORE Sample Results," in *Hypertext '91 Proceedings* (New York: Association for Computing Machinery, 1991), 1-14.

37.   Nicholas J. Belkin and W. Bruce Croft, "Retrieval Techniques," *Annual Review of Information Science and Technology* 22 (1987): 109-145.

38.   Jung Soon Ro, "An Evaluation of the Applicability of Ranking Algorithms to Improve the Effectiveness of Full-Text Retrieval. II: On the Effectiveness of

Ranking Algorithms on Full-Text Retrieval," *Journal of the American Society for Information Science* 39, no. 3 (1988): 147-160.

39.    Gerald Salton, *Automatic Text Processing: The Transformation, Analysis, and Retrieval of Information by Computer* (Reading, MA: Addison-Wesley Publishing Company, 1989).

40.    Belkin and Croft, "Retrieval Techniques."

41.    Ian H. Witten et al., "Indexing and Compressing Full-Text Databases for CD-ROM."

42.    Gerald W. Lundeen and Carol Tenopir, "Text Retrieval Software for Microcomputers and Beyond: An Overview and a Review of Four Packages," *Database*, 15 (August 1992): 51-57.

43.    For further discussion of text-retrieval systems see: Charles T. Meadow, *Text Information Retrieval Systems* (San Diego: Academic Press, 1992); and Peter Gillman, ed., *Text Retrieval: The State of the Art* (London: Taylor Graham, 1990).

# WHAT CAN THE INTERNET DO FOR LIBRARIES?

Mark H. Kibbey and Geri R. Bunker

## INTRODUCTION

About five years ago, the Internet suddenly appeared in the library literature. Since that time, it has increasingly dominated networking discussions; the flow of articles hit new highs with recent discussions about the National Research and Education Network (NREN). This development has raised a number of questions about the relationship of the NREN to the future of libraries. The largest issue may be the question of whether the NREN will serve society in general or only the chosen few. Either outcome is still possible because the Internet is still evolving. However, it will take action by librarians who understand the Internet and what it can do for society, working with their institutions and communities, to bring about a positive future. This paper is designed to help actualize that future.

The first section of this paper provides a selected short history of the Internet, and it defines various terms. This section provides basic

**Advances in Library Automation and Networking, Volume 5, pages 73-103.**
**Copyright © 1994 by JAI Press Inc.**
**All rights of reproduction in any form reserved.**
**ISBN: 1-55938-510-3**

background information for readers who are less familiar with the Internet and networks in general. The rest of the paper suggests a strategic plan for using the Internet to help create an open, national electronic library.

## WHAT IS THE INTERNET?

The Internet is an international network that is composed of many different computer networks. The best analogy is that the Internet is like a data highway system. As such, it is hard to separate the Internet from the services it provides. As a result, different people often have very different views of the Internet based on their network applications. To really comprehend the Internet requires an understanding of how it is built, what services run on it, and who funds it.

Like the U.S. highway system, the Internet is not a single entity, but it can appear as one to its users. It is a group of computer networks that are physically linked by computer switches and functionally linked by common adherence to a range of standards—the most prominent standard being TCP/IP (Transmission Control Protocol/Internet Protocol). These protocols are designed to allow computers from different manufacturers to exchange information over long distances. One way to understand this concept is to take a brief historical look at how such networks developed and how they differ from the networks in many libraries.

### Historical Development of the Internet

Libraries have used the word "network" for many things, but none of them are quite like the Internet. Traditional library computer networks linked terminals to one or more central computers. These library networks existed both in single organizations, as part of local library systems, and nationwide, as vendors such as OCLC built networks spanning the country. These networks generally ran at speeds below 9,600 bits per second, supported dumb terminals, and were wired in a star pattern, with all traffic flowing to and from a few central computers. In many ways, they looked like phone systems, with each user having a direct line to the central exchange. The key feature of these networks was that they were very centralized.

All the computing was done on a few big machines, and users had fairly simple display terminals. This type of network still dominates dedicated library systems.

Starting in the late 1970s, computing began to fundamentally change. System planners realized that the future of computing involved many distributed computers. Soon, users would have real computers on their desktops. In that environment, networks would have to link many computers, and communication could occur between any combination of them. There would still be some large central computers, but the distributed computing environment would dominate the scene. For this developing environment, new types of local area networks were designed. Besides supporting many computers, these networks also had to support new kinds of data traffic. Since computers were now talking to computers, whole files or large programs, rather than just short screens of data, might be transmitted.

Initially, the need to network microcomputers was not obvious to many people. Early microcomputers were usually installed as stand-alone machines, but, over time, users began to demand networks for a variety of reasons. Simply passing files around on floppy disks eventually becomes problematic, especially if you need to send them to several people. In the Macintosh environment, the development of the laser printer—too expensive to dedicate to a single user—drove early networking efforts. In other cases, networks were installed when services such as electronic mail were moved from expensive mainframes to microcomputer servers. Not all computers are yet networked; however, as microcomputers take over more computing tasks, the need to share data and services has made networking a big business. In most cases, data transfer on networks is from computer to computer and no large central host exists.

As a result, the structure of modern networks is radically different from the structure of earlier networks, which used point-to-point links. Usually, each local area network functions like one wire, with all messages flowing past every computer on the network. Instead of just sending data, the network must address each message with a "to" and "from" addresses so that only the correct machine(s) read it. The message, plus addressing and error correction data, came to be called a "packet." Although packets may include only a single character, they are more efficient when they contain more data.

Quite a few protocols were developed to handle local area networks. Today, Ethernet is the most common high-speed packet network protocol. Token Ring and other protocols still exist, but they are not as prevalent as Ethernet.

As microcomputers proliferated, local area networks increased in number. Since every message goes over the entire network, however, a single local area network cannot handle a large numbers of computers. To increase capacity, several local area networks are connected by special switching computers that keep local traffic on the local network and let long distance traffic cross onto another network. Simple links, called bridges, can connect two similar networks. However, to link networks of different types, complex high-speed switching computers called routers are needed. Routers require a well-developed protocol and an addressing scheme such as TCP/IP.

TCP/IP was developed for the original Advanced Research Projects Agency Network (ARPANET), which was sponsored by the U.S. Department of Defense. It originally linked approximately a dozen sites nationwide that were engaged in computer science research. The number of nodes grew as the technology matured; finally, the ARPANET was divided into military and research networks. The research side was taken over by the National Science Foundation (NSF), which has supported the research and development of the NSFNET backbone. Because this backbone is a critical piece of the national network, the U.S. portion of the Internet is often called the NSFNET.

The present NSFNET has three levels of organization. Each institution supports its own local network(s) to which users connect. Each local network has a connection to a regional network. Regional networks range in size from one such as BARRNet (Bay Area Regional Research Network) that covers only the San Francisco Bay Area to multi-state organizations such as NorthWestNet, which services six states. Each regional network has a link to the national backbone, the NSFNET. The distinction between the regional networks, NSFNET, and the Internet is important organizationally, but it is invisible to users. Normally, the term "Internet" is used unless there is a need to specify some particular aspect of network financing or governance.

The NSFNET now connects over 630 colleges and universities representing about 35% of the nation's four-year institutions of higher education. This covers 70% of the national student body enrolled in four year colleges and 90% of the federally funded research projects performed by higher education. Worldwide, the NSFNET is linked to other networks to form the Internet. The Internet now connects over 750,000 computers used by five million people in almost one hundred countries.

The current Internet growth is about 25% *per month*, whether measured by number of users or by density of traffic. This exponential growth supports the idea that distributed computing has matured and that "the market has now absorbed the basic technologies, consumers have learned enough to put these to good use, and the infrastructure has begun to emerge and provide reliable network service for a worldwide community."[1]

The current national plan is to use the present NSFNET as the foundation for developing the NREN. The NREN will carry U.S. networking into the twenty-first century with a range of research and development efforts. The backbone will operate at speeds of one billion characters per second by the mid-1990s, and new software services will be developed to improve security and access to information.

To use the NSFNET as the foundation for expanding the NREN, funding must be identified at all levels. The concept that current communications technology is the chief bottleneck in the continued success of U.S. computing was crucial to the passage of the National High-Performance Computing and Networking Act. (This is the legislation that supports continued development of the NSFNET.) Federal support is focused on the backbone, networking research, and pilot projects. However, while the emphasis is often on federal funding, most of the NREN's cost is local. For every federal dollar spent on the network, regional networks and institutions spend between $30 and $100. To some academic libraries, the Internet looks free because the institution is supporting it, but even then it has a significant impact on the institution's budget. For other libraries, the cost of Internet access is very real and very localized; usually, the biggest costs are getting wiring to the desktop and maintaining staff to support TCP/IP.

## A User's View of the Internet

Users seldom see the Internet's organizational hierarchy. Instead, it looks like a larger version of a local network, providing file sharing, electronic mail, and electronic bulletin boards. The Internet's address system resembles that of the international phone network: addresses are hierarchical, like phone numbers with country and area codes. Many of the present Internet users already had some form of electronic mail before their institution was connected to the Internet. Some even had international mail on networks such as BITNET. The biggest change for these users is the ability to do real-time log in and terminal emulation with programs such as TELNET. TELNET allows anyone on the Internet to log into a remote computer and to enjoy computing performance approximating that of a local connection. This has made the use of remote library catalogs increasingly popular. It has also allowed vendors such as RLIN and OCLC to offer services on the Internet that are much better than those that are normally available through dial-up methods.

On the other hand, many of the information services on the Internet are very crude by library standards. If you know the name of a file in a public server, there is a tool that may give you the address from which it can be retrieved. But if you want to find information on an unfamiliar topic, you had better have help! That is not to say help does not exist on the Internet, but there is little in the way of coordination. NorthWestNet has recently published an Internet guide.[2] The author claimed that 95% of the information was found by searching the Internet itself—but it took him years to learn how to find it.

The TCP/IP protocols used by the Internet are already used by most research organizations to link internal networks. For users at these sites, the Internet simply looks like an extension of their local network. All the tools work in essentially the same manner, but with the Internet a library catalog search can extend from New York to New Zealand.

## The Internet Community

Because the Internet developed from a research environment, its culture is different from that found in almost any library. The Internet was built to solve leading-edge problems, one step at a time. Pilot projects abound, and standards usually result from actual development efforts rather than from extensive and consensually written proposals. Solutions to problems are proposed as RFCs (Request for Comments) and then built and tested. Changes are based on real experience, with decisions being made by small technical committees. A solution that works usually becomes a defacto standard. If it remains the best answer for a few years, it may be incorporated into some more formal standard. This is far more action-oriented than, for example, the ISO networking model, which first developed an overall architecture. (At present, there does not appear to be any trend toward migrating the Internet to an ISO implementation. Instead, ISO services are being examined and, in some cases, implemented on the Internet.)

A key cultural quality common to both the Internet community and libraries is the concept of resource sharing. Almost always, computer programs to implement RFCs are shared. In fact, it took years before any commercial services appeared on the Internet; there is still strong support for cooperative projects. Bulletin boards and electronic serials are evidence of this trend.

Though the sharing component is quite compatible with library traditions, an action-based, iterative test approach is not. As librarians work in this environment, there will be increasing use of pilot projects, and this will require a change in our usual mode of operation.

## A VISION FOR THE INTERNET

### Planning for the Future

The real purpose of having a vision is not to see the future, but to have some control over it. As Greek tragedy illustrates, if the future were certain and unalterable, there would be little point in knowing it. In studying the Internet, the need is to understand the forces shaping the future and to direct them to our advantage. A useful vision must describe not only realistic goals, but also a pathway that leads to them. Strategic planning is commonly used to achieve this end.

The first step is to define a mission and to set goals that provide direction. Then the current environment and future trends are studied. These factors are the framework in which actions must take place. The next step is to outline the strengths and weaknesses of the organizations involved. Finally, an attempt is made to identify opportunities in the environment, while noting the presence of any threats to success in achieving the goals.

### Articulating the Mission

One of the most commonly held visions of the future is that of an electronic library that brings desired information from anywhere in the world directly to a user's desktop computer through some kind of network.[3,4] A reasonable mission statement can be gleaned from the short, but effective, common vision statement written by the Network Advisory Committee of the Library of Congress. This statement calls for a networked information system to support users with "access on a timely basis to the information they require without being faced with costs beyond their own or society's means."[5]

While this is a very attractive concept, there is a growing recognition that the biggest weakness of this vision is the lack of a clear pathway to reach it. At the RLG-sponsored meeting cited above, over 60 library directors and chief academic officers described the "wired desktop" as a universally desired future. At the same time, the conference report also noted that "another significant observation concerned the widespread lack of vision about how we get there from here."[6] If the NREN is even a partial tool for achieving this future, how can we employ it?

### Library Goals for the NREN

Additional NREN development has been funded as part of the National High-Performance Computing and Networking Act sponsored by Senator Al Gore. In support of his legislation, Gore stated, "Most important, we need to build the high-speed data highways. Their absence constitutes the largest single barrier to realizing the potential of the information age."[7] For some groups, this means the ability to transmit medical X-rays or images created by supercomputer simulations in realtime. Educators talk about using the NREN to bring the world's resources into every school in the country. There is even the hope that electronic journals will solve libraries' massive problems of space and preservation, plus end the spiraling costs of journals that threatens the present tradition of scholarly communication. With such sweeping promises, how can anyone oppose this development?

In fact, the broad claims of NREN supporters have given rise to concern. John Barry said in an editorial, "I fear the NREN because I fear that we will allocate vast resources—tax money—to the creation of a giant network of use and relevance to a very small group."[8]

More macabre visions of a networked future can be found in science fiction. For example, William Gibson's *Neuromancer* paints a picture of a highly networked world in which all the social problems of today have spiraled out of control. With the passage of legislation supporting the NREN, it seems clear that the Internet will continue to grow, and its current success suggests it will be a major factor in future information systems.

The question remains how much of this will really impact libraries. Major technological changes require that organizations—and even whole industries—examine what they really do, or they risk losing much of their market. Does the development of the Internet really represent a change of this scale? If so, how do we harness it? Periods of rapid change offer both the greatest challenges and the greatest opportunities. In this section, we will look at some of the present trends and examine ways to direct change towards meeting library goals.

The first step in realizing any vision is to develop specific goals. If we are to make the vision of an open, national electronic library a reality, at least three fundamental goals are necessary.

## Goal One: Universal Access

If the NREN is not to exacerbate the split between the "haves" and the "have-nots," it must be widely available. This goal also implies that the NREN must involve the entire library community. Equal access is not just a philosophical nicety—it is critical for success. Continued NREN development is going to require broad public support and a large electronic market, needed to keep costs low. These things will happen only if there is widespread use of the NREN and growing public demand for access to it. Not everyone will use the NREN directly, even in its broadest form; however, they must view it as essential to the community for the support of schools, libraries, medical facilities, and other community agencies.

The Internet is designed to reach institutions. To bring it to all citizens, it must connect schools, hospitals, and public libraries.[9] Through the public library, average citizens can get access. Community libraries can utilize the rich networked resources that are available. Over time, commercial networks will grow and provide many of these services directly to individuals and firms who can pay. Without access in public libraries, networked information will be exclusively commercial, and it will only underscore the major divisions in our society.

The task at hand is significant. While the current NSFNET reaches 70% of the students at four-year colleges, the remaining 30% represent two-thirds of the colleges—these colleges are usually small and they are sometimes geographically isolated from major communications centers. The percentage of community colleges with Internet access is even smaller, and few schools or public libraries are connected.

*Objective: Link Public Libraries.*   Since the Internet is designed to link institutional networks and is not designed to service individuals directly, public libraries are the key to bringing access to the general public. No other institution comes close in terms of its mission. Also, these libraries have introduced other technologies to the public. The first public photocopier and the first public terminal were often at the local library. Certainly many citizens' first use of a computer database has been on a public library CD-ROM. Providing general access through the public library as part of national and state programs can bring new resources and new life to these libraries.

*Goal Two: Affordable Information*

There should be a wide range of electronic information resources on the network to meet every information need. These resources include both traditional reference works and new types of information, such as local city information. Much of this will happen if the NREN expands significantly, but the goal of making information affordable is complex and requires serious study.

Information is never free in the strictest sense, but networking allows it to be shared with low distribution costs. The NREN is expanding the electronic marketplace by encouraging new products and pricing structures. Although creating the NREN and providing broad access is a critical factor in stimulating the information marketplace, additional action is needed.

*Objective: Establish New Marketing Models for the Electronic Marketplace to Identify Funding for Open, Public Access.*   Models for cost recovery in an electronic environment have been a major topic of discussion.[10] A larger market allows more services, it and encourages information providers to try new marketing plans. With a bigger pie, even a small slice can be worthwhile.

*1. Attracting more customers is a big factor.* The Internet has already increased the size and scope of the market for electronic information enormously. Suddenly, millions of people have direct, low cost (usually free to the end user) access to a high-speed network. The NREN will continue this trend for smaller organizations. An interesting question is whether most services will be marketed to individuals or to their organizations. Bibliographic search services are the most common commercial service on the network. The database market has grown rapidly, but much of the growth has been in CD-ROMs and locally mounted databases. The Internet gives centralized online information providers the ability to equal local systems' performance, and it opens up competition.

*2. New marketing schemes are emerging.* While the increased market size generates vendor interest, the changed environment encourages new forms of information marketing and pricing. The Internet is institutionally based, organizations join and pay—not individuals. Individuals, however, are the users. This fact encourages vendors to change to pricing structures that allow organizations to subscribe for their users.

Both OCLC and RLIN are trying new pricing schemes as part of their marketing strategy. RLIN sells licenses based on the number of simultaneous users, and OCLC sells search cards that can be distributed to users. Both models are well suited to libraries since they allow costs to be monitored and, if desired, controlled. This reduces the risk of trying such a system.

Vendors are also adding new services, particularly document delivery. As the market grows, more players will enter the marketplace; this will bring new mixes of services and a range of pricing models. The theoretical pricing models range from the establishment of electronic rights brokers to the utilization of a shared-cost distribution system, which is used by many present electronic newsletters. A key difference in these models is their assumption about the need for remuneration. This is a critical issue because of the current serials crisis and the Internet's tradition of sharing. We need to try to develop pricing models that can reduce the financial burden of academic libraries. Any change will not be easy. Not only do commercial publishers depend on this revenue, but many scholarly societies do as well. The important point is that there is now a window of opportunity for experiments—even radical ones.

*Goal Three: Usable Systems*

A wide range of usability issues exist. Depending on the subject area they are searching in, users will range from beginners to experts, and their information needs will range from specific factual questions to broad topical research. All the problems of traditional reference work (i.e., matching users to appropriate information sources) remain in the online environment.

*Objective: Integrate Systems for Easier Use.*   Library experience has shown that users want one easy-to-use system that is available locally. If the user has computing equipment, this means integrating systems at the desktop. Even more challenging is the notion that desktop integration includes copying data into applications such as word processors and bibliographic formatters.

*Objective: Broaden the Role of Librarians as Educators and Consultants.*   Support for a system is critical to its usability. Support includes training, documentation, and on-demand consulting. No single method will work for all users or all institutions, but it is clear that users don't want to be referred from one staff member to another. One contact point for all help questions is the ideal.

These three goals are critical to widespread network use and the development of electronic information as a public good. With these goals in mind, the next step is to look at the current and future environments. What trends can be observed? What resources already exist?

## ENVIRONMENTAL ASSESSMENT

The next area of the strategic plan is a review of the current environment. This review highlights the technical, political, and social trends that are important in identifying current opportunities and challenges. The breadth of the goals set above requires some understanding of a wide range of events in electronic information and scholarly communication, not just networking. There is no simple pattern to these trends; some overlap and others conflict.

## The Continued Growth of Computing Systems

### NREN

Computing systems have already altered significant elements of the information economy. The last critical piece for an information revolution is digital networking—the ability to send complex information, including sound and graphics, over a network. The NREN is key to this development.

The most common analogy used to describe this technological trend comes from the development of the automobile. Initially, the car simply replaced the horse for most uses, but slowly people began to travel more than they had before. To support increased travel, many more roads were built, and, eventually, superhighways were put in place. The resulting road system allowed the development of transportation-intensive environments such as the suburbs, which could not have been spawned without cars.[11] In many ways, the Internet is an early "data superhighway," and we may consider the NREN to be our interstate highway program.

### More Electronic Media

*1. Present media are converting to digital formats.* The increasing use of digital technology is happening in all areas, from technical information, to entertainment, to education. Digital technology is becoming the medium of choice for the capture, editing, storage, and transmission of information in all media formats. In music, compact discs have almost eliminated vinyl records in just a few years. Digital tape and digital television are the next wave.

The Internet is designed to handle large amounts of digitally encoded information, not only the dense data sets of physicists, but also non-scientific textual and graphic data that include all types of information. Before modern networking, bulk transport of digital information involved mailing a magnetic tape, a CD-ROM disc, or a similar physical item. Magnetic tapes and other physical storage formats will still have their place, but now a whole new communication channel is available; the rapid growth of network traffic and the burgeoning number of network users suggest that people are more than ready for it.

*2. New electronic information formats are appearing.* These new information formats range from fairly ephemeral bulletin board messages to peer-reviewed electronic journals. A good summary of recent developments is provided by Linda Langschied.[12]

With increased use of computer bulletin boards, information overload is becoming a serious problem, and the lack of filtering tools to handle large volumes of information is problematic.

Electronic newsletters are like edited bulletin boards. By reading these publications, subscribers can keep up with current topics. The low cost and informal nature of these newsletters fills a gap between totally open bulletin boards and formal publications. Electronic newsletters are done by volunteers, but some of them have been around for years. In most cases, these newsletters lack any formal structure, and they depend totally on volunteer authors for their existence.

With regard to electronic journals, at present the trend is not to duplicate present paper journals, but rather to take advantage of networks to explore new journal formats. Article submission and review is generally done via e-mail. Electronic journals typically have a more rapid publication timetable than print journals. Frequently, the information is also less formal, being more like a preprint than like a traditional journal article; however, some refereed electronic journals publish articles that are like traditional articles.

One of the most famous electronic journals is *PSYCOLOQUY*, a refereed journal that is sponsored on a trial basis by the American Psychological Association.

Another journal of special import to the library world is *The Public-Access Computer Systems Review*, edited by Charles Bailey, which creates a more formal companion to the LISTSERV, PACS-L. (To subscribe to PACS-L, send a message "SUBSCRIBE PACS-L First Name Last Name" to the address: LISTSERV@UHUPVM1.UH.EDU.)

*More Users*

As the Internet grows, so will the overall electronic marketplace, increasing the number and type of library users on the network.

Depending on the type of library, this increase will be felt in different ways. However, at least one of the following factors will apply to almost every library.

*1.    There are a growing number of users.*    New services bring new users, and most electronic services are very good at attracting users. This effect is not limited to the Internet; local databases and CD-ROM systems are very popular today.

*2.    There is a wider range of user experience and comfort with sophisticated platforms.*    While high-end users in research centers are rapidly migrating to graphical interfaces such as X Windows that run on high-speed networks, some users still have dumb terminals and dial-up connections. (In fact, some of them are high-end users operating at home instead of at work.) Computing developments are likely to continue at a fast pace for at least another decade, and this will increase the disparity between high-end and low-end users.

*3.    There is a broader distribution of users.*    Anyone in the world is now a potential library user, and many of the world's libraries are potential service providers. This has been true to some extent for a long time, but the network now makes it much easier to use remote library systems and services. In addition, some institutions are establishing programs that require libraries to support remote users. Academic institutions are increasingly adding evening programs and distance learning programs. This may even expand as networking allows institutions to sell their services more effectively over great distances—and library services will often be part of the package. Several states have been building statewide resource sharing programs with varying levels of incentives to get libraries to join. Recently, programs in North Carolina and New York have included Internet access as the means to link libraries.

Such changes generally increase both the size and heterogeneity of the active user population, which then impacts facilities, equipment, and staffing. Perhaps the most difficult challenge is the training and support this growing user population will require.

## Scholarly Communication is Increasingly Computerized

Formal printed journals are very resistant to change, but most scholarly communication has always taken place outside of journals.

*Scholarly Communication is Increasingly Multimedia.*   In the area of technical information, the results of research now often produce complex databases or multimedia presentations that cannot be accurately published in any print format. Increasingly, computers are used to produce results as images rather than as large tables of numbers. For example, instead of a table of binding values, a conference presentation may include a computer simulation of the active site of an enzyme during binding. As was discussed earlier, all media are moving towards digital technologies.

*More Research Involves Groups.*   An early role of the Internet was to meet the changing needs of scholarly research and communication. More recently, an increasing number of collaborative projects, particularly those using large and expensive resources, require that these resources be shared. Such resources include supercomputers, major telescopes, and large databases.

Sharing these resources has always been difficult, but the Internet has permitted significant improvements to occur. Now, we are even beginning to see research efforts that are deliberately designed to use networks and distributed computing facilities. The Human Genome Initiative (HGI) hopes to completely analyze human DNA, and the work will be done at hundreds of sites. The entire database may never be collected at one site.

Few examples are of this scale, but it is clear that "groupwork" is an increasing trend. Although this drive started in the sciences and is strongest there, it is happening in other fields. As the humanities gather large text files and historical databases, they are increasingly using networks both for building and providing access to shared text collections.

*Scholarly Communication is Increasingly Time Sensitive.*   Another change is the need for ever faster communication in the sciences and medicine. The most well-known example of the breakdown of traditional paper publishing came in 1987 with the discovery of superconductivity at higher temperatures. Journals were quickly flooded with articles, delaying publication. Scientists used electronic mail for regular communication, and they published articles for formal recognition of their work.[13]

*The Invisible College is Going Online.*   The general increase in networked communications is already causing some broader effects. The famous "invisible college" has become much more visible and accessible in the Internet environment. Bulletin boards and mailing lists are more open than personal meetings at conferences.

*The Pressures on Traditional Scholarly Publishing will Increase.*   The effect of the Internet on scholarly publishing is fairly indirect, but it cannot be ignored. This is particularly true in scientific and technical areas where the present journal publishing system is strained—if not broken—at least from the viewpoint of academic libraries. The serious problems with the present system make both librarians and publishers more willing to look at new—and maybe risky—alternatives such as document delivery and electronic journals. These alternatives often involve the Internet, so a basic review of scholarly publishing and its future is important for Internet planning.

The immediate problem is, as usual, related to money. Libraries feel pressed to the wall by constantly increasing journal prices. These price increases are due to several factors, including the commercialization of publishing and the increasing number of articles. The number of published articles has continued to grow at about 13% each year. It now totals over 6,000 articles per day. Often describing a small research step, journal article publication seems more driven by authors' recognition needs than by scholars' information needs. The increasing race to claim credit and to earn promotions and grants generates more articles each year. Some of this pressure to publish is transferred to libraries as faculty want the journals they publish in to be available. The push to purchase what is published, rather than what is read, leads to very low journal use rates.[14]

On the other hand, the importance of the print literature for communication is decreasing. Published journals have never been the sole source of information for scholars; however, as discussed earlier, the use of electronic alternatives seems to be growing. The Internet is increasing this growth by allowing more and more scholars to bypass journals in answering their specialized information needs.

This split between electronic communication and formal print publication exacerbates journal pricing problems.

The severe problems of the present system are encouraging publishers and libraries to consider electronic alternatives to traditional journal publishing. Publishers feel pressured both by subscription cancellations and by the knowledge that they must get into electronic publishing eventually. In the long run, publishers are fairly certain that electronic articles will become widely accepted. As scholars communicate electronically, it seems inevitable. If a publisher is not ready to move when the time comes, it could go out of business. So, there is a need to develop electronic alternatives, and the Internet seems to bring the time for action much closer.

*The Internet Supports Document Delivery.*   Can the Internet also help with some transitional technologies to make change easier or less risky? Certainly, document delivery is aided by the Internet. Historically, "access" meant interlibrary loan, usually under fair use provisions. ILL is normally far too slow to be considered a good replacement for ownership, and users with ILL experience are often suspicious when libraries proclaim access as a goal.

With the Internet, a new level of access is possible. If a table of contents can be browsed online and documents printed locally within hours, reasonable access might really be achieved. CARL started offering a document delivery service in 1991, and OCLC plans to market a Faxon service starting in 1992. These services pay use fees to publishers through the Copyright Clearance Center.

In theory, this has some benefits to both libraries and publishers. If a library can no longer afford a subscription to everything, it can still buy needed articles. For libraries, such a purchase meets user demands without a requiring a subscription. For publishers, it is some revenue as opposed to none. However, document delivery is not a long-term solution unless its use rapidly expands, profits increase, and user costs drop. Libraries' materials budgets will simply be split between subscriptions and on-demand purchases.

If publishers charge higher prices, they will simply force more ILL traffic (and encourage scholars to get copies from their colleagues). Only if overall demand increases will more revenue be generated.

## Changes in Online Information Systems

Research into new retrieval systems, such as WAIS (Wide-Area Information Servers) and "knowbots," will increase the demand for all resources, network bandwidth, processing power, and document delivery.

### Direct Sales to Users

Encyclopedias, magazine subscriptions, and book clubs have already targeted the home market. Now, multimedia computers and CD-ROM bookshelf packages are aimed at the same market, and they are beginning to compete with pay-per-view cable and satellite systems. These other services may have an uneasy relationship with libraries, raising new questions about tax-supported institutions competing with the private sector. On the positive side, the growth of the electronic market is critical in making electronic scholarly and specialty publishing viable. The CARL system option that lets you enter your VISA number is clearly aimed at users. Faxon also is looking at sales both through libraries and direct to users.

## Impact of Networking on Libraries

The development of the Internet also has some direct effects that are peculiar to libraries.

### The Internet Increases Pressure on Catalogs

As more services become available on the Internet, decisions about what a catalog should be become critical. There are several aspects to these decisions.

*1.   How should a library handle materials it has access to, but does not own or control?*   For example, some libraries have already taken the step of loading tapes for the Center for Research Libraries' (CRL) collections.

Another example is that ten libraries in a consortia each buy part of a large microform collection and agree to have reciprocal borrowing privileges. A magnetic tape is available with complete catalog records. Should all sections be loaded in each local catalog? Should only a summary record be loaded for the sections held by the other members of the consortia? If a library also has the ability to mount databases other than the catalog, should some of these collections be mounted as separate databases?

*2. What cataloging should a library provide for new forms of electronic material such as bulletin boards, CD-ROMS, and locally mounted databases?*   How about archiving? These issues go beyond the first question because the new formats include information that is much harder to control. The catalog has been the heart of the library. Automated systems have underscored this as integrated systems subsume what were once separate files for item and serials check-in records. But it is well known that this heart has serious problems. Perhaps only 3% of the item-level information of a collection is available. This percentage will be increased by both locally mounted databases and network access to remote databases. Present technology forces us to make these separate databases.

During the 1980s, progressive sites expanded their online access with locally mounted databases. In some of these sites, the catalog already accounts for a minority of all searches. The catalog, in fact, becomes more and more a locating tool for known items, and subject searching becomes concentrated in other files. By 1995, basically every commonly used index will be available in multiple electronic formats; every local catalog of holdings will have this status.

Because economics do not favor locally mounting all desired files, the big quest for the 1990s will be to develop common interfaces across disparate systems. In some cases, consortia will be an approach, but even the largest state systems seem currently unable to license all needed files.

## Access to Split Collections

Experience with split catalogs and index information in online and paper formats shows that users seldom venture into paper backfiles. If we don't put something online, users will often utilize a less appropriate— but more available—resource. At some point in the growth of online indexing, any paper index may have a very high per-use cost.

## Library Networks Versus the Internet

A number of library vendors have their own networks, and they need to recover costs for these networks. At the same time, Internet regional networks are making strong pitches to institutions and their libraries to use the Internet for connectivity to these vendors. For many research libraries, the Internet is already a viable substitute for library networks such as OCLC. Can the Internet serve all library needs, and, if so, how should a migration to the Internet take place?

## Organizational Pressures Will Increase

### Budgeting During Transitional Times

The Internet will require libraries to do much more serious planning for future electronic services. One comment in the RLG study was that provosts felt strongly that libraries would have to propose changes in their operations in order to support new activities because budgets would basically be flat. Since academic libraries can no longer afford all the journals desired by the faculty, they are examining a range of alternatives.

Although discussions of "access versus ownership" have gone on for years, the time has come for academic librarians, university administrators, and faculty members to negotiate some hard compromises, especially with regard to the "publish or perish" reward system and its inherent (and seemingly insatiable) appetite for journal subscriptions. As new services become possible, key questions about where resource and staff dollars are to be spent must be made.

### The Internet Model is NOT a Traditional Library Model

As noted above, there is somewhat of a culture clash between the Internet model and that embraced by traditional libraries. To reconcile these two models, differences need to be recognized and respected while the best efforts at compromise are made on all sides.

In addition to "the pilot project" versus "the fully mature product" conundrum described above, another difference is that the Internet has a rapidly changing technical base. It is not possible for anyone to keep up with it all; work groups must usually include both technical staff and managers—usually from different units. This is often viewed as requiring matrix management, which certainly does not fit within the traditional library hierarchy.

*Leveling Effect of E-Mail*

Research about e-mail use indicates that a leveling effect occurs that greatly weakens traditional hierarchies.[15]

This is likely to affect organizational communication and possibly enhance certain organizational structures. The message seems to be that rigid hierarchies don't fit well with electronic mail.

This change seems likely to be permanent since the telephone did similar things, "The phone overnight cut right through the nineteenth century etiquette that you don't speak to anyone unless you've been introduced."[16] If we have a long period of e-mail use before voice mail use becomes widespread, we may have to learn to write again.

*We Are Not Autonomous*

The Internet is not a library network, nor a supercomputer network, nor a medical network. No single type of network use is likely to dominate, and the most effective network projects will include many different groups working together.

## The Internet and Society

The growth of high-speed networking will also have some general and far-reaching impacts on our nation and our society. Many of the long-term effects will depend on the success libraries have with making the technology work for the good of society. Other effects, however, are already present, and the network simply increases the pace of change.

*Copyright, Ownership, and Networking*

Information has become a big market, with electronic products providing much of the growth. This has resulted in international discussions on software piracy, users rights, and "look and feel" lawsuits—all of which involve fundamental questions about when information should become property. This question of information as property goes well beyond libraries, and its answer will affect society even more critically as we really do enter an information age.

For information to become marketable property, it must be embodied in something that can be measured and charged for, and there must be a way to do this economically. Traditionally, information was something physical such as a book, film, or disk; however, this is changing: "The printing press ... converted thought into things. With a little help from copyright, these things became property. The Network de-materializes thought, and converts it instead into an event."[17] With computer networks, it is necessary to control distribution—not production—if you wish to market information. This is because anything on the network can be reproduced at almost no cost. Since a basic precept of the Internet is to facilitate communication, any real physical control becomes very difficult.

From a publisher's viewpoint, copying has been a problem with software and photocopies, but electronic articles are even more difficult to control. Any computer can make a copy, and the copy can easily be disguised so that it must actually be examined to know that it is a copy. Every computer on the Internet is a high-speed copier with abilities that dwarf most contemporary photocopiers. Distribution is equally open. If someone wishes to send a document, it is very hard to stop them without reading and analyzing every file that is transmitted on the network. Although work is being done on software to control copying, it seems unlikely that any form of document control will be more successful than controls on copying software were.

If technical solutions are not viable, any control system will depend heavily on institutional enforcement and individual cooperation—or the Internet as we know it will be destroyed by efforts to police it. User cooperation is critical, but how likely is it? It is almost certainly a function of cost. If users can get something cheaply, they are less likely to bother going around legal channels. High costs encourage black markets, as they always have.

## Privacy Issues in a Networked World

It seems likely that increased communication will tend to remove the last few shreds of privacy that remain. It is possible that this will bring about increased demand for some forms of privacy. The growing volume of electronic mail and junk fax may result in users wanting the network equivalent of unlisted numbers. Some predict that "mail filters and automatic call screening will be sure bets in the decade ahead."[18] If any significant number of users try to build one-way walls around themselves, much of the benefit of the Internet's present openness will be lost; however, some kind of privacy tools will be necessary.

*The NREN and National Sovereignty*

Open communication has raised a number of issues as nations consider information to be an increasingly important resource. With the Internet, national borders simply disappear for users. The positive side of this is well understood; however, if countries decide to protect research results paid for with tax dollars, trade wars could break out or governments could become involved in other ways.

## ISSUES AND OPPORTUNITIES FOR LIBRARIES

### Training and Support for an Increasing Number of Users

As networked access reaches libraries, there will be an increasing need for librarians to be trainers and educators. As "lifelong learning" becomes the watchword of the decade, it is clear that librarians will be called upon to share the wealth of networked information with the millions of citizens engaged in their own continuing education efforts.

With this new range of users and new range of services comes a new range of support issues. As noted previously, libraries have dealt with the introduction of new technologies to society before. Networks pose a new level of challenge because the users and systems may both be located at a distance from the library. For example, a public library offering Internet dial-up access could have a phone question from someone trying to access a remote catalog.

Again there are several large issues:

*1.    Who provides support and how can this be shared with Internet regional networks, vendors, university campuses, and others?* It must be assumed that many of these patrons will not be affiliated with an organization that provides such access and support. Public libraries are not currently funded to provide such deep and wide support; indeed, they suffer budgetary cutbacks and constraints all the time. Support should include: (1) how to get into a system, (2) use of basic Internet tools, (3) searching remote systems, (4) downloading records, and (5) reformatting citations into usable form.

*2. How should we train the support personnel?* In this area, application-dependent tool skills have a very short half-life! Staff who do well with systems they can see may have trouble with users who are describing a problem from outside the library. An "electronic conceptual framework" becomes a prerequisite to providing network support.

*3. How much emphasis do we put on help functions, documentation, and training?* It is clear users want immediate answers to questions. Is this possible, particularly if it is necessary to have a range of tool skills such that some questions require a specialist?

The Challenge of Organizing Networked Information for Access

The Internet is a bibliographic mess and the need for tools is widely recognized. At the same time, traditional library processes will not suffice. Working with developers in other disciplines, librarians have a chance to design tools that can be used to provide better access to rapidly changing material that cannot be centrally cataloged. How do 50,000 people collaborate to produce a common catalog? Traditional library tools have not kept up with tracking these new forms of information. This is not something new, but the trend is growing. Pat Battin reported years ago how a reference librarian spent days tracing down a database that described the protein sequence of a single enzyme. This work was reported in dozens of articles and a database had been built, but no one knew how to get access to it. Naturally, the answer was found right on campus—but only after phone calls to the research sponsor.[19]

Standards are Critical to an Open Market

Librarians have spent a lot of time formulating standards, but they have been much less effective in implementing standards. Communications, data, and other standards are critical to opening up the network market, making access easy, and reducing the cost of information as vendors are forced to compete.

*Standards Will Permit New Forms of Publishing*

A complete set of standards would allow new forms of publishing to be built on the network. A variety of basic services are needed to support electronic publishing. Using standards, each service could be performed by multiple vendors. Needed services include: document production, database indexing, online searching, document supply, credit/billing, white and yellow page services, peer review, subscription services, and archival storage.

The Internet world offers a new model for standards based on pilot projects and incremental solutions. This is an area where libraries and system developers can cooperate to produce publicly available shared code that really puts standards into practice. If the network community wants a retrieval standard, we should build a few applications and give them away. This will be more powerful than any standard-related plans, discussions, or joint proposals. We can learn a lesson from Sun Microsystems about how to set standards. Sun was a vendor who started too small to enforce any standards: "Sun learned to establish defacto standards by giving the source code away.... For example, Sun virtually gave away licenses for its Network Filing System networking scheme, which had lots of bugs and some severe security problems, but it was free and so became a defacto standard overnight."[20]

Z39.50, the NISO retrieval standard for machine-to-machine communication, is perhaps the best example of an in-progress standard being designed by computer and library professionals to meet the need for a standard protocol. It is designed to allow a search interface on a local computer to search any remote database. At present, each remote system may have its own interface, causing significant training and support issues. Perhaps the easiest way to see the value of Z39.50 is to look at some of the options it would allow under a common local interface:

- Mount five years of MEDLINE on a local computer and "bulk" purchase the backfiles from a national vendor.
- Mount INSPEC locally and trade five "ports" on this system for five ports on another system that has MEDLINE mounted.
- Mount the new Faxon journal database locally, but buy documents from CARL and ISI.

Clearly, this range of purchase options begins to put databases in an environment where we can decide to get a service based on subject content, and then choose the media based on price and level of service.

## ACTION PLAN

The Internet clearly has the potential for significantly changing information access in the United States. The NREN legislation offers us an opportunity to help direct this change. Given the current environment, how can we select reasonable pathways to achieve the library goals outlined earlier?

### Lessons from Failed Visions

*No Viable Action Plans*

Perhaps the biggest lesson from past library exercises in networking is that viable action plans are critical. In reporting on the failure of the National Commission on Library and Information Services's (NCLIS) network plan, Barbara Markuson notes that, "Perhaps plans that generate support, rather than action, are the most tyrannical of all."[21] Statements of support without action do not accomplish anything, but they mislead people into believing that something was accomplished.

*Library Plans Are Not "User Centered"*

Another factor is that many library developments have been focused on the library, not the user. Even if the goal was increased user services, the focus was on library operations, and the programs were developed by librarians. Future visions must be sold not by librarians, but by users. Technology therefore must be viewed in terms of end-user services, and it is vital that libraries decide what services they will provide to meet user needs.

### Strategies to Go the Distance

By itself, the library community cannot begin to implement the ambitious program outlined in this paper. Such a program is possible, however, through coordinated action with other partners. The excitement of the NREN is already contagious, and it can be built upon. Action coalitions are the key to progress. Recently, segments of the library community have been making great strides in such collaborative efforts. Some issues surrounding health sciences library partnerships were discussed at this year's OCLC Library Directors' Seminar in Portland, Oregon.[22]

*Basic Principles for Libraries*

1.　Collaboration and partnership with users, network specialists, and information providers are critical. The exact team members needed will depend on the type of library involved.
2.　Libraries will need to focus on teaching more and doing fewer mediated searches.
3.　Librarians need to get outside of libraries and become knowledgeable about their institutional environment.
4.　Libraries need to decide the nature of their business. In particular, libraries need to move away from being largely "accumulators and transporters" to becoming architects of tools and systems that help institutions solve problems by improving each library user's ability to productively utilize information resources.

*Build Coalitions*

In order to be effective, coalitions must comprise not only academic libraries, but entire universities; not public libraries, but local governments; and not school libraries, but whole educational districts. The key will be to forge consensus around basic goals but to compromise on everything else!

There are already several examples of these kinds of coalitions, and they are organizations we can work with. The broad initiatives required to reach this exciting future will not come from libraries alone.

As late as 1988, the word "networking" in a library publication meant library networks. To engage in the information business, we must join with other providers to create the kind of coalitions that can build pilot projects and develop broad support. No one solution will accomplish everything mentioned here; many solutions are needed. We already have some successful examples.

The IAIMS (Integrated Academic Information Management System) program of the National Library of Medicine exemplifies successful cooperation among information organizations. Its purpose is "to assist health-related schools, organizations and libraries in planning, developing and implementing computer systems that make it possible for health care workers to gain access to the information they need for problem solving and learning."[23] The University of Washington Health Sciences Center has recently joined the IAIMS Consortium. This consortium includes the medical centers of Columbia University, Duke University, Georgetown University, the Oregon Health Sciences University, the University of Cincinnati, and the University of Michigan.

The goals that we set earlier came from library organizations, but they are reflected in similar goals within NSFNET planning. FARNET (Federation of American Research Networks) is an organization composed of regional networks, communications vendors, and computer vendors. Eric Hood, Executive Director of the Northwest Academic Computing Consortium (NWACC) and current president of FARNET, has stated six principles for the development of the NREN.[24] Paraphrasing, they are:

1. Secure the right of equal access to our nation's information resources.
2. Provide ubiquitous access and universal connectivity to our nation's information resources.
3. Give priority to network reliability, performance, and end-to-end usability.
4. Relax unnecessary restrictions on the delivery of commercial services across the NSFNET and the emerging NREN.
5. Conduct further research on high performance computing, including key technologies, as a high priority.
6. Continue close collaboration with industry, government, and academia; this is critical to realizing the NREN vision.

Access to electronic information within libraries is becoming critical to their continued success, and, possibly, to the entire concept of an informed citizenry. If electronic information becomes a strictly commercial entity with no general access, we will have lost our birthright. Is the Internet the right tool to use in providing this access? The answer seems to be "Yes"—if we study the present Internet and work together to articulate a common vision for, and a path for reaching, an open, national library without walls.

## NOTES

1.  Stephen C. Hall, "The Four Stages of National Research and Education Network Growth," *EDUCOM Review* 26 (Spring 1991): 21

2.  Jonathan Kochmer, *User Services Internet Resources Guide* (Bellevue, WA: NorthWestNet Academic Computing Consortium, Inc., 1991). Order from: NorthWestNet, NUSIRG Orders, 15400 SE 30th Place, Suite 202, Bellevue, WA 98007; $20.

3.  Robert J. Spinrad, "The Electronic University," *EDUCOM* Bulletin 18, nos. 3/4 (1983): 4-8.

4.  Richard M. Dougherty and Carol Hughes, *Preferred Futures for Libraries: A Summary of Six Workshops With University Provosts and Library Directors* (Mountain View, CA: The Research Libraries Group, Inc., 1991), 11.

5. Henriette D. Avram, *Library of Congress Network Advisory Committee: Introduction to NAC and Areas of Concern*, Network Planning Paper 18 (Washington, DC: Network Development and MARC Standards Office, Library of Congress, 1989), 14.

6.  Dougherty and Hughes, *Preferred Futures for Libraries*, 11.

7.  Al Gore, "Infrastructure for the Global Village," *Scientific American* 265 (September 1991): 151.

8.  John N. Berry III, "NREN and the Information Explosion," *Library Journal* 117 (1 February 1992): 6.

9.  Eric Hood, "Developing NREN" (Paper presented at the University of Washington Computer Fair, 18 March 1992).

10.  *Serials Review* 18, nos. 1-2 (1992).

11.  Thomas W. Malone and John F. Rockart, "Computers, Networks and the Corporation," *Scientific American* 265 (September 1991): 133.

12.  Linda Langschied, "The Changing Shape of the Electronic Journal," *Serials Review* 17, no. 3 (1991): 7-14.

13.  Melvin Kranzberg, "Interdependence of Scientific and Technological Information and Its Relation to Public Decision Making," *The Annals of the American Academy of Political and Social Science* 495 (January 1988): 37.

14.  Langschied, "The Changing Shape of the Electronic Journal," 9.

15.  Lee Sproull and Sara Kiesler, "Computers, Networks and Work," *Scientific American* 265 (September 1991): 116-123.

16.  William Grimes, "Ahoy! The Great Mystery of the Simple 'Hello' Is Solved," *New York Times*, 6 March 1992, sec. B, 1.

17.  Robert Kost, "Technology Giveth …," *Serials Review* 18, nos. 1-2 (1992): 69.

18.  Paul Saffo, "Personal Computers Will Make Solitude a Scarce Resource," *InfoWorld* 13 (23 December 1991): 37.

19.  Pat Battin, "The Electronic Library—A Vision for the Future," *EDUCOM Bulletin* 19, no. 2 (1984): 12-17, 34.

20.    Arnold Hirshon, "Vision, Focus, and Technology In Academic Research Libraries: 1971 to 2001," *Advances in Library Automation and Networking* 2 (1988): 215.

21.    Barbara Evans Markuson, *Issues in National Library Network Development: An Overview*, Network Planning Paper 12 (Washington, DC: Network Development and MARC Standards Office, Library of Congress, 1985), 11.

22.    Sherrilynne Fuller, "Innovations in Health Sciences Libraries: Present and Future" (Paper presented at the OCLC Library Directors Seminar, 3 March 1992).

23.    "UW Accepted Into IAIMS Consortium," *Vital Links* 2 (April 1992): 3.

24.    Hood, "Developing NREN."

## AN INTERNET BIBLIOGRAPHY

### Compiled by Dorothy D. Smith


Anderson, Bart, Bryan Costales, Harry Henderson, and The Waite Group. *UNIX Communications*. 2nd ed. Carmel, IN: Howard W. Sams, 1991.

Britten, William A. "BITNET and the Internet: Scholarly Networks for Librarians." *College & Research Libraries News* 51 (February 1990): 103-107.

Comer, Douglas. *Internetworking with TCP/IP: Volume 1: Principles, Protocols, and Architecture*. 2nd ed. Englewood Cliffs, NJ: Prentice-Hall, 1991.

Farley, Laine, ed. *Library Resources on the Internet: Strategies for Selection and Use*. Chicago: RASD/MARS, American Library Association, 1991. Available by anonymous FTP from dla.ucop.edu; directory: pub/internet; file name: libcat-guide.

Frey, Donnalyn, and Rick Adams. *!%@:: A Directory of Electronic Mail Addressing and Networks*. 2nd ed. Sebastopol, CA: O'Reilly and Associates, 1990.

Kalin, Sally W., and Roy Tennant. "Beyond OPACS ... the Wealth of Information Resources on the Internet." *Database* 14 (August 1991): 28-33.

Kehoe, Brendan P. *Zen and the Art of the Internet: A Beginner's Guide to the Internet*. Chester, PA: 1992. Available by anonymous FTP from ftp.cs.widener.edu; directory: pub/zen.

LaQuey, Tracy. L., ed. *The User's Directory of Computer Networks*. Bedford, MA: Digital Press, 1990.

NSF Network Service Center. *Internet Resource Guide*. Cambridge, MA: Network Service Center, 1989. Available by anonymous FTP from nnsc.nsf.net; directory: resource-guide. Subscription requests should be sent to: resource-guide-request@nnsc.nsf.net, or contact the NNSC at (617) 873-3400.

Quarterman, John S. *The Matrix: Computer Networks and Conferencing Systems Worldwide*. Bedford, MA: Digital Press, 1990.

Raeder, Aggi W., and Karen L. Andrews. "Searching Library Catalogs on the Internet: A Survey," *Database Searcher* 6 (September 1990): 16-31.

Stoll, Clifford. *The Cuckoo's Egg: Tracking a Spy Through the Maze of Computer Espionage*. New York: Doubleday, 1989.

# ELECTRONIC DOCUMENT DELIVERY:
## AN OVERVIEW WITH A REPORT ON
## EXPERIMENTAL AGRICULTURAL PROJECTS

John Ulmschneider and Tracy M. Casorso

## OVERVIEW

Libraries traditionally store, manage, and deliver physical packages, such as paper documents, maps, audio disks, and video cassettes. This orientation to physical packages profoundly and intimately shapes libraries' organizational structures and services. Yet, in the past three years, powerful new electronic technologies have opened the way to redefining this orientation to physical packages, particularly in interlibrary loan and document delivery services.

Until quite recently, electronic technologies have been used in libraries chiefly to access physical packages (e.g., online catalogs and citation databases). Applications of electronic technologies to materials themselves have evolved more slowly. The principal examples have been experimental, seeking to answer fundamental questions about the usefulness of electronic technologies, such as CD-ROM,

**Advances in Library Automation and Networking, Volume 5, pages 105-144.**
**Copyright © 1994 by JAI Press Inc.**
**All rights of reproduction in any form reserved.**
**ISBN: 1-55938-510-3**

network-based publishing, scanning, and videodisc technologies, for the storage, distribution, and preservation of library materials. This work is ongoing and accelerating; however, electronic materials still represent a small percentage of library collections. Nevertheless, electronic formats have become important to librarians for a number of reasons. In particular, commercial and library-based document delivery systems have concluded that electronic document formats make ideal information delivery mechanisms, which meet speed and quality requirements better than any other means.

## What Is an Electronic Document?

It is useful to establish guidelines to distinguish between electronic documents and other electronic entities. It is important at the outset to recognize that no consensus exists about the definition of an electronic document. For example, ongoing efforts within the library and computing communities to develop a universally unique document ID consider all electronic entities residing as files on computers (e.g., compiled programs, graphical images and sounds, source code, text files, and video) to be documents that are eligible for document IDs.

In general, we consider electronic documents to fall into four classifications or types. These classifications exclude computer programs and other electronic entities that act upon or transform other electronic entities, but include most other types of electronic files.

1. *Facsimile:* Group III and Group IV facsimile are digital technologies. Fax machines contain scanners that capture the document image through digitization, transmit the image through analog translation, reconstruct the image, and print it digitally. Consequently, whenever a document is held in a fax machine, it exists as a digitized image. Many facsimile machines take advantage of the image's digital format: they provide buffer memory to store received documents or queue up outgoing documents for optimal transmission times. They also can connect to computers or local area networks to receive facsimile transmission directly from computers.

2. *Full-text:* For many librarians, systems and files containing the complete text of documents in ASCII format epitomize the concept of an electronic document. In such systems, full-text means

that the document contains only characters that can be expressed through the ASCII character set (or modest extensions of the ASCII character set). They do not contain formatting information, images, or sounds. Full-text files represent the lowest common denominator for electronic documents. They are supported by the most basic terminal devices, they can be imported into the native file format of nearly all application programs used on desktop computers, and they can be transmitted within an acceptable time through ordinary analog telephone lines. Because most libraries require this lowest common denominator access to electronic documents to meet their users' needs, many commercial and nonprofit full-text electronic document initiatives have created a substantial body of ASCII material over the past decade.

3.  *Digitized text:*   In the document delivery context, digitized text has come to have a very narrow and specific definition. Digitized text generally refers to the machine-readable picture of a printed page that results from scanning printed materials and capturing the output as a bit-mapped image. Insofar as scanned pictures are bit-mapped images and are not structured or in ASCII format, they might be classified as facsimile-like in format, although they differ in important ways from facsimile images. Digitized document pages capture all the elements of a printed page: graphs, pictures, tables, and text as well as all of the special formatting used in the presentation of the text. But since the digitized page is a picture (a bit-mapped image), it cannot be treated as textual data for search and retrieval purposes.

4.  *Compound documents:*   The content of compound documents is unrestricted (not limited to ASCII text). The characteristics of compound documents are captured through highly structured file formats and formatting languages. Compound documents combine the complete data content of digitized documents with information that distinguishes various elements in a document. For example, text is distinguished from other elements such as graphs and pictures. Consequently, compound documents permit computer programs to treat the different elements in appropriate ways (e.g., to build retrieval indexes using a document's textual elements). In many cases, compound documents can be printed, but they also may exist in a form that does not allow paper expression (e.g., they may contain hypertext or image elements).

There is growing technical and procedural agreement about standards for the structure and content of documents, coalescing around the Standardized General Markup Language standard (SGML). However, there is little maturation evident in the development of similar standards for the typographical appearance of documents for printing (although there are efforts underway in Editable Postscript, Page Interchange Language, and others) or for capturing images, video, sound, and hypertext attributes. Consequently, not all documents are accessible without special (or even proprietary) hardware and software.

As pictures of pages, digitized images fall into a category of materials readily understood by libraries: image data. Audio data, maps, micrographics, photographs, slides, and video are all image data resembling digitized images, but they are recorded in analog form (except for audio CDs). These materials represent particular difficulties for users, because they generally require that the user travel to the library to use them, and they often require special equipment only available in the library.

By contrast, the designers and users of digitized images and other electronic documents have been guided by the requirement for remote access and the need to support standard equipment that is widely available to users. For this reason, as digital formats expand to include traditional image materials such as photographs, libraries will be able to apply systems designed for delivery of electronic documents to these materials as well.

## Why Develop Electronic Document Delivery?

Despite the paucity of available materials in electronic form, the use of electronic technologies for the delivery of library materials has evolved quickly and has become a highly visible library service for patrons. Commercial vendors have aggressively pursued electronic delivery of materials, and libraries also have begun to invest in the hardware, software, and human resources needed to support electronic delivery services. In the last three years, two major commercial document delivery services based on electronic ordering and facsimile delivery (augmented by some direct electronic delivery) have emerged, with several others announcing their intention to enter the market during 1992 and 1993. Library projects related to electronic delivery of materials have proliferated rapidly. Three motives underlay this rapid expansion and fuel the intense interest that libraries have in these developments.

## Economic Motive

Almost every description of the future gigabit National Research and Education Network (NREN) that appears in the popular press starts off with something akin to the following quote in the *New York Times*: "Scientists will have instant access to computerized libraries the size of the Library of Congress."[1]

Commercial suppliers of documents for the science and technology research communities have responded to this vision of access to research information, and have vigorously pursued the electronic ordering and delivery of materials. They recognize a market opportunity because scientific and technical research, particularly private sector research, depends on and can pay for rapid delivery of information in high-quality formats. Libraries are subject to similar economic pressures to deliver high-quality materials rapidly to the research communities they serve. In addition, the high costs of periodical literature, particularly in science and technology disciplines, mandate efficient utilization of purchased materials and effective arrangements for sharing materials. Electronic document delivery strengthens ILL arrangements with much faster, more flexible delivery of materials in high-quality formats.

## Service Motive

The confluence of the demand for prompt delivery of library materials to researchers, the emergence of powerful desktop computers and high-speed telecommunications networks, and the evolving sophistication of researchers in the application of computers to research problems have created a demand to make the access and delivery of library materials a seamless component of the scientist's research function. Rapid access to research information and the delivery of this information directly to the researcher's workstation in a value-added, machine-readable format will only increase the demand for libraries to provide such services.

The delivery of source documents is largely contingent on the responsiveness of the document supplier, whether it is a lending library, a local library, or a commercial service. Electronic document delivery helps to remove obstacles that prevent the effective delivery of library materials from the library to the researcher and from one library to another. However, for users to realize the full benefits of electronic document delivery services, ILL and document delivery services must address persistent inefficient internal processing procedures that have historically accounted for long turnaround times.

### Collection Development Motive

Although physical materials overwhelmingly dominate library operations today, librarians recognize the importance of and growth potential for electronic documents. A number of journals, including peer-reviewed journals of considerable importance to their subject fields, are now published electronically as ASCII text files.[2] Experimental publication efforts aim to expand scholarly electronic publishing beyond the limitations of ASCII text, employing markup languages such as SGML, hypertext extensions, and graphical elements to create wholly new mediums that literally cannot exist on paper.[3] These materials will increase their presence in library collections during the next decade, and their importance to users likely will be greater than their numbers indicate. Libraries require tools to store, retrieve, and distribute these materials. Research and development efforts involving electronic documents are intended to create just such tools.

### Evolution of Technology

The rapid evolution of electronic storage and transmission technologies are the principal catalysts for new electronic document delivery initiatives. In 1985, early capabilities for digitization, distribution, and utilization of materials by the end user did not hold much promise for large-scale implementation. However, by 1988 (just three years later), data communication, optical storage, and scanning technologies had evolved to the point that organizations could undertake serious, large-scale experiments with electronic storage and delivery. In particular, the unexpectedly rapid growth of and improvement in global computer networks, culminating in the Internet, provided electronic delivery channels with the bandwidth and speed to rival local data communication systems.

## What Is Electronic Document Delivery?

Electronic document delivery comprises three essential components.

1. *Electronic finding and ordering service:* The delivery of items via facsimile or computer networks only modestly improves delivery times over paper-based delivery methods because it cannot speed up either the time needed to find a desired item or the time required to order it. Effective electronic document delivery requires use of a system that permits users to quickly identify needed items and conveniently order them. It combines: (1) advanced finding tools to locate items in local or remote online catalogs, citation databases, and other sources; (2) authentication and validation mechanisms; and (3) accounting systems. The goal is to create virtual collections of library materials that allow users to locate relevant materials, regardless of source or location, and to electronically order these materials.

2. *Electronic delivery mechanism:* The most widely used electronic delivery mechanism is Group III facsimile, primarily because of its wide availability. However, facsimile has two serious disadvantages. First, it is primarily a black-and-white imaging technique designed for textual business documents. Pictures, graphs, illustrations, and diagrams are poorly rendered, and color is not supported at all. Second, the facsimile format is not used or supported by most desktop computers (e.g., it is not used by OCR programs or graphics editing software). These disadvantages are unlikely to be overcome in the near-term future.

An ideal document delivery architecture provides delivery mechanisms that are well suited to the format of the material. The quality or intellectual content of some types of electronic information (e.g. compound documents) would be compromised by print or facsimile reproduction. Since they permit electronic information to be sent directly to user workstations, campus information systems provide a good way to deliver of this type of information.

3. *Library materials:* The delivering agent must have access to the needed materials. Most materials are stored in conventional media like print and come from library collections. A tiny, but growing, fraction of materials are available in machine-readable form in library collections or in the computers of the delivering agent.

To locate and provide requested items quickly, recent commercial efforts have concentrated both on implementing electronic finding and ordering services and on creating virtual collections of library materials. They chiefly rely on facsimile as their delivery mechanism. By contrast, library-based experiments have concentrated on implementing more sophisticated delivery mechanisms through network-accessible computer systems.

## THE AGRICULTURAL RESEARCH ENVIRONMENT

Given the publication practices of agricultural researchers and the monetary value of the research literature that they produce, agricultural research information is particularly well suited to storage and delivery using electronic technologies. In terms of its financial and general activity levels, the agricultural industry in the U.S. is massive. It is important to every state in the union, accounting for 14.9% of the gross national product (or a total of $727 billion) in 1989. This enormous economic contribution is supported by an extensive research and development structure. The U.S. government alone spent over $2.1 billion for agricultural research services in 1989, and private sector expenditures for research and development mounted into the hundreds of millions of dollars. In the state of North Carolina alone, the agricultural industry accounts for 25% of the state's gross product (about $25 billion), and the state expended $52 million on agricultural extension services in 1989. At the academic level, North Carolina State University alone spent over $66 million on agricultural research in 1989. Clearly, agricultural research represents a significant expenditure of both private and public funds, making it an attractive market for commercial publication interests and an important support service for land-grant university libraries.

The distributed nature of the agricultural research effort underscores the intense demand for high-quality, timely document delivery. Numerous agencies nationwide conduct federal and private sector research projects, including federal and private laboratories, agricultural research stations, colleges, and land-grant universities. The body of literature generated by this distributed agricultural research structure remains diverse and difficult to access. Subject areas range from agricultural economics and foreign trade to aquaculture, engineering, and the physical sciences.

Much of this research literature is published in the form of technical reports and papers. Consequently, commercial indexing services do not cover large parts of the literature. Researchers are often located at field research stations or other remote locations, far from research library collections that contain needed materials. For these reasons, the supporting information delivery system, composed of institutions as diverse as the National Agricultural Library (NAL), land-grant university and college libraries, veterinary medical school libraries, forestry libraries, USDA field libraries, and special libraries in agribusiness and industry, is highly motivated to investigate and implement new techniques and technologies to support access to the rapidly growing research literature.

Agricultural science researchers have limited options for locating and acquiring research literature. Depending on a researcher's affiliation, either traditional interlibrary loan procedures or the Regional Document Delivery Service (an ILL service extended by NAL to USDA field researchers) provide materials. In both cases, document ordering is a manual process, and document delivery depends on the U.S. mail, courier services, or facsimile. These delivery methods poorly support researchers in the agricultural sciences, and, unfortunately, a substantial body of research materials are only available this way.

## THE NATIONAL AGRICULTURAL TEXT DIGITIZING PROJECT (NATDP)

In the mid-1980s, the escalating costs of acquiring, processing, indexing and abstracting agricultural literature as well as the emergence and rapid maturation of optical storage technologies served as catalysts for the National Agricultural Library to initiate a systematic investigation into the use of digitizing and networking technologies to improve access to agriculture literature. The National Agricultural Text Digitizing Project (NATDP) is an experimental investigation into the use of optical disk technology to distribute U.S. and world literature on agricultural research and applications. The project is a cooperative initiative coordinated by the National Agricultural Library that includes 42 land-grant libraries nationwide. The project and its achievements have been discussed in more detail elsewhere.[4]

NAL undertook the NATDP and related projects to address the difficulties attendant on supporting a growing investment in agricultural research. The results from these projects substantiate high user demand for innovative document delivery systems that take advantage of computer technology. Even with the limited range of materials provided by the NATDP (data on areas such as aquaculture, Agent Orange, and acid rain) and the drawbacks of the CD-ROM delivery mechanism, survey instruments reported a very positive reception for the products, a strong demand for much broader subject coverage, and a desire for utilization of more advanced delivery technologies. In addition, services supplying particular regional needs, such as access to tobacco research literature in North Carolina, have shown strong interest in delivery mechanisms that overcome the limitations of the postal service and facsimile transmission.

## Brief History of the NATDP

The NATDP began in September 1986 as a experimental investigation into the use of optical disk technology as a way to distribute U.S. and world literature on agricultural research and application that was both timely and resistant to deterioration. The project was soon expanded into a systematic three-phase investigation into the use of digitizing and networking technologies for improving access to agriculture literature.

Phases one and two of the NATDP were an optical publishing effort to create CD-ROM disks containing scanned, digitized copies of printed agricultural research materials and to distribute copies of these CD-ROMs to institutions within the agricultural community. Efforts focused on the issues of data capture and the publication of selected full-text and image collections.

Phase one concentrated on technical requirements for carrying out the project, and it evaluated a proprietary scanning system for capturing text and images in digital format for publication on CD-ROM discs.

Phase two used the digitized collections of documents created in phase one to evaluate different indexing and retrieval software packages in order to identify the most appropriate package for retrieving both text and image data. Phase two was recently concluded, and a final report is expected during the fall of 1992.[5]

The initial NATDP study design in June 1987 recognized a need to examine alternative delivery methods for digitized images other than optical technologies. Phase three of the NATDP mandated the evaluation of alternative means of distributing digitized images to remote sites given the significant drawbacks of CD-ROM technology. As part of phase three, Clifford A. Lynch, University of California, conducted a survey of state-of-the art telecommunications options for the transmission of full text. The Lynch report considered both architectural and technical system design issues for accessing and delivering digitized text and images, and it examined the role of networking in NAL's interlibrary loan and document delivery efforts.

Recognizing NAL's role as a national resource within the agriculture community, Lynch recommended that it take the lead in investigating the application of network technologies to document delivery. In a related paper outlining the strategic issues in platform selection for the production phase of the NATDP, Lynch stated that the guiding principle for the NATDP initiative should be to use nonproprietary hardware and software base.[6]

## THE NCSU PILOT PROJECT

In early 1988, following the general design of the NATDP and the recommendations of the Lynch paper, NAL opened discussions with the NCSU Libraries and the NCSU Computing Center about an evaluation study to investigate the electronic transmission of digitized images. The participants designed a study that would put into place a demonstration project to test the technical feasibility and the administrative structures necessary to successfully capture, transmit, and receive machine-readable text at remote sites through the Internet.

This pilot project was intended as the first step of a larger investigation to determine the effectiveness of computer and network-based document delivery mechanisms for agricultural information, so it emphasized a systematic approach to the questions identified by the Lynch study. The participants anticipated that they would use the findings of the pilot project to develop a grant proposal that would expand the study to a representative subset of the land-grant community.

## Pilot Study Technical Design

In September 1989, the USDA provided the NCSU Libraries with a \$57,000 grant to carry out the evaluation study, which was supplemented by hardware, software, and human resources from the NCSU Computing Center and the NCSU Libraries. The pilot study design called for the creation and transmission of digitized images from NAL via the Internet to computers located in the NCSU Libraries. The technical design specified the utilization of nonproprietary, widely used, standard-based technologies as well as the use of established national and local networking infrastructures. It included five components:

1.  *Hardware:*  The pilot project specified a desktop computer, scanner, and PostScript-compatible printer located at each site participating in the project. NAL used its DOS-based system supporting the NATDP's high-speed scanning and printing system; NCSU used Macintosh computers, Abaton scanners, and Apple LaserWriter printers.

2.  *Standard image format:*  The project participants examined several options and agreed upon the Tagged Image File Format (TIFF) as the file format standard. TIFF is widely supported by scanning, digitizing, and image editing software as well as by optical character recognition software. Early on in the course of the NATDP, NAL had established a high-throughput, production operation for scanning and producing CD-ROMs containing images of the scanned materials. Although capable of high speed and exceptional quality, the equipment and software was proprietary and did not support the standard image format identified by the pilot project. The primary contractor for the equipment provided software to translate the proprietary format of the scanned images into TIFF.

3.  *High-speed data communications link:*  Both NAL and the NCSU Libraries required high-bandwidth connections from the libraries to their local Internet nodes to accomplish the transfer of scanned images. The participants agreed to use existing Internet links between North Carolina and Washington, D.C. to transfer images.

4.  *A host computer at the recipient site:*  To ensure round-the-clock availability, sufficient disk storage, and access from all sites on campus, the NCSU Computing Center established one of its VAX computers, running under Ultrix, as the receiving node for images

from NAL. From that node, computers in the NCSU Libraries could pick up the images at any time and from any location on the campus network.

5. *Compression:* The participants initially transferred uncompressed image files to test the time required to transmit scanned images of entire journal articles. Since the average journal article consisted of eight megabytes of scanned data, even high-speed transmission of the files took an unacceptable length of time. The participants selected a DOS-based shareware archiving and compression package to compress the scanned pages of articles into a single archive file. Since the Macintosh could run DOS software, using a DOS-based program did not prove an obstacle. Because of the large amount of white space in textual materials, archiving and compression commonly achieved 80 to 90% compression; on average, compressed journals articles required about 800 KB of storage.

Using a DOS-based scanning workstation at NAL, staff captured printed material in electronic form and transferred it to temporary storage on a WORM disk. The images files were then translated to the TIFF format, compressed, and transmitted via the Internet to the Ultrix file server at NCSU. There the images were retrieved, uncompressed, displayed, and printed using standard Macintosh computers in the NCSU Libraries.

To implement the appropriate network connections to transfer the large image files, the project established a T-1 link between NAL and the SURAnet node at the University of Maryland. SURAnet, the Southeastern Universities Research Association Network, is the largest regional network in the national Internet. The NCSU campus was already connected to SURAnet. The project team provided the NCSU Libraries with Internet access by connecting the Libraries' Apple-based local area network to NCSU Computing Center's Ethernet-based network. Because the LocalTalk medium reached almost every DOS and Macintosh computer within the central library complex, the Libraries had considerable latitude in the location of workstations and the distribution of images. However, the low bandwidth of the twisted-pair LocalTalk medium (240 kbps) proved a hinderance in moving large files from the higher-speed campus Ethernet backbone.

## Conducting The Pilot Study

The initial stages of the pilot project were devoted to testing network connections by transmitting digitized files between NAL and the NCSU Libraries. Efforts also focused on identifying and resolving technical issues related to compressing, transmitting, previewing, manipulating, and printing images.

The study design assumed that the electronic delivery of digitized images between libraries would have no impact on their procedures for receiving and processing borrowing requests. However, the integration of electronic document receipt into existing workflows did require these workflows to be changed. These changes could not be fully evaluated in the limited environment of the pilot project.

### Why Not Fax?

The early stages of the pilot project coincided with the rapid, nationwide expansion of facsimile use. Given this trend, numerous observers questioned the need to use digitization technology. The project participants decided to devote substantial efforts to investigate and articulate the differences between facsimile and scanned images.

First, the project reviewed existing studies on the use of facsimile in libraries. Several prominent studies on the use of facsimile have been conducted since the advent of the Group III facsimile standard in 1980.[7] Notable projects include the national programs conducted by the National Library of Canada in 1986 and the NAL Telefacsimile Evaluation Project in 1985. There also have been a number of statewide studies conducted by networks of academic, special, and public libraries. While the studies cite advantages to facsimile, disadvantages are universal. These disadvantages primarily center on copy quality, particularly the blurred text and poor image resolution characteristics of facsimile. Graphical information (e.g., line graphs and many type faces), pictures, and scientific and mathematical notations are poorly reproduced. The time required to transmit lengthy reports exacerbates these problems. The NAL study noted deep frustration with the use of facsimile to distribute research documents. In general, the literature seemed to conclude that, even though the use of facsimile had become widespread in libraries, significant drawbacks compromised its use in research settings.

*Note:* In this figure a portion of a page from the August 19, 1991 issue of the journal PC Week is reproduced using facsimile transmission (shown on the left) and digitized image (shown on the right). The facsimile image was created through Group II facsimile standard; the digitized image was scanned at 300 dpi using half-tone scales.

*Figure 1.* Facsimile and Digitized Image Comparison

Second, the pilot study directly compared facsimile with digitized transmission of documents. It selected specimen pages containing graphical, notational, and textural information and transmitted each page using Group III facsimile and digitized TIFF images. TIFF images always resulted in textual and graphical information that was significantly more readable than facsimile images. Figure 1 presents sample specimen pages reproduced from a TIFF image and a facsimile transmission.

These comparisons revealed two substantial technical differences between scanning and facsimile.

1.   *Resolution:*   Most facsimile machines conform to the CCITT Group III standard, which specifies 200-dots-per-inch resolution during scanning. The de facto resolution for digitization through computer-based scanning is 300 dpi, a 50% increase in resolution. The difference is substantial for the reproduction of technical illustrations and photographs.

2.   *Shading:*   Group III facsimile is a black-and-white standard, designed to transmit textual business documents. Every pixel is either black or white, depending on the intensity of the reflected light from the scanner. Facsimile has no facility to capture differences in the intensity of black and white data (gray-scale) or color data. Nor can it use dithering to simulate gray-scale data. (Dithering is a printing technique used to simulate gray-scale data using patterns of black and white dots; newspaper pictures, for instance, are dithered renditions of actual photographs).

Third, the pilot study affirmed that facsimile is unlikely to become prominent in the research environment because it does not support the data communications and format standards essential to scholarly work. Numerous attempts to join facsimile with desktop computers, including commercial hardware and software solutions, have failed to produce an acceptably smooth integration. DOS, UNIX, and Macintosh software for image manipulation, text recognition, word processing, and other common tasks use standard formats such as TIFF, but they do not support Group III facsimile formats. Progress towards network transmission of facsimile standards (such as Group IV) remain some years away. Furthermore, investments in desktop computer and network technologies for research far exceed investments in facsimile; laboratories and research stations are much more likely to install desktop computers and network connections than facsimile machines.

## Results Of The Pilot Study

The pilot study successfully transmitted digitized document pages between computers at NAL and NCSU. Particular achievements include:

1. *Conclusively demonstrated the superiority of transmitted images over facsimile transmission.* The pilot study demonstrated the shortcomings of facsimile and the contrasting value of digitized materials. The study confirmed that, in addition to its technical shortcomings, facsimile exists as a largely stand-alone technology. As such, it has decreasing applicability in a research environment that is increasingly dependent on networked desktop computers to gather, analyze, and distribute data.

2. *Established the ability to operate in dissimilar computing environments.* The project showed that it is possible to integrate dissimilar computing environments by using data format and data communications standards and industry-standard computers and software.

3. *Identified the administrative and procedural issues involved in carrying out computer-based document delivery within the existing support matrix for ILL activities.* A major goal of the pilot study was to use existing ILL procedures to receive requests from users, place requests with NAL, and receive and deliver scanned materials in response to those requests. The pilot study concluded that the electronic delivery of digitized images need not change ILL procedures for receiving and placing requests. However, ILL procedures may require considerable adjustment to cope with delivering materials in electronic formats directly to users.

4. *Identified and, in most cases, resolved important technical issues.* The project was able to provide technical solutions to most problems concerned with compressing, previewing, manipulating, and printing images; using local networks linked to national networks; and minimizing network bandwidth requirements. The project did not resolve problems with printing speed in a PostScript environment, an issue that still remains problematic.

# THE DDTP PROJECT

The pilot study successfully established proof of concept and articulated the technical and administrative requirements to implement electronic delivery of digitized documents on a larger scale. Building on the findings of the pilot study, the NCSU Libraries proposed an expanded investigation to further explore the issues involved in bringing digitized document delivery to a substantial community of researchers. In early 1990, the NCSU Libraries submitted a Title II-D Research and Demonstration Grant proposal entitled *Transmission of Digitized Text: Improving Access to Agricultural Information* to the U.S. Department of Education's College Library Technology and Cooperation Grants Program. The proposal called for installing graphics-capable, networked workstations that used commercially available hardware and software at up to eight land-grant campuses to test and evaluate a full-scale digitized text delivery system. This system would serve a representative subset of the total land-grant library community. The goals of the expanded initiative were fivefold:

1.  To investigate the administrative, procedural, technical, and user issues involved in bringing digitized document delivery to a substantial community of researchers.
2.  To further establish libraries as stakeholders in the development of a NREN.
3.  To expand the use of networking technologies by the agricultural research community.
4.  To investigate the implications of copyright law for electronic document delivery services.
5.  To examine issues related to selecting hardware platforms for delivering graphics-based materials over established networks.

*Brief Project Chronology*

The project was divided into three phases. Although some aspects of the project timetable were modified because of the participant base was expanded, the project team has been able to adhere to the original timetable submitted in the Title II-D grant proposal.

Phase one (October 1990 to April 1991) was devoted to purchasing, configuring, and installing the project equipment; testing local network connections among the 14 participating libraries; and developing operational procedures. Each site designated a local project coordinator. Because a project goal was to explore the issues involved in integrating the DDTP system into the existing interlibrary loan infrastructure, the project team strongly recommended that the individual appointed as local project coordinator be intimately involved in the local interlibrary/document delivery operations.

Phase two (April 1991 to February 1992) began with a two-day training workshop for the project participants; over 35 people participated. The focus of the workshop was on interlibrary loan protocols, data collection, problem reporting mechanisms, and training. The workshop was not structured to address networking or other related technical issues.

Prior to transmitting actual library borrowing requests, fabricated library requests were processed through the system so as to test the agreed upon operating procedures and network linkages. By July 1991, sites were transmitting actual interlibrary requests.

Initially, participants used four software packages (i.e., scanning, compressing, transmitting, and printing software) that required an unacceptable level of manual intervention. The project management team recognized (and stated the need for) a front-end system that would link and/or integrate the four software packages.

In phase three (March 1992 to October 1992), the sites will continue production operations. The project team will begin a systematic evaluation of system performance. Using the automated data gathering feature of the system interface, the project team will evaluate both workstation functionality and network performance under production conditions to determine throughput rates across local and regional networks. The project's final report will identify and address factors that impact the successful integration of the system into the current matrix of ILL delivery options. The project team will conduct a conference on the project in late 1992.

The first two phases of the project are discussed in more detail below.

## The Selection Process

Anxious to be positioned to quickly proceed with the investigation, the Libraries began to screen and select project participants in the spring of 1990. The project team employed the nomination and review mechanism established for the NATDP to solicit applications from the land-grant community. Three participating libraries were explicitly identified before the selection process: the NCSU Libraries; NAL; and the North Carolina Agricultural and Technical University (Greensboro, N.C.), which represented historically black colleges and universities.

The grant proposal specified that other participants meet certain minimum criteria: (1) the library had to have demonstrated technical expertise for project support, (2) the parent institution had to have access to Internet (applications were preferred where libraries had direct high-speed connectivity), and (3) institutions had to show a high interest in the project and a willingness to commit sufficient resources.

In May 1990, the NCSU Libraries sent out applications to the entire land-grant library community soliciting information from interested participants. A total of 75 applications were mailed or faxed; over 33 applications were received. The project team refined the initial selection criteria to include:

- Responsiveness during the first two phases of NATDP.

- High-speed connectivity from the interlibrary loan processing area.

- Library systems support for troubleshooting network problems and operating networked, graphics-oriented desktop computers.

- Cooperative relationship between the library and the campus computing community.

Using these criteria, the project team divided the 33 applications into three groups.

*Group 1:*   This group of candidates had access to the Internet from desktop computers within the library, had demonstrated technical support sufficient for the project, and had carried out joint projects between the library and campus computing services.

*Group 2:*   This group stated it would have access to the Internet by the required deadline (December 1990) and met the other criteria to varying degrees.

*Group 3:*    This group had limited access to the Internet via slow-speed lines and met the other criteria to varying degrees.

The criteria and the groupings were submitted to the United States Agricultural Information Network (USAIN) Technology and Networking Committee for review on June 22, 1990 at the ALA Annual Conference. From this information, the USAIN Technology and Networking Committee (UTNC) developed a ranked list of 15 institutions for participation in the project. They expressed concern about the large number of interested parties in relationship to the small number of proposed participants. For three reasons, the UTNC strongly urged the project team to expand participation to add at least five additional sites to the eight sites initially proposed:

1.    A larger participant base would increase the accuracy of data analysis and help ensure that the project discovered and solved all likely technical problems.
2.    A small number of participants could compromise the important project goal of establishing libraries as stakeholders in developing the NREN.
3.    A larger participant group would improve the commitment of the participants and communicate a more substantial sense of purpose to them as well as to those institutions unable to participate.

Between July 1990 and October 1990, the project team designed a final selection process to choose project participants from the ranked list developed by the UTNC.

The funding level awarded ($178,707) fell short of the $235,386 requested, and this required the project team to reduce equipment funding to support the participating sites. For this reason, the project team decided to seek a commitment from candidate sites about the financial commitment each site could make for equipment purchases, and the team used this information, along with the rankings provided by the UTNC, to select the final participants. In October 1990, the NCSU Libraries mailed to all minimally qualified institutions a summary of selection factors and a request for additional information that would show the institution's commitment to purchase equipment for the project and its ability to do so.

Based on the recommendations of the UTNC, the ranked list of candidates, and the replies from candidate sites to the October 1990 letter, the project team decided to add 12 participants to the three participants already selected, bringing the total number of participants to 15. The participants were divided into two groups:

*Level One:* These five institutions made up the top five institutions in the UTNC's ranked list of 15 institutions. Level one institutions received funds to purchase a scanner and a laser printer; they agreed to provide the desktop computer and all network support.

*Level Two:* These seven institutions were selected from the remaining candidates in the UTNC ranked list based on their response to the October 1990 letter. Level two institutions received funds to purchase a scanner; they agreed to provide the desktop computer, printer, and all network support.

Participating institutions were notified of their selection in December and invited to attend an orientation meeting for the project on January 14, 1991, during the ALA Mid-Winter conference. The project team delivered a full briefing on the selection of participants to the UTNC meeting on January 11, 1991. The UTNC approved the final selection of candidates, but they were concerned because the project would only have twelve additional participants.

The 12 land-grant institutions participating with NCSU and NAL in the Digitized Document Transmission Project were: Clemson University, the University of Delaware, Iowa State University, the University of Maryland at College Park, Michigan State University, the University of Minnesota, North Carolina Agricultural and Technical State University, the Ohio State University, Pennsylvania State University, Utah State University, Virginia Polytechnic Institute and State University, and Washington State University.

## Technical Design

The technical design for the project was based upon the findings of the pilot study, with appropriate modifications for the circumstances of each participant. Specifications for hardware, software, and network connections reflected both the requirements for scaling up the pilot design and the problems that occurred in the pilot.

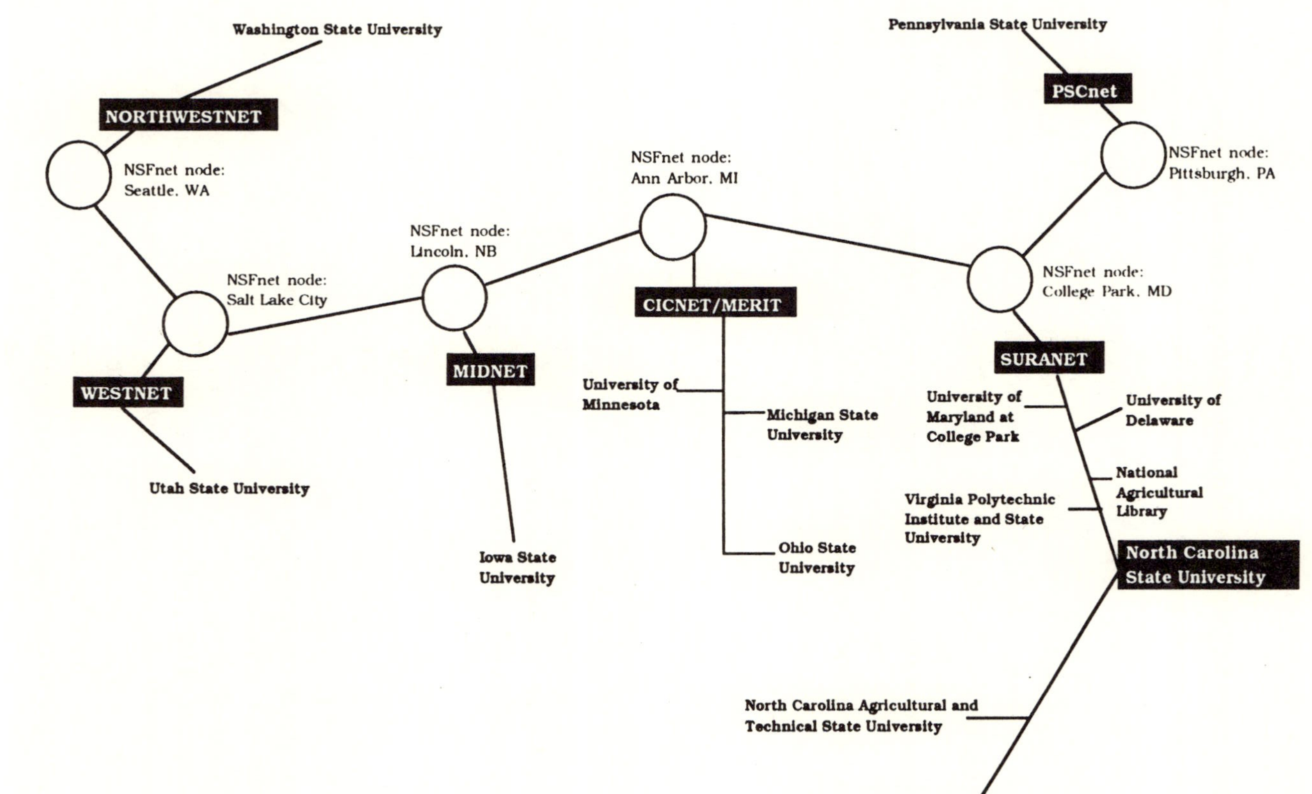


*Figure 2.*   DDTP Participants Logical Schematic (June 1991)

127

*Network Specifications*

The pilot project demonstrated that high bandwidth was required for transfer of large files in a reasonable amount of time. During the pilot, the comparatively low-speed LocalTalk medium used for the NCSU Libraries' AppleTalk network proved a hinderance to file transfers. Since LocalTalk permits AppleTalk speeds up to 230 kbps, this clearly ruled out the participation of sites whose Internet connectivity consisted of 9.6 kbps modems and it threw in doubt the participation of institutions with 56 kbps lines, both common mechanisms to connect libraries to campus networks and the Internet. Consequently, the project screening criteria gave preference to sites with Ethernet bandwidth available in the interlibrary loan area, where the workstation would reside and with T-1 links from the campus to the Internet. The NCSU Libraries upgraded its LocalTalk medium to Ethernet medium in the spring and summer of 1990, permitting it to run AppleTalk protocols at Ethernet speeds (EtherTalk), and bringing it into compliance with the preferred criteria.

For the purposes of the project, a direct connection to the Internet was defined as the ability to perform Telnet/FTP operations directly from the desktop computer used for the project. At the beginning of the project, few sites had a direct connection to the Internet; most performed Telnet/FTP functions through an intermediate Internet-connected computer that was connected to desktop computers by networks or asynchronous links. Participants otherwise meeting the project requirements agreed to install a direct connection to the Internet prior to beginning the project.

The design permitted two configurations for receipt of images. Participants could specify a host computer, usually a UNIX or IBM mainframe machine on the Internet, as the machine for receiving transmitted images or they could use an Internet-connected Macintosh. The preferred configuration was to establish a single central computer as a server host for the campus. This computer received and stored images transmitted to the participating library for later retrieval by library staff. The project team saw powerful advantages to using a server host computer:

1.  *7x24 availability:* Most host computers are located in computer rooms and available up to 24 hours a day, seven

days a week. Desktop computers are subject to more interruptions in service.

2. *Campus distribution:*  Once image files arrive on the host computer, they can be picked up from any computer connected to the host computer. This would facilitate branch library support and direct delivery of image files to users. Host computer storage would permit the project to explore the direct delivery of electronic documents from library collections.

3. *Disk space:*  Desktop computers generally have limited disk space compared to host computers. A host computer would be able to receive and store many image files before it ran short on space, whereas even a large hard disk on a desktop computer would be consumed by a relatively small number of image files.

4. *Reliability:*  Experiments by the project team had shown that host machines performed FTP receipt better and more reliably than desktop computers.

About half the participants established a host machine for receiving images. Two important obstacles prevented remaining participants from using a host machine. First, few libraries owned a host computer to serve as the FTP-receive site. Second, computing center managers were often reluctant to provide FTP-receive capability on host machines for library-related projects, citing security concerns.

*Desktop Computer Specifications*

The project team examined several desktop computer options to serve as the platform for the project. The foremost consideration was the use of nonproprietary equipment and software. In the initial stages of the project, few resources were available for customized hardware or software, so each desktop configuration was required to perform all project functions with commercially available hardware and software. Other considerations included strong network connectivity options, support for graphics programs to visualize scanned images, low training and maintenance overhead, and processing power sufficient for the needs of the project.

After examining DOS, Macintosh, and UNIX options, the team decided to use Macintosh computers for the following reasons:

1. *Network connectivity:*   Network options are included as part of the Macintosh operating system and are well integrated into the Macintosh environment. The project team believed that built-in networking would reduce training and maintenance overhead, and it more closely approached the functionality of high-end UNIX workstations, which assume network connectivity as part of their normal operations. DOS computers require much more customization and attention to the local environment to perform network operations.

2. *Consistent graphics support:*   The Macintosh supports a high-resolution graphical imaging model consistent across Macintoshes and across all monitors and monitor boards that might be used in the project. In general, individual applications do not anticipate, require, or even know about specific graphics hardware on a Macintosh, and they use any Macintosh display device without modification. Because of this consistent imaging model, the project team could ignore the details of monitor type (e.g., large screen, small screen, or color), monitor boards, and the number of monitors used on an desktop computer. Instead, they could concentrate on using applications, manipulating scanned images, and the like. DOS computers do not offer a consistent graphical imaging model.

3. *Low training overhead:*   The project team thought that Macintosh computers, particularly at project start up (prior to the release of Windows 3.0), offered less training overhead than alternatives.

4. *HyperCard:*   All Macintosh computers are equipped with HyperCard as part of the operating system software. The team decided that HyperCard offered the best environment for the limited software development envisioned for the project.

The January 1990 grant application proposed a different model Macintosh, but, at the time of the award in October 1990, Apple introduced new products at reduced prices, and it discontinued the Macintosh model proposed by the grant. The IIsi model offered more processing power at less cost than the IIcx model proposed by the grant.

The team settled on the Abaton scanner after examining a number of commercial scanners. The Abaton supported all existing standards and offered resolution and gray-scale rendering comparable with other scanners on the market, but at considerably less cost. In

*Figure 3.*   Workstation Configuration

---

*Hardware*
Macintosh computer
40 MB hard disk
8 MB RAM
Ethernet connection to the Internet
Abaton Scanner
PostScript Printer
*Software*
System 6.0.5 (or greater)
Abaton Scanning Software
HyperCard 2.0.1
MacTCP 1.0.1
StuffIt Deluxe 2.0.1
NCSA Telnet for the Macintosh 2.4.4 (or higher)

---

addition, scanner drivers for the Abaton were well integrated with the Macintosh and easy to use.

Figure 3 shows the configuration of workstations used in the DDTP Project.

## Phase One Software

The grant application proposed two approaches to software for the project. During the initial phases of the project, participants used existing, unmodified applications programs for Macintosh computers to scan (Abaton scanner desk accessory), compress (StuffIt Deluxe), transmit and receive (NCSA Telnet), and print (SuperPaint) images.

The use of independent software components permitted participants to carry out project operations, but required great care and an unacceptable amount of time. The time required to simply start up each program for each step of scanning, compressing, transmitting, receiving, uncompressing, and printing compromised productivity levels. In addition, participants had to carefully follow instructions for each step in order to perform them in the correct sequence.

## Phase Two Software

During the second phase of the project, the project team designed and implemented a HyperCard application that streamlined and simplified the entire process. Four principles guided the application design.

1. *Reduce manual operations:* The application should automatically perform as many of the existing operations as possible. The first release of the application should concentrate particularly on automating and handling the transmission and receipt of image files.
2. *Flexibility:* The application should be designed so that the addition of new capabilities was anticipated and included as part of the initial architecture of the application.
3. *Low Cost:* The application should not require additional investments in hardware or software.
4. *Open:* The application should not confine library staff to transmitting and receiving only scanned articles; it should be open to all forms of digitized information.

The first release of the application allowed users to perform most operations with a single click of a mouse button. It included a directory of sites participating in the project, including their IP addresses, and other information for performing FTP operations and controlling the receipt of scanned images. Scanning itself was not integrated into the HyperCard stack. Instead, when users clicked the scan button, control was transferred to the program used in the previous environment to scan documents, and users scanned documents and otherwise controlled the scanner as before. The stack directly controlled all other operations.

This release of the HyperCard stack solved some, but not all, throughput and productivity problems. The project team decided to strengthen the application by incorporating direct control of the scanner, making performance improvements, and adding other extensions. The current release of the program (see Figure 4) incorporates major improvements over the initial release and provides important capabilities beyond simply scanning and transmitting images.

The revised program had the following new capabilities:

1. *Multiple document sources:* The HyperCard stack directly supported and controlled scanning of journal articles; however, it distinguished scanning from compression and transmission. Consequently, it could import, compress, and transmit any file

*Figure 4.*   Hypercard Interface for DDTP

(regardless of its source), including database, sound, video, word processing, and other file types. To use data other than scanned images, the user clicked the import button.

2.  *User-controlled address book:*  The stack contained a user-defined and user-maintained directory of transmission addresses. The directory could contain any FTP-receive site on the Internet. Users could add local, regional, or national FTP-receive sites at any time. For instance, library staff could deliver scanned journal articles directly to any user's computer simply by entering the user's IP address into the directory, provided that the user had an IP-connected computer with FTP receive enabled.

3.  *Direct control of scanning:*  The stack contained its own drivers to directly control the scanner. Previous releases used a commercially supplied scan driver, which required the application to initiate the scanning program and then suspend its own operations until the user completed the scanning. It also required the user to manually supervise the scanning process. The new drivers automated page counts, file naming, and other aspects of the scanning process.

4.  *Strong recovery and diagnostic procedures for transmission and receipt:*   The stack included thorough diagnostic procedures to detect problems during transmission of materials. It also provided for error recovery and retransmission in the event of problems.

5.  *Comprehensive logging for statistics:*   Notably lacking in most Internet-based experiments are useful ILL statistics. The stack provided comprehensive logging of data related to scanning and transmission, ranging from the size of scanned items and the time required for scanning to error rates and transmission times. The measures were stored in files that were formatted for easy import into spreadsheet or statistical analysis programs.

The first release of the application reduced the number of steps required to digitize and send a document from 33 to six, and achieved a greater than 60% reduction in the time required. The second release included significant performance improvements as well as adding new capabilities; it achieved a further 50% improvement over the earlier release. Preforming all steps in fulfilling a request, from scanning to transmission, now requires 25% of the time needed at the beginning of the project.

## DDTP UTILIZATION

The project participants agreed on basic operational and procedural guidelines at the project training workshop in April 1991. For management purposes, project participants elected to flag selected borrowing requests for electronic delivery rather than have the supplier determine how the filled request would be delivered. The group agreed on a 24-48 hour turnaround time for responding to and filling article requests. They also agreed to procedures for following up on common processing problems, such as missing pages.

### The Document Delivery Process

Once the borrowing library verified the request, the request was transmitted via the OCLC ILL Subsystem to the lending library. A phrase in the *maxcost* field of the OCLC record flagged incoming requests to indicate that the filled request was to be delivered electronically.

Upon receiving the borrowing request, the lending library retrieved the document from the collection, electronically scanned the material, and stored the OCLC workform into an electronic folder. The folder was identified using the OCLC ILL Subsystem request number. This naming convention allowed for easy identification of incoming materials and provided an electronic trail for both the lending and borrowing libraries. Once scanned, the document was automatically compressed and transmitted to the designated intermediate host machine at borrowing site.

Staff at the borrowing site periodically checked their host machine by activating the retrieve function of the system interface. Files were retrieved individually or in batch; the auto-feature of the HyperCard interface automatically decompressed and printed the files. The system deleted the file(s) both on the host machine and the workstation once a file was printed, downloaded, or delivered via campus networks to the researcher.

## THE ELECTRONIC DOCUMENT DELIVERY SERVICE

As it was originally conceived, the DDTP design called for direct links to faculty and student users of agricultural and industrial research materials via computers located in the branch libraries at the North Carolina State University. The technical design of the project anticipated direct document delivery by establishing server-based TIFF image repositories for images from other participants and by providing for network-based printing and delivery of image files.

The end-user network delivery component of the project design was eliminated from the Title II-D grant request to reduce the total project cost, but it was later resurrected as a related study with equipment support from Apple Computer, Inc. In February 1991, the NCSU Libraries received two complete desktop computer systems from the Apple Library of Tomorrow (ALOT) grant program to investigate issues related to the direct delivery of digitized research materials to researchers via campus networks. NCSU contributed funding for personnel resources to manage and conduct the project.

In collaboration with the NCSU Computing Center, the project team developed a new service called the Electronic Document

Delivery Service (EDDS). EDDS allowed researchers on the campus network to retrieve their requested library materials electronically. EDDS supported workstations running the DOS, UNIX or Macintosh operating systems. Using the EDDS, researchers submitted their document requests via the campus electronic mail system to the Libraries' Interlibrary Loan department. Requests were filled, through the DDTP sites, by obtaining a scanned electronic version of the article (or an original electronic document). Filled requests were received and stored on the NCSU document server computer, which automatically notified the researcher that the digitized document was available and provided retrieval instructions for electronic pickup by the researcher.[8]

The NCSU Libraries are pilot testing the EDDS, and they anticipate testing the system at two other DDTP sites. Direct delivery to the researcher raises numerous technical, management, user computer literacy, and training issues. These issues will be identified and project findings reported in a final EDDS report scheduled for late 1992.

## COMPARISON WITH OTHER ELECTRONIC DOCUMENT DELIVERY PROJECTS

Two other projects have tested the feasibility of electronic document delivery systems using fax-over-the-Internet distribution systems: the Committee on Institutional Cooperation Network's (CICnet) Network Facsimile Project and the Research Libraries Group's (RLG) Ariel system. Both projects use digitization technology and the Internet as the primary means of delivery. The CICnet and RLG systems can be understood as point-to-point, platform-dependent, print-over-the-Internet systems. They rely on transmitting to identical platforms, and they have a single input device (a scanner) and a single output device (a printer) that are directly attached to the workstation.

The Network Facsimile Project essentially aims to use the Internet to deliver facsimile images generated by standard fax machines. The technical design for the project is summarized in Figure 5. Operators scan documents requested through normal ILL channels using a standard fax machine. They then transmit the image to a desktop computer equipped with a facsimile circuit card by a local phone call or a direct connection (using a special cable). The computer stores

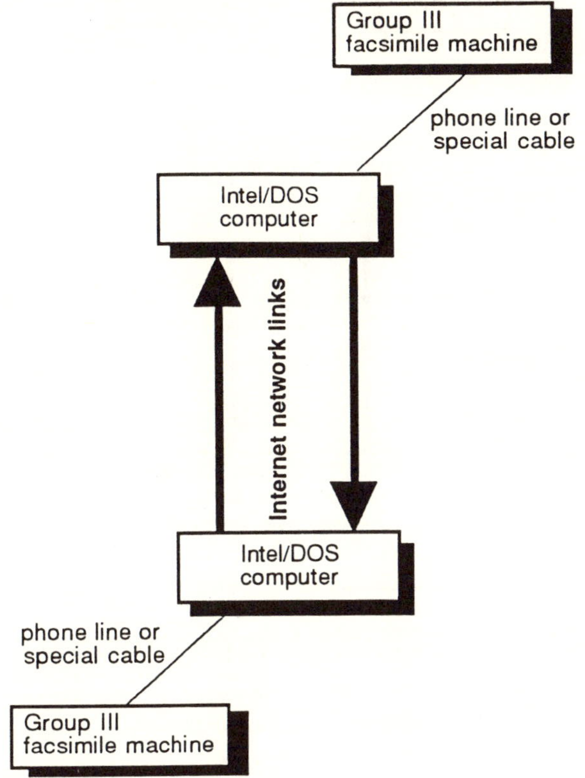


*Figure 5.*   CICnet Transmission Schematic

the image in Group III format, and it then contacts to the computer at the requesting institution via the Internet. It arranges to transfer the facsimile image to the remote computer using FTP and special software written by CICnet. After receiving the image, the remote computer, using a facsimile circuit card, transmits the image to a standard facsimile machine for printing by either a local phone call or a direct connection.

The CICnet design offers the advantage of complete integration with existing ILL procedures, requiring little change and preserving high throughput production levels. It also eliminates long distance phone charges.

It has two principal disadvantages. First, it requires Group III facsimile, which is marginally acceptable for some materials and not

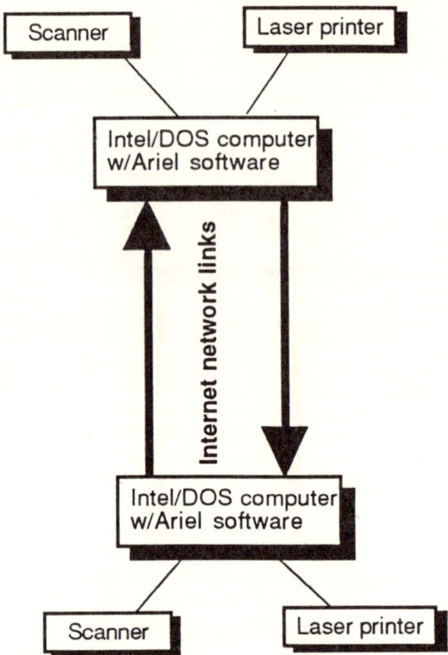


*Figure 6.*    Research Libraries Group—Ariel
Transmission Schematic

at all acceptable for others. Second, it requires customized software and runs only on DOS-based computers, making it difficult to use or integrate into university networks that are characterized by use of dissimilar computing platforms.

Ariel started as a research initiative by the Research Libraries Group (RLG). The Ariel project evolved into a substantial software engineering project. RLG released the first commercial version of its software in October 1991.

The Ariel system is promoted as a replacement for facsimile. The technical design for the project is summarized in Figure 6.

The system consists of hardware and software to scan documents, transmit them on the Internet, and receive and print them at the requesting site. The hardware consists of a DOS-based desktop computer, specific commercially available scanners and printers, and network connectivity that permits FTP directly to the desktop computer. The printer is equipped with a hardware accelerator board to improve print performance. The Ariel software directly drives the scanner, compresses scanner output, and transmits the scanned articles to a receiving Ariel station. The Ariel software on the receiving station takes receipt of the image, uncompresses it, and prints it.

The Ariel system provides a production environment that is capable of high throughput and integrates well with existing ILL procedures. The scanned images are stored in a standard image format accessible to desktop computer software. With suitable changes, Ariel might be used to transfer the images to other computers rather than printing them.

Ariel's principle disadvantages are two-fold. First, it requires customized hardware and software in very specific configurations. Second, the system design emphasizes printing documents. There is no provision for the integration of the Ariel system into campus networks to allow the transfer of the images to other types of network computers or printers.

The DDTP system design contrasts sharply with both the Network Fax Project and Ariel (see Figure 7). The project team has not envisioned the DDTP system design as a replacement for facsimile, although the software has the functionality required for this. Instead, the design provides for multiple sources for documents, including network sources and files from applications other than scanning, and multiple delivery options, including network delivery and diskette delivery. It also supports printing to any network-accessible PostScript printer.

It also has two principal disadvantages. First, it only runs on Macintosh hardware, although it will support virtually any Macintosh-compatible scanner and printer. Second, because it uses only unmodified, commercially available hardware, performance varies according to the hardware employed by each site, and it is generally below that of Ariel or the Network Fax Project. Memory, disk space, printer configuration, enhancements (e.g., use of an accelerated PostScript printer), and network reliability all affect performance.

## IMPACT OF ELECTRONIC DOCUMENT DELIVERY SERVICES

Electronic document delivery is but one part of the changing reality challenging traditional interlibrary services. Sophisticated access mechanisms, spiraling serials costs, new technologies, and growing researcher needs and expectations are all driving libraries to reassess

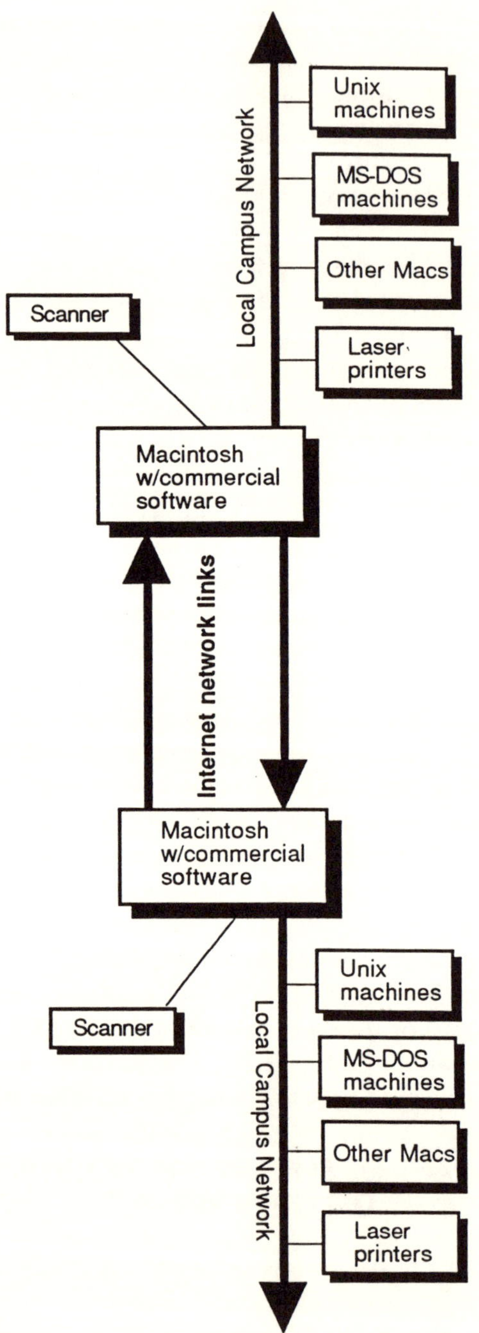


*Figure 7.*   DDTP Transmission Schematic

basic assumptions about interlibrary and document delivery. Electronic document delivery can provide a faster, value-added alternative to traditional approaches; however, the successful integration of this service into the research process demands a holistic—versus an ad hoc—examination of document delivery services from an institutional perspective and a thoughtful analysis of workflow issues from an operational perspective.

## ILL Workflow Implications

Implementing an electronic document delivery service requires a solid network infrastructure: broad-based, high-speed network connectivity; trained staff to operate networked, graphics-capable desktop computers; and local systems staff to install and maintain networked devices. The successful operation of an electronic document delivery system requires changes to current ILL operations in order to integrate and fully utilize it.

The DDTP transmission system is an easy-to-use, icon-based system that is no more difficult to use than conventional library systems, such as OCLC or RLIN. This delivery option does not require a change in the level of ILL staffing. As stated above, an electronic document delivery system between libraries does not impact on procedures for receiving and placing requests. Other than specifying electronic delivery as the delivery option of choice in the borrowing request form, no other changes in workflow are necessary. Even this step could be avoided through borrowing agreements that specify that all incoming requests will be automatically filled via electronic delivery.

However, the delivery and receipt of digitized materials do require workflow changes. From the lender's perspective, digitization represents another option for creating a facsimile of the original material besides photocopy and telefacsimile. Digitized document delivery requires similar workflow changes that occur when flatbed telefascsimile machine are used. Managers must also track the actual delivery of electronic documents and insure corresponding updates on OCLC.

From the borrower's perspective, the receipt of materials is analogous to checking one's electronic or print mail. The document is then retrieved from the intermediate computer and automatically decompressed and printed. The mechanisms for addressing incomplete documents, blurred images, and other problems already exist; these problems are not particular to the digitized transmission.

Utilizing the DDTP import file feature allows for the delivery of electronic documents that exist only in machine-readable form (e.g., hypertext or multimedia). This not only raises staffing issues, but also larger organizational issues that ultimately reflect institutional priorities. It will demand that the ILL department forge partnerships with the reference and systems departments to help identify and obtain electronic documents from other libraries.

## Cost Effectiveness

Network-based systems shift the direct delivery costs incurred by the lending library, which are variable, to the borrowing library in the form of indirect overhead costs.[9] The elimination of direct delivery expenses by the lending library will alter formulas for calculating document delivery costs. Currently, most libraries do not pay to use the Internet. Such access is generally considered an integral component of the university's research infrastructure, and it is absorbed as an overhead cost. It is conceivable that universities may develop charge-back mechanisms for Internet access or use. For the time being, this is not the case.

Will this digitized document delivery be cost effective compared to traditional delivery mechanisms? Studies of facsimile transmission show that a minimum of 600 to 1,000 pages per month need to be transmitted to break-even.[10] The costs of faxing have ranged considerably. Current fax-over-the-Internet transmission systems, such as the Ariel and the CICnet, systems are too new to accurately predict costs. The shifted, direct, indirect, and hidden costs of digitized electronic delivery will be examined in the third phase of the NCSU project.

## CONCLUSION

The full benefits of an electronic document delivery system cannot be realized until all three components of the process—discovery, ordering, and delivery—are integrated. Fundamental questions about the structure and operation of such a delivery service remain to be answered. These questions fall into three major areas:

1. *Administrative:* What operational changes will be required to implement convenient document delivery for users? What staffing changes will be needed? How will such services be charged back or otherwise be financed? Who will be allowed access to these services?

2. *Technical:* Once a user finds a desired citation, how will the system locate the requested item? How will electronic document delivery systems fit into the existing interlibrary loan arrangements between libraries? What authentication and authorization mechanisms will be required?

3. *Legal:* What are the implications of existing copyright law for electronic document delivery? Should libraries be treated similarly to commercial services with respect to copyright?

The library community needs to conduct ongoing research and development efforts that systematically address issues in these three areas of concern. Although libraries will make progress in deploying integrated electronic document delivery systems during the next five years, such systems will be successful only to the extent that they speak to these fundamental issues.

## NOTES

1. John Markoff, "Creating a Giant Computer Highway," *New York Times,.* 2 September 1990, 1.

2. Michael Strangelove, Diane Kovacs, and Ann Okerson, *Directory of Electronic Journals, Newsletters and Academic Discussion Lists*, 2nd edition (Washington, D.C: Association of Research Libraries, 1992).

3. Clifford A. Lynch, "The Development of Electronic Publishing and Digital Library Collections on the NREN," *Electronic Networking: Research, Application and Policy* 1 (Winter 1991): 6-22; and Charles W. Bailey, Jr., "Network-Based Electronic Serials," *Information Technology and Libraries* 11 (March 1992): 29-35.

4. Pamela Q. J. Andre and Nancy L. Eaton, "National Agricultural Text Digitizing Project," *Library Hi Tech* 6, no. 3 (1988): 61-67; and Pamela Q. J. Andre, "In the Field of Agriculture, CD-ROM Delivers!" *CD-ROM EndUser* 2 (July 1, 1990): 26.

5. Nancy Eaton et al., *Final Report: National Agricultural Text Digitizing Project*, forthcoming. (Includes text of Lynch report.)

6. Ibid.

7. Havelin Amand, "Interlibrary Loan and Document Delivery Using Telefacsimile Transmission: Part II. Telefacsimile Project," *The Electronic Library* 5, no. 2 (1987): 100-107; Anthony Aguirre, "Libraries Fast-Fax for Physicians,"

*American Libraries* 18, no. 1 (1988): 61-62; Eve J. Davis, "Fax Goes Far in Montana," *American Libraries* 18, no. 1 (1988): 62-63; Mary Jackson, "Facsimile Transmission: The Next Generation of Document Delivery," *Wilson Library Bulletin* 62, no. 9 (1988): 37-43; and Mary Y. Moore, "Fax It To Me: A Library Love Affair," *American Libraries* 18, no. 1 (1988): 57-59.

8.    Eric Lease Morgan and Tracy Casorso, "Digitized Document Transmission Using Hypercard," *Macintoshed Libraries* 5 (1992): 47-53.

9.    Bruce Morton, "Rapid Document Delivery via Digitized Documents: The Pacific Northwest Land Grant Universities Project," Library Hi Tech 5, no. 2 (1987): 79-84.

10.    Mary Jackson, "The Online Environment in the 1990's: A Challenge for Resource Sharing," in *IOLS' 90 Integrated Online Systems: Proceedings*, comp. David C. Genaway (Medford, NJ: Learned Information, 1990), 91-101.

# CAMPUS-WIDE INFORMATION SYSTEMS

Judy Hallman[1]

---

## INTRODUCTION

Campus mainframe computers are the repository for a wealth of information, but faculty, staff, and students have not traditionally had easy access to this information. Most people have not had easy access to the computers; they did not know the commands needed to find information, nor did they have the security clearance to explore the data in the campus computers.

While the increase in microcomputers on campuses and significant improvements in computer networking have facilitated access to mainframe computers, mainframe operating systems and the need for security for data have not changed significantly. What has evolved is a new set of tools for providing access to campus information, collectively called campus-wide information systems (CWISs).

A CWIS provides campus information of general interest, online, accessible from virtually every workstation on campus that has communications capability. The systems are menu driven, but

**Advances in Library Automation and Networking, Volume 5, pages 145-176.**
**Copyright © 1994 by JAI Press Inc.**
**All rights of reproduction in any form reserved.**
**ISBN: 1-55938-510-3**

provide short cuts for experienced users. A typical system contains the campus directory, event schedules, guides, policies, and other documents.

Several issues are emerging, including the following ones:

- A variety of software is in use. Their screen displays and menu presentations vary as do their means for navigation. What are the similarities and differences between them?

- How can the displays and access mechanisms be improved to help people find the information they need?

- How do people know that these services exist and what information they have access to?

- The definition of "public information" is being questioned; which data can be freely displayed, which should have restricted access, and which can and should be censored?

- Text formatted for the printed page usually won't display exactly the same on a computer screen. What guidelines should be followed to preserve the design of the authors and editors?

- Should data be changed after it enters the CWIS to keep it current or should it faithfully represent the source document?

- Who should be responsible for maintaining data in the CWIS—the authors and editors or the people running the CWIS software? And who should run the systems—computer specialists or librarians?

- How can CWISs be linked together so that people on one campus can easily access information on another campus?

These are issues that require the combined skills of librarians and computer specialists.

CWISs make a significant contribution to the availability of information. This paper first examines the emergence of CWISs as viable systems of information distribution, tracing the contributions of key individuals. Next, practical problems facing those starting a CWIS are addressed, followed by a discussion of possible future directions for CWISs. Appendices describe an electronic discussion group, called CWIS-L, which has been invaluable to those who provide CWISs, and how to try out some of the CWISs available on the Internet.

## CURRENT SYSTEMS

### What Is a CWIS?

A CWIS provides campus information of general interest, online, accessible from virtually every workstation on campus that has communications capability. This definition excludes Student Information Systems, which provide students with personal information concerning their records. Similarly, it excludes visitor information systems that are not available on the campus computing network.

Most CWISs require a userid, and some also require a password, but they vary in access control. Some CWISs only display information, some allow anonymous user input, some provide access to special data (such as medical records) to special users, and some provide access to all campus computing facilities and services. Most campuses provide a userid and password for visitors to look at information in the CWIS, but access to services, such as electronic mail, are limited to registered users.

### What Information Is Provided by a CWIS?

The types of information provided by most CWISs include the following:

- event calendars, including sports, music/film/theater, lectures/ seminars/workshops, academic calendars;

- promotional/expository information, including books, pamphlets, newsletters, directories, primarily describing campus functions and services;

- lists, such as job openings, available housing, class schedules, buy/sell bulletin boards, rides needed/offered;

- grant and funding opportunities, current research activities, faculty publications;

- access to the online library catalog; and

- e-mail/forums/discussion groups/digests.

Further, some systems also include community information, an inclusion that has been subject to discussion. While some campuses feel their time is best used expanding the campus database, others see local events and activities as important to the campus community. Some campuses include bus/train schedules, weather forecasts, fortunes, community guides (including movie schedules and restaurant information), agricultural extension information, and news feeds.

One of the most interesting services provided by CWISs is psychological counseling. Since 1986, Cornellians have been asking Uncle Ezra, an online counselor, for help with their problems. Questions are asked anonymously through electronic mail. Professional counselors then post both the questions and their responses in CUINFO where anyone can look at them. This service has been valuable to people with problems, and fun and interesting to people who use CUINFO. Cornell has even published a book called *The Best of Uncle Ezra*. Other campuses, such as Appalachian State University, have adopted this service.[2]

## What Are the Benefits of CWISs?

CWISs provide a variety of benefits, including the following:

- All the information is in one place. CWISs provide one-stop shopping for quick answers to simple questions, like how many students there are on campus or what time the basketball game starts. If you are already online, it might be faster to look up a phone number in the database than to find your printed copy of the phone book.

- Information is available around the clock.

- Information may be more current than printed copies. Campus directories are a good example. Online versions are likely to be updated frequently while the paper version may only be printed once a year.

- Information can be accessed from afar. While CWISs service the local campuses, they are especially valuable for remote users. Campus directories and course catalogs are likely to be used by people off-campus. When you get home from a conference and discover you want to discuss something with someone you met at the conference, you can look up his or her phone number and electronic mail address in that campus' phone directory. Similarly, you might want to see if a university has a course in a particular subject and who teaches it.

- Information can be accessed by more people. A CWIS expands the audience for newsletters, course catalogs, and even postings of events. For example, the University of North Carolina at Chapel Hill (UNC-CH) posts the publications of the Institute for Academic Technology and a list of library-related events of interest to librarians worldwide.

- CWISs have educational benefits. They are a lot like cookbooks; you may start off looking up one thing and end up reading a lot of unrelated information. It is easy to browse a variety of publications on the local campus and on other campuses on the Internet.

- CWISs can provide online archives. At UNC-CH, old issues of newsletters are kept in the system.

- CWISs have the potential for saving paper. It is reasonable to think that in the future, campus directories, class schedules, and course evaluations, for example, might only be available in electronic form.

- Having facts in a CWIS can reduce phone calls and save personnel time.

### How Did CWISs Get Started?

It is difficult to determine exactly when CWISs got started or who had the first one. For example, mainframe logon messages, sometimes called the "message of the day," date back to the early days of mainframe computers and provide a crude announcement service. The University of Illinois at Champaign-Urbana provided information about their campus in the early 1970s using PLATO, a system developed on that campus to provide self-paced instruction in a variety of subjects using touch-screen terminals.[3] Stanford had a similar system in the 1970s using SPIRES, software noted for its excellent full-text search capabilities and marketed by Stanford.

In the 1970s and 1980s several campuses experimented with providing documents to users of mainframe computing services. However, Rita Saltz of Princeton questions whether anything can really count as a real CWIS prior to the micro revolution that put electronic access on the desktops of a large part of the campus.[4]

Certainly Cornell had one of the first CWISs as we know them today, championed by Steven L. Worona. According to Worona,[5] CUINFO at Cornell began to take shape in Spring 1982. Two commands were made available on their IBM computer system: ROSTER to display the University's course roster and EXAM to display the final examination schedule. Worona notes that these schedules "were invariably obsolete even before they reached students' hands. Since both of these documents were prepared for publication on the central computer system and regularly updated (although not reprinted), the possibility for electronic access to current information was tantalizing." The CUINFO command (installed in October 1982) was created as a generalization of EXAM and ROSTER.

As Worona points out,[6] at the time these CWISs began, campus computers were used for number crunching and data analysis and the users were technically oriented. CWISs expanded the audience to all members of the university community, including many who never had reason to use a computer before. Several CWISs came into being during 1986-87.

## What Software Is Currently in Use?

CWISs run on a wide range of computers (often hardware already on campus) and the software is still evolving. Like the evolution of word processing software, the process will probably result in some outstanding systems that will dominate, establishing consistency in menus and ways of moving around. Right now there is no clear standard. Current systems present similar menus, but vary in navigational methods, resources they access, and the difficulty in installing data.

The basic concepts of these systems are essentially the same. The user is presented with a menu and chooses an item by entering its number or part of its name. Some choices lead to other menus. Eventually the user reaches text that is displayed one screen (or page) at a time. Users can move forward or back, one page at a time, they can return to the last menu displayed, or they can return to the initial (main) menu. Short cuts are provided for moving directly to information of interest, and indexes or maps tell users the keywords to use in the short cut method. How menu choices are made, the commands and key sequences for paging through text, and the short cut methods vary.

The following describes systems currently in use with the design goals of some of their developers. Three samples of opening menus are included to show different menu presentations. See Appendix B for information on how to obtain a file that tells how to connect to CWISs on the Internet, what the systems contain, who to contact for more information, and for an easy way to browse through some of the services.

**CUINFO:** According to Steve Worona of Cornell, CUINFO (written in IBM system 370 assembler language) was originally developed for use under the VM operating system that runs on IBM mainframes. While CUINFO could not be easily transported to other operating systems, "a complete re-implementation would not be a formidable task."[7] Yale also runs CUINFO.[8]

Figure 1 shows Cornell's opening screen (February 1992).

```
       C U I N F O - Cornell University's Electronic Information Source

                              MAIN MENU
   Select... For items such as...

       NEWS          Weather, Announce, Grad. Bulletin, Safety Reports, Updates
       EVENTS        Calendars, Athletics, Colloquia, Theatre, Music, Movies
       DIALOGS       Drug IQ Network, Mr. Chips, Uncle Ezra, Auntie Em, Suggest
       SERVICES      Computing, Support, Housing, Transport, Food, Careers, Jobs, OEO,
                     Directories, Volunteer, Library

   Or select a more general category like...

       ACADEM        Information about Cornell instruction and research
       ADMIN         Items from and about Cornell administrative offices
       ITHACA        General information for and about the Ithaca area

   Or type the name of any specific CUINFO entry such as WEATHER, DIRECT, or EZRA.
   (Type INDEX for a list of available items, or DETAILS for descriptions.)

              Please select a topic or type HELP for hints. (Blank to exit.)

   -->
```

*Figure 1.*   CUINFO Initial Screen

Worona describes the CUINFO user interface as follows:

The CUINFO interface is based on activities with which everyone is familiar—selecting from a list and flipping through pages—and we have yet to encounter a person who doesn't immediately understand the system. What we find more and more surprising is the wide variety of information that can be distributed effectively by this mechanism. The key is taking the trouble to organize the data before putting it online.

The approach of many information retrieval systems is to provide the user with powerful searching tools, utilizing keywords, free text, boolean logic, and anything else the designer can throw in. These tools are then applied by the user to a data base whose internal organization is unknown or invisible. In this context, powerful tools are almost a necessity. But the rules for using powerful tools tend to be difficult to learn and easy to forget. The standard solution for this problem—online "HELP"—is not so much a solution as proof that the problem exists.

CUINFO takes the opposite approach. The searching tools are extremely simple, but therefore usable by anyone. The burden is on the information providers and system administrators to structure their data in such a way that it can be readily processed by these simple tools.[9]

**VTX:**    VTX is a product of Digital Equipment Corporation (DEC). It runs on DEC VAX computers and is available in the Education Software Package. Campuses using this software include Appalachian State University, Clemson University, New Mexico State University, North Carolina State University, Pima County Community College, the University of New Hampshire, the University of North Carolina at Chapel Hill, the University of North Carolina at Greensboro, the University of North Carolina at Wilmington, and Western Carolina University.[10]

One special feature of VTX is the ability to link services together using DECNet. The University of North Carolina uses DECNet to link together the services at Appalachian State University, North Carolina State University, the University of North Carolina at Chapel Hill, the University of North Carolina at Greensboro, the University of North Carolina at Wilmington, and Western Carolina University.[11] VTX also supports voice output using DECTalk.[12]

Navigation in VTX relies on use of function keys and some key sequences. New Mexico State University modified the user interface allowing users to type commands (like Q for quit). Several of the campuses that use VTX have applied the modifications from New Mexico, but these modifications are not supported by DEC. Further, they only work for VT100 terminal emulation, not for users emulating IBM 3270 terminals. DEC is addressing these problems in a new version of VTX, version 5.0.

**PNN:** Howard Strauss is responsible for the development of Princeton News Network (PNN). Princeton runs it under VM/CMS, UNIX,[13] and HyperCard (on Macintoshes). All versions are available to universities at no cost. Several campuses use this software, including: Arizona State University's PEGASUS and ASEDD (under VM/CMS), Northwestern University, Notre Dame (under VM), San Diego State University (on a Sun SPACstation 1 running SunOS), and University of Colorado at Boulder (running on both VMS and UNIX).[14]

Strauss says that the major design goal for PNN was to provide an intuitive, user-friendly interface for a variety of platforms. For example, to scroll forward to the next page, F8 works (for the CMS users), PgDn works (for the PC users), abbreviations of FORWARD work, tabbing to the word FORWARD displayed on the command line and then pressing return works, and entering the number 22 to scroll ahead 22 lines works. Macintosh users can use scroll bars and they can use the mouse to point to commands.[15]

**Indiana's AIE:** Unlike CUINFO, VTX, and PNN, Indiana University's Academic Information Environment (AIE) provides access to computing resources.[16] Indiana wrote their own software (in Pascal) to run under VMS. They paid particular attention to the user interface; the screens were designed by a standards team consisting of a graphic artist, an editor, a programmer, and a CAI consultant.[17]

Figure 2 presents the AIE menu (March 1992).

**MUSIC/SP:** Some campuses, including McGill, Lafayette, and Lehigh, are using software called MUSIC (Multi-User System for Interactive Computing/System Product) for their CWISs. MUSIC was developed at McGill University in Montreal, Canada, and is distributed by IBM.[18] According to Roy Miller, one of its developers, MUSIC "includes a full-function CWIS system that supports menus, full-text keyword searching, direct updating of sections by the data providers, electronic feedback from viewers to data providers, and access to external systems through TCP/IP."[19]

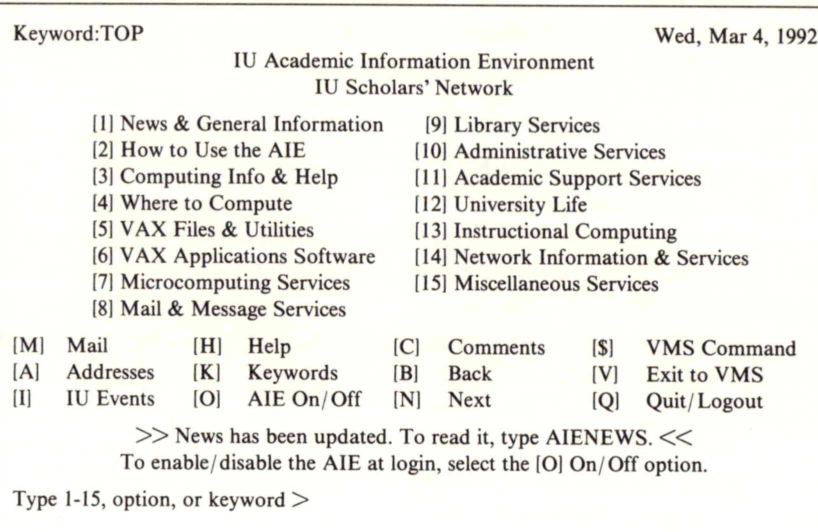



*Figure 2.*   AIE Initial Screen

**TechInfo:**   MIT developed TechInfo which runs on a MacPlus with one megabyte or more of memory, System 6.0.3 or better, and licensed MacTCP drivers. Source code is available free. Campuses running this software include Mississippi State University and the University of Pennsylvania.[20]

Tim McGovern says that one of the design goals of TechInfo was to distribute the responsibility for content to the information providers. Thus, MIT designed tools that information providers could use over the network to enter new information and to maintain information.[21]

**Other systems:**   There are several new systems under development that utilize client/server architecture to present information so that users can navigate through it using the tools they have on their workstations. Each database is presented by a server, and the user's interface to the databases is controlled by client software run on the user's workstation. Thus the user interface is different for each type of client and is natural to the user.

## Linking Information Systems

There are at least three implementations of software that facilitates logging onto remote services: LIBTEL (a UNIX script), LIBS (an implementation that runs under VMS and UNIX), and Hytelnet (a hypertext system for UNIX and VMS). These products provide menu access to libraries, CWISs, and other information systems worldwide. You simply select the service you would like to connect to and the software makes the connection for you. You do not need to know the Internet address for the service or the appropriate terminal emulation (VT100 or TN3270). With current implementations, once you connect to a service, the way you navigate is determined by the service you are using. Perhaps before long, there will be a single user interface to similar services, so that online catalog searches, for example, are done using one command language, regardless of the software used by libraries being searched. Appendix B describes how to use the LIBTEL software at UNC-CH.

The Internet Gopher developed at the University of Minnesota uses client/server architecture. Gopher is described by Mark McCahill, of the University of Minnesota, as a distributed document delivery service that allows access to documents residing on multiple hosts. Users can look at documents from menus or prepare queries and receive a list of documents that match the search criteria. You can access the Gopher system as a VT100 client via Telnet.[22]

Another approach to linking campus systems is the Campus-Wide Information Systems Protocol (CWISP), described by Strauss as a protocol (based on Z39.50 standards) that will allow users of a CWIS to access data of other CWISs while preserving the user interface of the local CWIS.[23] However, Strauss says that deciding to use the Z39.50 protocol added complexity to CWISP and it was taking a long time to implement . Meanwhile Gopher appeared on the scene and has become the defacto CWISP. He says that work on CWISP is on hold.[24]

WAIS (Wide-Area Information Server) is a protocol, evangelized by Brewster Kahle of Thinking Machines Corp., that allows users to perform searches of multiple databases at remote sites worldwide. Queries are simple English sentences or phrases. Matches are assigned usefulness values (based on criteria such as the number of matches in the selection) and listed at your workstation by value. Once a good document is found, you can use relevance feedback to find more documents like it, and you can then easily retrieve items of interest on your workstation. Currently, text and graphics can be retrieved; inclusion of sound and full-motion video is anticipated in the near future.[25]

WAIS also utilizes client/server software. Unlike current implementations of Gopher, WAIS uses the Z39.50 communications protocol. Perhaps one solution to the CWISP problem would be to implement Gopher in WAIS.

Another approach to presenting information is the wide-area hypermedia initiative called World-Wide Web (WWW or W3). Initiated at CERN, the European Particle Physics Laboratory in Geneva, Switzerland, W3 displays vary depending upon the type of workstation you are using. While for a VT100 it displays text with imbedded numbers and if you enter one of the numbers you get more information, for more sophisticated workstations it displays multifont text; linked text is underlined or boxed as a button and you can point-and-click to follow the link. Another function of W3 is an index search. According to Tim Berners-Lee of CERN, "Some documents are tagged as 'index cover pages'. When you get one of those, you can do a search by typing in keywords (like WAIS)."[26] Further according to Berners-Lee, other systems, like WAIS and Gopher, "can be represented as a combination of hypertext links and searchable indexes."[27]

Figure 3 shows the WWW opening screen (April 1992) as displayed for a VT100 terminal.[28]

```
                                    The World Wide Web project (23/50)
                        WORLD WIDE WEB

    The WorldWideWeb (W3) is a wide-area hypermedia[1] information retrieval initiative
    aiming to give universal access to a large universe of documents.

General Project Information

    See also: an executive summary[2] of the project, Mailing lists[3] you can join, Policy[4],
    latest W3 news[5].

    Project Status[6]      A list of project components and their current state. (e.g. Line
                           Mode[7], X11 Viola[8], X11 Erwise[9], NeXTStep[10], Daemon[11])

    People[12]             A list of some people involved in the project.

    History[13]            A summary of the history of the project.

    How can I help[14]? If you would like to support the web..

Technical details

1-26, Back, Up, >RETURN< for more, Quit, or Help:
```

*Figure 3.*    World-Wide Web Initial Screen

Regardless of the particular software used, we can expect to see more information accessed directly on the computer on which the data is maintained; there will be less copying of information to change its location or format.

## OPERATIONAL ASPECTS

### Who Initiates the CWIS?

Early systems were defined by imaginative programmers (like Steve Worona of Cornell and Howard Strauss of Princeton) who observed the difficulty of getting information to the people who need it, when they need it. They were encouraged and supported by the people responsible for the information. Those who came later liked what they saw and wanted to provide similar services on their own campuses.

On some campuses (North Carolina State University, UNC-CH, and Northwestern University, for example), implementation of the campus information system was initiated by a high-level university administrator. On many campuses, implementation of the service was driven by information providers wishing to get specific information, such as calendars of events and class rosters, to students, faculty, and staff in a timely manner.

### Getting Support for the CWIS

In an interesting discussion on CWIS-L about the driving force behind the implementation of a CWIS, Strauss said that "developing a system is often the easy part. Getting anyone to use it or support it can be orders of magnitude more difficult." He started a list of criteria for a CWIS,[29] which was enhanced by contributions from Worona[30] and Terry Mathias of Southern Illinois University at Carbondale.[31] They made the following points:

- Try out a few CWISs before developing a new one.

- Start by defining the services your users want and then finding the tools to provide those services.

- Make sure that the CWIS contains the information people want to see and that it is presented clearly.

- Make the system entertaining and have things that people want to know so that they will use the system. If people use the system, it can also inform and educate them. A daily police blotter, for example, is compelling, informative, and educational.

- Don't overlook useful information outside the university. CWIS users have lives that extend outside their offices and classrooms.

- The CWIS must be easy to access, for example, from public terminals in a variety of locations around the campus.

- A CWIS needs an assertive, resourceful person who can tap a variety of campus information structures.

### Who Maintains the CWIS?

Most CWISs are operated by the campus computer centers. Northwestern University is an exception; there the library is responsible for the CWIS. According to Brian Nielsen, Assistant University Librarian, "The Library more or less allied with administrative computing, arguing that current surplus capacity on an IBM mainframe should be utilized to build a more centralized utility; the Library argued that some 'editorial responsibility' was required to make a CWIS that was easy to use by any student/faculty member/staff, and agreed to take on such responsibility itself."[32]

The work associated with maintaining the database is distributed between the information providers and the organization responsible for the CWIS itself. On some campuses the information providers install the data themselves; on others, the organization responsible for the CWIS installs the data.

### Advisory Committees

Many campuses have established committees to assist in establishing policies. At UNC-CH, the original steering committee consisted of a student, a computer science faculty member involved in text research, a journalism faculty member with experience with videotex systems, three librarian/programmers (one of whom had experience with a CWIS), and the three people from the computing center responsible for developing the system. The steering committee met several times during the planning stages of the service, helping to determine policies and define the menu structure.

Some of the outcomes were:

- The committee reviewed menu proposals, tested the prototype, and recommended significant changes.

- The committee recommended a topic orientation instead of an object orientation; subjects from books were used as menu items rather than having the books themselves as menu items.

- The committee helped establish the CWIS management position as publishers, not writers or editors.

## Policies

Timothy J. Foley (Lehigh) has described the need for a clear computing and information policy that addresses possible legal liabilities, censorship, resource management, information ownership, and user responsibilities.[33] Policies need to be established for determining what campus information is considered to be public information. Some campuses are having difficulty obtaining permission to install in the CWIS some information that appears in print on campus: campus directories, for example. Advisory committees can be extremely helpful in this area.

Policies also need to be established for how the information will be organized and how the work of installing information is divided between the information providers and the organization responsible for the system.[34] Some campuses have documents describing policies and procedures for entering data into the CWIS.[35]

## Cost

Computer hardware and software costs vary widely. Many campuses run their services on hardware that was already on campus; some have acquired new, relatively inexpensive workstations. Some campuses use free software, others use proprietary software, and some develop their own software.

The majority of the cost of a CWIS is personnel time to monitor the database; add, delete, and change information in the database; train information providers; acquire and add new sections to the database; and to keep university faculty, staff, and students informed about what is in the database and how to use it.

## Putting Information into the System

The following aspects of entering text into the database are addressed by the information providers and/or the service providers:

- *Converting the information from its current form to a file on the CWIS machine.*

  The majority of the information in a CWIS comes from a computer file, but the difficulty in moving it from one system to another will vary depending on the software and hardware used on each end. Computer programs may be needed to convert the formatting codes used by the originating word processor to something useful on the CWIS machine. Note that this step could be eliminated in the future by CWIS software capable of accessing information directly on the machine where it is maintained.

  Some information, such as announcements for special events, may come to the service providers as phone calls or printed announcements and need to be keyed into the system.

- *Preparing the file for display on a computer screen.*

  Files prepared for the printed page usually need reformatting for a computer screen. The first steps are to change the font and character size so the characters are monospaced (all the same width) and the size they will be on a computer screen, for example, Courier font at 12 points, and to change the line length to something like 65 (screen displays are usually a maximum of 80 characters).

  The next step is to create an ASCII file; that is, one with no special characters in it. There usually is an option in the word processing software to do this, but some do a better job than others. (You may have seen e-mail messages that have a capital R instead of an open quotation mark and a capital S instead of the close quotation mark.) Regardless of how it is done, bullets, em dashes, en dashes, true (curled) quotation marks, and accent marks should be changed to standard keyboard characters.

Tabs can present a problem, depending upon the word processing software used. When saving an ASCII file, some software inserts blanks to preserve spacing, but some leave the tab character. When displayed on the user's terminal, tabs at best will not provide the spacing the editor intended.

Tables may be too long for the computer screen and need to be split. Pie charts and bar charts need to be retyped as tables. Sometimes tables or forms are omitted from the CWIS and readers are referred to printed copy.

Footnotes often need to be relocated within the text.

● *Changing menus.*

Menu structures need to be evaluated and changes made, as appropriate.

● *Adding highlighting.*

Some CWIS software provides highlighting features, such as bold, flashing bold, and inverse video. While it can be useful to highlight headings and footers, highlighting has its hazards; how it looks on a particular screen depends on the terminal and the terminal emulation software. For example, at UNC-CH, inverse video is used to display the title and date of the source document in the bottom line of the screen. However, many terminals on campus do not have inverse video capabilities, and the source identification in the footer is often difficult to distinguish from the text itself.

● *Installing the data and checking it.*

Procedures are followed to install the data in the database and check each screen.

At UNC-CH, a lot of time is spent converting files from their original form to the format for the database, adding highlighting and the commands to actually install the data, and checking it after it is entered. There was a time when the time-consuming nature of this activity at UNC-CH was questioned. Then in an e-mail message to CWIS-L, David Millman (Columbia) expressed curiosity as to how Howard Strauss and Rita Saltz handled the day-to-day maintenance of their CWIS,[36] and Rita Saltz (Princeton) responded with her famous "groan" message, describing how her staff takes information in whatever form they can get it in and installs it in their database.[37]

In an interesting discussion of ways to put weather reports in CWISs, several campuses admitted to calling weather stations, taking notes, and typing in the reports. But Gary Anderson (Virginia Institute of Marine Science, College of William and Mary) described automatic procedures for obtaining weather and updating their CWIS several times a day. He noted that "The 4am posting has been especially helpful to those about to put out to sea for a day of fieldwork!"[38]

In fact, most campuses have developed some programs and scripts to aid in installing data. Strauss strongly encouraged CWIS managers to work on the maintenance problems, saying that the problems of maintaining a CWIS can be solved, and that "Arizona State University is running a version of PNN and has highly automated the update procedures."[39]

## CWIS Managers as Publishers

Most who provide CWISs think that their task is to gather existing, edited and reviewed publications and present the information in a useful fashion. One question that arises regards how much fixing should be done before information is put in the CWIS. Should spelling and punctuation errors be corrected? Should printed publications be changed to keep them current?

When a publication is put in the CWIS at UNC-CH, the name and date of the publication is provided in a footer that appears on each screen. At the beginning of a document, a note is usually included containing at least the department and a phone number of the department responsible for the document. As a matter of policy, the documents in the database contain *exactly* the same information as the printed documents. If a document is changed, permission is sought from the editor of the document and/or a note is included explaining what was changed and why.

UNC-CH has a rather unique problem of multiple sources for information because publications are divided and the information is organized by subject. For example, there is overlap between *The Undergraduate Bulletin* and the student handbook, called *The Source*. The information providers for both documents agreed that information in *The Undergraduate Bulletin* takes precedence over that from *The Source*. Thus, if you look at the section on "Grades" under "Academics," you see the section from *The Undergraduate Bulletin*.

## Taking Information Out of the System

Most campuses have addressed the need to remove information when it is out of date; old information looks bad and takes disk space. In many cases, the software allows specification of an expiration date that is carried with the text but hidden from the viewers, and the text is automatically deleted after the specified date. But there are some interesting issues associated with removing information, particularly events, from the system.

It is not always clear how much text should be associated with the expiration date; for example, should a sports schedule (such as a football schedule) be treated as one text that is removed at the end of the season or should each event be removed the day after it happens? If an event spans several days, do you take it out after the first day or the last? Exhibits that span several days should be kept in the system through the last day, but information about workshops is not valuable through the last day because people who missed the first day probably cannot participate.

For seasonal events, should the entry remain on the menu after the last event of the season, before the next schedule is available, or should the menu be changed to remove the selection? If the menu selection is left in the system, what message should the user see when there are no more events in the season?

At UNC-CH, events are removed the day after they happen, menu choices are left for schedules even if no events are listed, and the message "There are no events to post at this time." is inserted by the software that removes events when it takes out the last in the schedule.

## Designing the Menus

Like many campuses, UNC-CH began designing its system by planning the menus. Existing systems were examined, items that might go into the database were identified, and a prototype containing just the menus (no data) was built .

The advisory committee tested the prototype. The main menu contained too much text; there were 14 items on it, each with a long description of what was in that area. It did not invite people to use the system.

UNC-CH initiated its service with a menu that had jobs and grant/ funding information under "News" and academics, student life, and services and facilities under "Ask INFO about...". Before long, categories much like those in the prototype were moved back to the main menu, because they most clearly represented the information in the database; however the items were shortened and presented in two columns.

The main menu for a CWIS presents political, practical, and design challenges, as many people want their information presented on the main menu. It is very handy to have an advisory committee to share in the decision-making process when questions arise about design, particularly the main menu.

Issues of breadth versus depth also challenge designers of CWIS menus. In the early days of its service, UNC-CH worked toward a set of menus designed to include all information on campus that might become available, but items were added to the menus only when the information became available in the database. Thus, users would sometimes have to move through menus of only one or two items each to get to the information they wanted. Even after a couple of years of development, there wasn't enough information available in the database to warrant the number of levels of menus, and users didn't seem to know what information was available to them in the database. After about three years of operation and continued development, UNC-CH redesigned its menus building them for the data already in the system or clearly on its way. The depth of menus was reduced, often by putting a large number of items in one menu.

When developing a new service, some campuses present full menus before all of the information is available. If a user selects an item that is not in the system, they get an appropriate message. Some campuses highlight information that is available. For example, both Appalachian State University and Western Carolina University use inverse video to highlight the item numbers of items in the system.

Another consideration associated with designing menus for a CWIS is how to construct menus for a large publication. Is it better to show the full table of contents, with the subheadings in a long menu that may exceed one screen, providing menu choices at logical points (more like hypertext), or should the menus be hierarchical, one menu of the major headings, and then several menus of subheadings? If menus are subject-oriented (as they are at UNC-CH), how do you combine those from several publications into a meaningful menu?

One last note on menus: If newsletter articles are presented as a menu, the newsletter editors should re-evaluate titles of regular monthly articles, such as "Recent and Relevant" and "Feature of the Month," to provide more informative titles.

## How Much User Documentation Does a CWIS Require?

A CWIS should require minimal documentation. Users need to know how to connect to it, how to move around, and what information is available in the database. Indiana University has paid particular attention to documentation needs. According to Marsha Snyder Waren,[40] Indiana's initial Academic Information Environment (AIE) came with easy-to-use menus, online help, and 115 pages of paper documentation (describing, for example, how to search the online card catalog and how to use Dow Jones News/Retrieval). AIE's documentation was then reduced to a handful of how-to sheets. Waren continues to evaluate CWIS documentation needs. In October 1991, she asked CWIS-L, "Do you encourage your users to survive on electrons alone? Or do you provide something on paper to get them started more comfortably?"[41]

Responses indicated that several campuses provide indexes or maps as part of the service itself, and some have an area in the CWIS describing new additions to the service. Some campuses also provide starter and overview information on paper.

## Feedback: How Useful Is It?

Most systems provide mechanisms for recording frequency of access to specific pages. Some CWISs (for example, Lehigh) provide usage statistics as part of the database.

But how are usage statistics used? If segments of the database are not used, does that mean the information is not useful or that people don't know the information is in the database or that people can't find it?

In these years when CWISs are still new, should CWIS managers take out information just because it isn't being used? There are still many people on campuses with CWISs that don't know the CWIS exists. As these services become more common and more useful, more people will learn about them. When a person looks for information in a campus database, they should find it, even if it is information that is not accessed very often. On the other hand, statistics do indicate what information is not being accessed so its placement in menus can be checked and advertising provided for it, if appropriate.

One way CWIS managers find out what the users want is from phone calls and e-mail messages. At UNC-CH, if jobs are not posted on time, users call and complain. People call when something is wrong, and they often send e-mail describing what they would like added or changed.

## FUTURE DIRECTIONS

The future for CWISs promises to be exciting. Sophisticated ways are being developed to link information systems; services are being expanded off campus to the community; and the idea of the library as the focal point for computer-based information systems is gaining force.

### Linking Information Systems

While text-searching capabilities across databases worldwide, as provided by WAIS, present attractive alternatives to menu-driven information systems, they do not exclude the desirability of menu-driven systems. Some people will want to explore menu-driven systems, while people who know what they are looking for are more likely to want to use text-searching facilities. Hopefully, the information in CWISs worldwide can be linked together for text-searching inquiries as well as being available via traditional menus. For example, high school students should be able to search university catalogs electronically. They should be encouraged to go to their public libraries or computer work rooms in their schools to access campus information systems and look at eligibility requirements, course offerings, student activities, housing, and tuition costs as they begin to select the colleges they might want to attend.

Similarly, it would be nice to be able to move easily from menu mode to text-searching mode and back again when looking at information. Consider the following scenario: A user works through some menu items and finds a section of interest on a local information system. The user then issues a command that says, "Show me more of these." If, for example, continuing education courses in public health are being displayed, the system might respond: "Would you like to see more continuing education courses in public health?" If the user responds "Yes," then text-searching software would search directories and present the user with a list of other selections.

As more information systems are linked together, it will be increasingly difficult to tell where the information you need is physically located, but where it is will become less important, as long as you can get to the information electronically.

Unless information providers are careful in how they identify information when they put it in databases, users may find a piece of text appropriate to their needs, but have difficulty identifying the source document. As Daniel Updegrove (University of Pennsylvania) pointed out in a message to CWIS-L, if everyone is committed to designing systems as Internet resources, there is a lot of information that could be shared. However, he also noted that content might need to be adjusted to provide more complete information, for example, adding areas codes to phone numbers.[42]

Further, information services will become more closely linked on the campus level. Some campuses already have one main menu for accessing mainframe computing services, the campus library, and the CWIS. Hopefully in the near future users will be able to make queries that would cross boundaries of information systems, such as the library holdings and the campus information system. This won't happen unless it is planned for and services using standard protocols like Z39.50 are developed.

### Expanding Toward Community-Wide Information Systems

Campus-wide information services are expanding into the general community in two ways: campuses are encouraging the use of their services by alumni and prospective students, and campus personnel are helping to establish community information systems.

Parents of currently enrolled students, alumni, prospective faculty and students, and journalists would benefit from access to campus information. Electronic mail services would be particularly valuable for parents of currently enrolled students. Electronic mail, bulletin boards, and news groups can be particularly valuable to alumni.

Some communities have established local public information services. These are free services offering electronic mail, discussion groups, and ask-an-expert services, as well as accessibility to event schedules, directories, brochures, and the like. These systems are run by the communities themselves, with volunteers doing most of the work, but most are affiliated with a local university. For example, Cleveland Free-Net is sponsored by Case Western Reserve University (CWRU), Cincinnati's TriState Online service is affiliated with the University of Cincinnati, Peoria's Heartland Free-Net is affiliated with Bradley University, and Youngstown Free-Net is affiliated with Youngstown State University. These universities provide campus information to the community system. Several more communities are in the process of establishing similar systems, and some campuses are moving toward putting their campus information systems into the community systems.

There are several different models of community information systems. The Public Electronic Network (PEN) offered to the residents of Santa Monica, California, has received much attention. PEN is based on the UNIX operating system and software called Caucus. It was introduced to the public (local residents only) in February 1989.[43]

Several communities are using the Cleveland Free-Net model, and Free-Net users have formed National Public Telecomputing Network (NPTN), similar to National Public Radio. NPTN will assist in the development of community information systems and disseminate information features in areas such as health, education, government, and law to its affiliates.

According to literature provided by NPTN, Cleveland's system began "in the fall of 1984 when Dr. Tom Grundner, then of CWRU's Department of Family Medicine, set up a single phone line, computerized, "bulletin board" system called "St. Silicon's Hospital and Information Dispensary" to test the effectiveness of telecomputing as a means of delivering general health information to the public."[44] The Free-Net software is written in the C programming language and uses the UNIX operating system.[45]

Most of the community services are accessible from the Internet. Appendix B describes how you can explore them.

## Roles for Libraries

Librarians should have central roles in expanding CWISs. While on most campuses the CWIS was implemented as a computer service, it is becoming increasingly clear that the task of overseeing CWISs belongs in the campus libraries. Librarians have traditionally gathered information, organized it, provided tools for locating it, and helped people find the information they need. Many of the issues facing providers of campus information have already been addressed by librarians; censorship, freedom of information, prohibition of keeping records of access by individuals, for example. It makes sense for computer centers to do the research and development work, to evaluate hardware and software, to develop tools for entering text, and to improve computer networking interfaces, but computer specialists are not well prepared for establishing policies regarding access to information. While campus libraries and computing centers have traditionally worked well together, there appears to be a need for closer interaction between the two.

Libraries are also in a better position to provide free computing for CWISs than most computing centers are. During the last few years many libraries have implemented their own computing systems and services and now have the resources to support the CWISs. Meanwhile computing centers typically charge for services and find it increasingly difficult to justify providing information services free when at the same time charging for other uses. Libraries traditionally provide free services.

Libraries are logical places to provide terminals for accessing campus and community information systems; people traditionally take their questions to the libraries. To help patrons use these services, librarians will need to continue to expand their knowledge of electronic information services.

Librarians are already providing information to their users through campus and community information systems. These systems provide the mechanism for innovative ways to provide library reference services and information about special collections.[46]

Further, community information systems will need people to run them. Most of the community information systems currently in place have at least one full-time staff position to coordinate the effort. These positions seem well suited to the skills of librarians.

The librarian's Strategic Vision Steering Committee could have been thinking about CWISs when they drafted the following vision statement:

## Strategic Vision for Professional Librarians

Establish the basis for librarianship in the 21st century in:

SERVICE

By selecting and delivering information that users need at the point and moment of need;

By creating and maintaining systems which provide accurate and reliable information;

By promoting the design of information systems that require little or no learning time for effective use;

By correctly analyzing users' questions and providing them with the information they need (which may not be reflected accurately in their questions);

By educating users to manage information;

By initiating contact with potential information seekers to ensure a widespread understanding of professional services available to them, including assistance for those who do not wish to use the library independently;

By furthering the development of the "virtual library," a concept of information housed electronically and deliverable without regard to its location or to time;

LEADERSHIP

By taking responsibility for information policy development, information technology application, environmental awareness, information research, and risk-taking in making strategic choices in the information arena;

By accepting accountability for the information services we provide;

By identifying and collaborating with strategic partners and allies in information delivery. ...[47]

These aspirations certainly reflect the requirements for making CWISs more valuable services in the future.

# APPENDIX A
# CWIS-L LISTSERVER

An electronic discussion group, called CWIS-L, has been invaluable to those of us who provide CWISs. When we have a question or a problem or are thinking about trying something new, we post a question to the list. During the next few days we receive advice from our colleagues worldwide and can adjust our plans based on the experience of others. The questions and responses can uncover aspects and legal considerations we hadn't thought about. Participants have been free with advice and take the time to compose messages to help others.

CWIS-L has provided much of the information for this paper. I subscribed to the list in January 1990 and since then have logged many of the messages I found particularly interesting. It has been fun to reread them while preparing this paper. Excerpts from several messages are included here. Further, members of the list have provided extensive help in preparing this paper.

Steve Middlebrook of Washington University set up the electronic discussion group, or "listserver," called CWIS-L in January 1990. CWIS-L has been maintained by Timothy Bergeron (c09615tb@wuvmd.bitnet) of Washington University since October 1990.

The stated purpose of CWIS-L is as follows:

> This list is for discussing the creation and implementation of campus-wide information systems. The term CWIS includes systems which make information and services publicly available on campus via kiosks, interactive computing systems and/or campus networks. Services routinely include directory information, calendars, bulletin boards, databases and library information.[48]

Entering its third year of operation in January 1992, there were over 1,000 subscribers. The discussions on this listserver are also available in the Usenet news group bit.listserv.cwis-l, so there are more uncounted participants.

To subscribe to this list, send to LISTSERV@MSU.EDU, the following message:

> SUBSCRIBE CWIS-L yourfirstname yourlastname

For example, SUBSCRIBE CWIS-L Judy Hallman.

Messages sent to CWIS-L@MSU.EDU are sent to everyone signed up to the list. If you reply to a message from CWIS-L, be aware that your reply will be directed to the entire list, not just to the sender of the message. Messages are archived; see your local computer people for information on how to use archives.

# APPENDIX B
# TRYING OUT SERVICES

Besides providing the conduit for electronic mail, the Internet allows us to connect to CWISs worldwide. Campuses that have systems up and running provide information on how others can access their services via the Internet and try them out. For people who are designing new services or contemplating major changes, it is really helpful to be able to explore someone else's design. For people planning new services, it is also valuable to be able to try out the underlying software using someone else's implementation and see what the capabilities of the software are from the user's point of view.

During the summer of 1990, I started gathering a list of services and occasionally posted it to the list. Art St. George (University of New Mexico), co-founder and maintainer of the *Internet Library Guide*, asked me to maintain this section for his publication. With the help of others on CWIS-L, I have done so. The first list was published in the *Internet Library Guide* in Fall 1990. Entries tell how to connect to the service, the hardware and software used, a contact person, and special items of interest in the system. You can pick up this list by anonymous FTP to ftp.oit.unc.edu; it is in pub/docs/cwis-l. See your local computer people for information on how to use FTP.

LIBTEL software makes it easy to explore CWISs; it displays menus of services and then will connect you to the service you chose. You can try LIBTEL at UNC-CH using the Extended Bulletin Board Service (EBB). Telnet to ebb.oit.unc.edu, logon as ebb. (Note: You cannot use EBB if your terminal is emulating an IBM 3270-type terminal.) You will receive some informational messages and be asked for your name. From the EBB menu, select item #9 (Libraries and information systems). If you then select USA, you will be asked to choose the state in which the service you want resides. After you select a state, you will get a menu of services offered in that state. For example, if you select NY, you can select CUINFO at Cornell. The EBB software will then make the connection for you, if you so choose; you do not need to know the Internet address of the service you want to use. Further, EBB provides the proper terminal emulation for you (Telnet or TN3270).[49]

# NOTES

1.   The author's e-mail address is: judy-hallman@unc.edu). Note that e-mail addresses can change. Those listed in this paper were valid in April 1992.

2.   For an extensive list of information provided by CWISs, see: Rita Saltz (rita@pucc.bitnet), "Report of CWIS-L Discussion Session at Snowmass," cwis-l@wuvmd.bitnet, 7 August, 1991. The message contains the working notes from the August 5 workshop session, "Operating and Maintaining a Campus-wide Information System," at the General Directors' Seminar/22nd Annual Seminar on Academic Computing, held at Snowmass Village, Colorado.

3.   David Lassner (david@hula.oit.hawaii.edu), "RE: Was CUINFO the First," cwis-l@wuvmd.bitnet, 14 January 1992).

4.   Rita Saltz (rita@pucc.bitnet), "Was CUINFO the First," cwis-l@wuvmd.bitnet, 13 January 1992.

5.   Steven L.Worona (slw@cornella.bitnet), *An Informal Overview of CUINFO* (*Cornell's Computer-Based Bulletin Board System*) (n.p., n.d).

6.   Ibid.

7.   Ibid.

8.   The contact person for CUINFO is Steve Worona (slw@cornella.bitnet).

9.   Worona.

10.   There is a listserver for VTX, VTX-L@NCSUVM.BITNET.

11.   Users on one UNC campus simply select another campus from a menu, as shown in Figure 4 from the UNC-CH system.

There is no noticeable degradation in response time when looking at data on another service regardless of the distance between campuses (for example, Appalachian State University and UNC-Wilmington are more than 400 miles apart). Eventually we hope to have all 16 of the University of North Carolina campuses on this link, making it easy for us to share information.

Besides access between UNC campus services at the main menu level, DECNet allows connection directly from any menu choice or by special "global" keywords. For example, a person on the Chapel Hill campus who selects "Publications" from the main menu and then selects the electronic publication "Postmodern Culture," will view the publication installed in the North Carolina State University database in Raleigh.

12.   Appalachian State University is currently using this feature which, according to Ernest Jones, "provides voice responses to an Alumni job opportunities file." Ernest Jones (jonesel@appstate.bitnet), "RE: CWIS and Voice Service," cwis-l@wuvmd.bitnet, 19 December 1990.

13.   UNIX is a Trademark of Bell Laboratories.

14.   The contact person for PNN is Rita Saltz (rita@pucc.bitnet). Direct system and development questions to Howard Strauss (howard@pucc.bitnet).

15.   Howard Strauss (D8897@pucc.bitnet). "User-friendlyness of CWIS," cwis-l@wuvmd.bitnet, 18 October 1990.

16.   Indiana's AIE is generally only available to registered users, but it is possible to obtain special permission to look at AIE by contacting Pete Percival (percival@iubacs.bitnet).

To connect directly (via DECNet) to the information service on another University of North Carolina campus, select one of the following services:

1.  Appalachian State University, VideoText System
2.  North Carolina State University, Happenings!
3.  University of North Carolina at Greensboro, Minerva
4.  University of North Carolina at Wilmington, SeaBoard
5.  Western Carolina University Information System

For information on how to connect to information systems worldwide, select the following item:

6.  How to connect to information services via the
    UNC-CH campus extended bulletin board

Commands: Help Quit Main Backup Find

   Enter menu choice number or command:

*Figure 4.*   DECNet Connection Instructions

17.   Caroline Beeb. "Friendly but Streamlined: Implementing an Integrated University Computing Environment," in *Proceedings, ACM SIGUCCS User Services Conference XVIII*,(NY: Association for Computing Machinery, 1990), 31-34.

18.   Direct inquires to Roy Miller (ccrmmus@mcgillm.bitnet).

19.   Roy Miller. "Comments on Your CWIS paper," E-mail message to hallman@unc.bitnet, 13 March 1992

20.   The contact person is Tim McGovern (tjm@mit.edu).

21.   Tim McGovern (tjm@eagle.mit.edu). "Re: Manpower Estimates and CWIS Data," cwis-l@wuvmd.bitnet, 4 January 1991.

22.   Mark P. McCahill (mpm@boombox.micro.umn.edu). "New Release of PC Gopher Client Software Available," cwis-l@wuvmd.bitnet, 19 September 1991.

23.   Howard Strauss (D8897@pucc.bitnet). "CWISP," cwis-l@wuvmd.bitnet, 19 October 1990.

24.   Howard Strauss (D8897@pucc.bitnet). "Status of CWISP???," e-mail message to hallman@unc.bitnet, 8 April 1992.

25.   A WAIS bibliography, prepared by Barbara Lincoln (barbara@think.com), is available for anonymous ftp from /pub/wais/wais-discussion/bibliography.txt@quake.think.com. The bibliography covers WAIS documents, WAIS-related articles/publications, and electronic services. Hard copies are available from Barbara Lincoln (barbara@think.com), Thinking Machines Corp., 1010 El Camino Real, Suite 310, Menlo Park, Ca, 94025, phone: 415-329-9300, fax: 415-329-9329.

26.   Tim Berners-Lee (timbl@info.cern.ch). "RE: Please Check Info for a Paper on CWISs," e-mail message to hallman@unc.bitnet, 6 May 1992.

27.   Ibid.

28.   The contact person for World-Wide Web is Tim Berners-Lee (timbl@info.cern.ch). He says, "There's more information in the web. You can pick up line mode, NeXT or beta test X browsers by anonymous FTP from info.cern.ch—also you could pick up a paper from the same node: /pub/www/ doc/ENRAP—9202.ps for example, or a version of the W3 'book' from /pub/ www/doc/the—www—book.ps.Z ( or .tex for LaTeX version)."

29.   Howard Strauss (D8897@pucc.bitnet). "Re: Drive Force Behind Implementing a CWIS," cwis-l@wuvmd.bitnet, 28 September 1990.

30.   Steven L.Worona (slw@cornella.bitnet). "Re: Drive Force Behind Implementing a CWIS," cwis-l@wuvmd.bitnet, 2 October 1990.

31.   Terry Mathias (ge0515@siucvmb.bitnet). "Driving Forces in CWIS Creation," cwis-l@wuvmd.bitnet, 2 October 1990.

32.   Brian Nielsen (bnielsen@nuacvm.bitnet). "Re: Drive Force Behind Implementing a CWIS," cwis-l@wuvmd.bitnet, 27 September 1990.

33.   See: Timothy J.Foley (tjf0@ns1.cc.lehigh.edu). "Developing a Campus Computing and Information Policy: Issue and Concerns," CAUSE/Effect 14 (Winter 1991): 25-29, 33.

34.   As part of her work toward a Masters in Communication and Information Studies at Rutgers, Hannah Kaufman, of Princeton, has prepared a report "Campus-Wide Information Systems: Factors Affecting Willingness to Contribute Information." A summary is available from her via e-mail to hannahk@pucc.bitnet. She notes, for example, that people seem to contribute "to provide information to a different (not larger) group" and because of "a belief in online information."

35.   Kansas State University, for example, has a document describing policies and procedures to be used for including information in their system, called UNICORN (UNIversity Central Online Resource Network). The document includes instructions for users to prepare and install their own information. For more information, contact Betsy Edwards (betsy@ksuvm.bitnet). UNC-Chapel Hill has a similar document; contact Judy Hallman (hallman@unc.bitnet).

36.   David Millman (dsm@cunixf.cc.columbia.edu). "Forced e-mail," cwis-l@wuvmd.bitnet, 2 October 1990.

37.   Rita Saltz (rita@pucc.bitnet). "Day-to-day Maintenance of PNN (Groan)," cwis-l@wuvmd.bitnet, 3 October 1990.

38.   Gary Anderson (gary@ches.cs.vims.edu). "Re: Weather," cwis-l@wuvmd.bitnet, 19 July 1991.

39. Howard Strauss (D8897@pucc.bitnet). "Re: Non-University Info," cwis-l@wuvmd.bitnet, 11 July 1991.

40.   Marsha Snyder Waren. "How Much Paper Do You Need to Support an Electronic Information System,?" Proceedings, ACM SIGUCCS User Services Conference XVIII, 1990, pp. 355-360.

41.   Marsha Snyder Waren (waren@unixpop.ucs.indiana.edu). "Paper Maps of CWISs.," cwis-l@wuvmd.bitnet, 24 October 1991.

42.   Daniel Updegrove (updegrove@dccs.upenn.edu). "CWIS as Internet Resources?," cwis-l@wuvmd.bitnet, 13 April 1990.

43.   Articles discussing PEN include: Gayle Hanson. "Making Waves Via Computer," *Insight*, (27 Jan, 1992) and Pamela Varley. "Electronic Democracy," *Technology Review* (November/December 1991): 42-51.

44.    From literature from NPTN. For more information about NPTN and Free-Net software, contact T. M. Grundner, Ed.D., President, National Public Telecomputing Network, Box 1987, Cleveland, Ohio 44106. Voice: (216) 368-2733. FAX: (216) 368-5436. Internet: aa001@cleveland.freenet.edu.

45.    Ibid.

46.    Anne K. Abate and Rosemary Young. "Community Access Bulletin Boards: Cincinnati Librarians Become Involved." *Special Libraries* (Spring 1992): 113-117.

47.    Sue Martin (skmartinΘvax.bitnet). "Draft Vision Statement," pacs-l@uhupvm1.bitnet, 17 January 1992.

48.    Timothy Bergeron (c09615tb@wuvmd.bitnet). "Re: Info on CWIS," cwis-l@wuvmd.bitnet, 7 November 1990.

49.    The Extended Bulletin Board is a development project of the Office of Information Technology, University of North Carolina at Chapel Hill, and is experimental. Services are often expanded, modified, or dropped as appropriate, and no service-level guarantees are made to the users.

# USE OF A GENERAL CONCEPT PAPER AS RFP FOR A LIBRARY SYSTEM:

## A NEW MODEL FOR LIBRARY SYSTEM PROCUREMENT

Mona Couts, Charles Gilreath, Joe A. Hewitt, and John Ulmschneider

## INTRODUCTION

The Triangle Research Libraries Network (TRLN) is a consortium of three research libraries, Duke University, North Carolina State University, and the University of North Carolina at Chapel Hill, located in close proximity in the Research Triangle Park (RTP) area of North Carolina. TRLN operates programs of cooperative collection development, reciprocal borrowing privileges, and access to collections; document delivery services; and, since 1983, a locally developed, distributed online catalog—the Bibliographic Information System (BIS). In 1989, the TRLN Board of Directors decided

Advances in Library Automation and Networking, Volume 5, pages 177-202.
Copyright © 1994 by JAI Press Inc.
All rights of reproduction in any form reserved.
ISBN: 1-55938-510-3

to discontinue development of BIS and to migrate to a commercially available system as soon as feasible.

In acting on this decision, TRLN adopted a novel approach to screening and evaluating candidate systems. Rather than using a typical RFP listing the desired functionality, technical specifications, and performance standards in great detail, TRLN distributed to vendors a concept paper describing a vision of future TRLN systems and the general qualities of systems and vendors that would match that vision. *The Concept Paper* was sent to some 30 vendors with a request to respond to the major themes and issues expressed in the document. These general responses were used to screen the number of candidate systems to two for intensive investigation and evaluation.

There were several elements in the rationale that led to this approach to systems procurement. First was the recognition that all systems are in a state of development and flux; any RFP that focuses on currently available functionality and feature sets artificially freezes a moving target, with potentially problematic results. The real issues in choosing a system relate to what it is expected to become in the future, how the vendor plans to achieve its goals, and the relationship that the vendor is willing to establish with key users to pursue mutual objectives. In short, the key points of emphasis relate to the future, not the present, and they have to do with qualitative characteristics of systems and vendors rather than those suitable for a standard checklist-based assessment procedure.

A complementary element in the rationale was the assumption that all systems, or at least those that have achieved some degree of critical mass in terms of customer base, offered a basic level of functionality that would be acceptable for the TRLN libraries for the present and for the immediate future. Another way of stating this position is that library systems under consideration for adoption should be assessed primarily as platforms for future development rather than fixed systems with a stable set of functionality and features available for immediate installation.

A third element of the rationale related to the need for TRLN to express a new strategic direction for its systems. The decision to cease local development was unquestionably sound economically. On the other hand, BIS was a familiar system and an excellent one in some respects, and it offered customized features that would not be duplicated in commercially available systems. Staff in the TRLN libraries had invested considerable effort in the development of BIS. While there seemed to be a widespread general understanding of the financial conditions and systems considerations that had led to the decision to discontinue local development, BIS still had its supporters and there was continuing uncertainty about the ability of TRLN to meet its long-term goals and maintain its unique qualities as a network while using a vendored system.

As a result of these contextual conditions, it was necessary to treat the system selection process at TRLN as part of a change in strategic direction rather than a mere procurement decision. Thus the systems selection process was intended to inaugurate a new way of looking at the future for a staff that had grown accustomed to a systems environment based on local development and control. It was obvious to those who wrote the *Concept Paper* that the strategic dimensions of systems selection were frequently deemphasized in standard procurement processes. The selection of a system for TRLN appeared to be a good opportunity to develop and test a new approach to systems evaluation, one that emphasized system selection as a strategic decision rather than a mere purchase decision.

This chapter reproduces the TRLN *Concept Paper*, further explicates its rationale, and describes the context in which it was used. The paper also reports and analyzes vendors' responses to the *Concept Paper* as an exploratory procurement instrument and assesses it as a potential approach for other libraries and consortia. Any process of system selection must be individually designed to meet the needs of the procuring organization; the *Concept Paper* is not presented as a model for others. However, it is presented as a case history of a library organization attempting to overcome the limiting assumptions governing standard RFPs for library systems. Perhaps it will also serve as a useful example for other organizations that hope to improve on this obsolete procedure.

## OBJECTIVES OF THE CONCEPT PAPER

The decision to discontinue development of BIS was based primarily on financial considerations. The TRLN libraries faced major hardware upgrades; large segments of functionality in BIS remained to be developed; existing software required increasingly substantial investment in ongoing maintenance; the system needed basic redesign and reimplementation to become more flexible in the current networking environment; the hardware was unique in the Triangle University environment; and TRLN was isolated from University-based system support groups familiar with the TRLN hardware. In short, the Universities simply could not support continued local development. The decision to discontinue BIS was self evident and inevitable.

As a result of the overwhelming weight of financial factors, little concrete exploration of alternatives to local development was made at the time of the decision to abandon BIS. It was taken for granted that TRLN would adopt a commercially available system, yet a systematic examination of the market for suitable replacement systems had not occurred. At the same time, the staffs of the TRLN libraries had not been directly involved in the decision to discontinue BIS development and it was necessary to explicate the context of this decision and to explain its rationale. It became evident that a single document that would present a general view of TRLN's current status and desired future direction would be useful both for the procurement process itself and as a means for informing the staffs of TRLN's strategic position. The *Concept Paper*, which was written originally as a report to the TRLN Executive Committee, was intended to meet the following objectives:

- To state briefly the rationale for discontinuing local systems development; for this reason the document at several points speaks to specific limitations in BIS and to disadvantages of TRLN's situation as a systems development organization. At the same time, strong features of BIS areacknowledged and incorporated as ultimate goals of replacement systems.

- To state a new underlying approach to future development of TRLN systems, including adoption of a vendored system and cultivation of productive working relationships with hardware and software vendors.

- To describe specifications and requirements of a new system in general terms with an emphasis on systems selection as a strategic decision; also to supply a supporting rationale for moving away from specific functional and performance checklist evaluation procedures.

- To suggest the general framework and content of a codevelopment relationship with a vendor which would serve as the basis for a future document developed after discussion and negotiation with vendors.

- To prepare the staffs of the TRLN libraries and potential vendors for a selection process based on the premises stated in the *Concept Paper*.

In the TRLN organization, the Associate and Assistant Directors of the constituent Libraries constitute a group called the AULs Forum that was established to advise the Executive Committee and the Board. This group has initiated a number of grant proposals and other TRLN projects. A subgroup of the Forum wrote the *Concept Paper*, the paper was approved by the full AULs Forum, and transmitted to the Executive Committee. After its adoption as an accurate description of TRLN's future directions, it was decided to make use of the document as a procurement instrument. In effect, TRLN decided to share with potential vendors a basic internal planning document and asked them to respond to the proposition that they might have a contributing role to play in its realization. The full *Concept Paper* is reproduced in the following section.

## CONCEPT PAPER: THE FUTURE ONLINE SYSTEM AT TRLN
## INTRODUCTION

The bibliographic information system (BIS) developed by the Triangle Research Libraries Network (TRLN) has served as an adequate online catalog for the TRLN libraries for six years. Like all online catalogs of its generation, BIS falls short of the ideal library retrieval system. BIS's particular pattern of strengths and weaknesses results from limited resources for development and necessary trade-off decisions made in the course of design and implementation. In spite of a number of excellent features, BIS does not represent a promising platform for developing the fully functioning library information system of the future, primarily for the following reasons:

1. the high cost of local development;
2. an expensive hardware platform;

3.    major gaps in retrieval and authority control functionality;
4.    software that is difficult to modify to incorporate features.

For these reasons TRLN has decided to adopt a new strategy to the implementation of the next generations of its online systems.

Briefly, the new approach involves acquiring systems from commercial vendors. In doing so, TRLN will of course consider current functionality and performance of systems, but its primary goal will be to establish mutually beneficial relationships with innovative software firms that share TRLN's vision of future library systems. At the same time TRLN will seek to establish a similar relationship with a hardware supplier with a strong commitment to library applications and to the educational and library market. This document describes this strategy in more detail and delineates TRLN's general vision of future library systems. It is not intended to serve as a specifications document for the evaluation of candidate systems.

## ASSUMPTIONS

The underlying assumption at this time is that TRLN will not identify a system that will meet all of its requirements. We share the perception of numerous librarians that state-of-the-art systems offered by commercial firms still do not fully meet research library needs. Many difficult trade-off decisions will have to be made with respect to the current functionality of systems evaluated.

Not the least of these decisions will relate to the extent to which TRLN must sacrifice the strengths and special features of BIS not commonly found in commercial systems in order to gain expanded functionality in other areas. Examples of the special qualities of BIS include:

1. the distributed network design;
2. a record validation system that is possibly the most advanced in the field;
3. superior capabilities for normalizing index terms and search statements, and indexing special characters;
4. refined capabilities for handling complex holding mixtures (different call numbers for multiple and the same location; accompanying materials, etc.).

It is acknowledged that the new strategy may result in the loss of some of the outstanding bibliographic qualities of BIS, at least in terms of current capabilities. However, these capabilities will be sacrificed only for the sake of larger strategic advantages that place TRLN in a more favorable position with respect to the transition to future generations of online information systems.

A prominent general assumption about future library systems is that interconnectivity and flexibility will be their most critical characteristics. Interconnectivity can be defined in several contexts; on each campus, the library system should be a major component, if not the integrating core, of a campus-wide information system; it should also serve as a gateway to external databases, including full text systems, as well as document delivery and information services of various types; and it must be easily interfaced with workstations to serve as the source of data for individualized electronic files and electronic document delivery systems. Flexibility implies, among other things, hospitality to records from many different sources, including OCLC, LC, GPO, indexing services, as well as locally created records. Through flexibility and interconnectivity, the system's primary data file will not only be more varied and expansive, but the system will allow users access to a variety of data sources beyond those representing the libraries' own collections. It is in this area that a new system should redress some of the major limitations of BIS. In the general assessment of candidate systems, the technical implications of this concern for interconnectivity and flexibility involve issues of standards, hardware compatibility, networking capabilities, and so forth, that may in some cases override issues of present performance in support of specific library functions.

A third assumption is that the local networking environment will continue to be a paramount consideration. The linked online catalog supports shared use of collections and programs of cooperative collection development that constitute the heart of TRLN collaboration. A principal criterion for judging candidate systems will be their potential for supporting these programs, either in terms of present networking capacity or negotiated agreements concerning future development. Support for networked architecture, however, does not require that TRLN mirror the existing configuration for operations, with computers and systems management staff at each TRLN site, but rather that the catalogs functionally and architecturally embody desirable network features, even if the implementation is on a single computer or several computers housed centrally. Of all current BIS functionality, the networking capability will be the one that must be preserved in some form in a new system.

A fourth assumption is that the future TRLN system need not be a fully integrated library system as traditionally conceived. Rather, the total system may consist of a series of interfaced components chosen on the basis of their performance in supporting specific functions (online catalog, acquisitions, serials control, etc.). Thus a major consideration in selecting systems may be their hardware compatibility and potential for interfacing with components already in place.

A fifth assumption is that successful acquisition and implementation of commercial systems will turn on the ability of the TRLN libraries to meet needs and build acceptance throughout the university communities. For this reason, system acquisition, development, and implementation will be done in cooperation with the university computing communities, in particular with the university computing centers. The libraries will draw on the particular expertise of the campus computing communities in hardware performance, application performance and efficiency, distributed computing and connectivity, awareness of standards and standards compliance, and operating systems. It is important that the libraries keep the computing centers, along with other campus constituencies, fully informed on progress and developments during the search and evaluation process. While the libraries must build strong connections with campus computing centers, the relationships they establish should ensure that final judgments and decisions on systems acquisitions and development priorities rest with the TRLN libraries.

The final assumption is closely associated with networking and flexibility. It is assumed that the appropriate arrangement with a software vendor will include involvement of TRLN in the design of future systems and some degree of codevelopment. It is anticipated that joint development efforts will present the opportunity to apply TRLN's software engineering expertise in networking and processing support as well as shape a significant library system of the future. Collaborative arrangements assume that vendors will be "in for the long haul"; vendors with stable market and financial histories will become principal candidates to supply systems support. Purchased systems and the vendor relationships that come with them will fill two roles: as a production platform for support of routine library operations, and as a dynamic, flexible development and experiment platform open to improvements as required by the TRLN libraries' constituencies. It is further assumed that the principal areas for TRLN participation will be in embellishing and customizing the system's capability for interconnectivity and flexibility, or development "on the fringes" of the primary applications software system. This assumption is based on a principle that we believe may well be the ideal goal of future library systems and library/vendor relationships: the acquisition of a general systems capability designed so that the user interface and interconnectivity with other local systems is largely under user control. The goal will be a cost-effective combination of standardization and customization. The vendors' level of interest in working in this direction will be an important criterion in the selection process.

The weight of these assumptions has strong implications for the systems evaluation process. Taken together, these assumptions imply that the decision of which system to acquire will be conceived as a strategic decision, not one based on close item-by-item comparison of current systems capabilities. It will be a decision with respect to how and under what conditions the TRLN libraries will proceed in the future to provide successive iterations of online systems rather than a choice between specific configurations of functionality and performance as they are currently offered in the systems marketplace.

## STATE OF THE ART AND FUTURE OPAC FUNCTIONALITY

The functionality of an OPAC is the extent to which the system meets programmatic requirements for a library's production environment. Commercial offerings judged most competitive for the research library market offer capabilities recognized as "state of the art" to meet those needs. "State of the art" in this sense means capabilities that have come to be regarded as essential features for research library systems. The TRLN libraries assume that TRLN cannot develop BIS in a cost-effective manner to provide such essential features commonly available in commercial systems.

Commercial products appropriate for research libraries provide "state-of-the-art" feature sets similar in scope, refinement, and capacity, but no commercial system provides a feature set that fully meets research library needs. Differences between these commercial offerings, while sometimes significant, do not change their relative ability to meet the programmatic requirements of the TRLN libraries. Because of their similarity, analysis of appropriate products will weight configurations of functionality and performance considerably less than previous reviews undertaken by TRLN. Factors that will assume a larger role include the vendor's accommodation for joint development, the degree to which a product's design and implementation permits changes to meet future system requirements, and the performance of "state-of-the-art" systems in life-cycle cost models.

## "State of the Art" Features and Considerations

1.  *Standards compliance:* Software and hardware comply with promulgated and de facto standards that are well established for library applications systems, and show evidence of compliance with emerging standards important to systems migration and peer- to-peer data communications. A partial and by no means exhaustive list of such standards includes:

- NISO Z39.2-1985 MARC format
- NISO Z39.58 Common Command Language (ISO/CCL standard)
- Other NISO Z39 standards as applicable
- SGML and other compound document standards
- ANSI RS-232C for serial communications
- TCP/IP support for remote network sessions
- "Glass teletype" and VT-100 for asynchronous terminal interface control
- ISO/OSI Open System Interconnect protocol suite
- SMTP or X.400 for electronic mail services

Compliance with network standards is particularly important in light of TRLN's commitment to collaborative collection development.

2.  *Well supported hardware platform:* The hardware platforms required by products are well represented and supported by the TRLN university community. This means that the university communities have such significant

investments in the selected platforms that the TRLN libraries will benefit from purchase and maintenance discounts, site licenses, special vendor arrangements, and communications infrastructure support. In addition, the hardware supplier will have a strong commitment to library applications and to the educational and library market.

3. *Financially secure, stable vendor:*   The selected vendor is stable, with sufficient installed base, financial backing or assets, and demonstrated organization staying power.

4. *Uses modern software engineering techniques:*   Vendors that use "state of the art" software engineering techniques to construct and maintain their products will be considered better prepared for support and development than vendors whose products represent or require older, less flexible, more expensive techniques. Few or no operational commercial products show thorough-going use of modern engineering techniques, but ongoing development of some products employs such techniques to varying degrees from vendor to vendor. Modern engineering techniques for large-scale software development and maintenance include:

- **Modular construction:**   Application system is organized as discrete modules well isolated from other system components. The application's interface to hardware isolates machine-dependent interactions to replaceable modules, and database architecture is as removed as possible (given optimization constraints) from hardware and operating system considerations.

- **Prototyping:**   Applications development relies heavily on CASE and I-CASE tools in a structured environment that employs rapid prototyping techniques as much as possible when defining and implementing functional specifications and requirements.

- **Quality control:**   Separate quality control systems independent of development systems that test and evaluate product functionality and reliability.

5. *Provide integrated access to information:*   Integration of data has come to mean modal access to data organized and presented as logically coherent entities to users. For instance,

users can see comprehensive bibliographic data on items in library collections while using the catalog section of an OPAC ("catalog mode"), comprehensive information on journal articles while using the external database section of the OPAC ("external database mode"), and comprehensive information on community activities while using the bulletin board section of the OPAC ("bulletin board mode"). The data for each section need not reside in a single database, on a single machine, or in a single product. In general, commercial systems access the collections of different libraries on the same product by a modal switch to their databases; the integrated union view of different catalogs provided by BIS is not available commercially.

6. *Authority control:*  Different products provide different degrees of control over catalog entry points. The strongest and most flexible control possible over all entry points is desirable. Good authority control will provide a suite of tools for maintaining consistency and integrity of catalog entry points, such as global change and replace for any entry point, automatic notification of consistency or integrity violations from incoming records or edits, and variant form dictionaries or thesauri to map non-standard to authoritative forms.

7. *Use of multiple class number schemes:*   It is not uncommon for libraries to use more than one classification scheme for their collections, for instance, Dewey and LC. Commercial systems support multiple classification schemes in different ways, some more desirable than others. The BIS approach of interfiling all call numbers is the least acceptable alternative.

8. *Multiple input sources for records:*   Commercial products generally support three minimally required input streams for record creation: tape load from different vendors, where the software is equipped to deal with small idiosyncracies in vendor data formats; direct record transfer from OCLC, from either a screen image or a MARC record transmitted to the system; and local creation of full MARC records. TRLN will prefer systems having the greatest flexibility in handling different record formats. TRLN will examine systems particularly respecting their ability to load records from the broad variety of existing bibliographic management systems

already in use by TRLN libraries (e.g., INNOVACQ, BIS, microfiche systems, etc.).

9.  *Real-time editing of changes:*   Commercial products reflect changes to existing records in two ways: immediately, by applying edits as they are made; or by holding changes in special files until stand-alone programs are run to make the changes in the production database. TRLN will prefer products that reflect changes to the production database as soon as possible after the changes are made.

10.  *Comprehensive searching capabilities:*   Basic indexing and searching features of commercial systems include author, title, publisher, subject headings, call number, and control number searches; keyword indexes for library-specified fields; and, in some systems, proximity string operators, phrase searching, author/title search, and other more sophisticated searching tools.

11.  *User-tuned interface:*   Existing products offer varying degrees of user control over the appearance and capabilities of the system interface. All products offer strong parameter-driven control over the text of most screen messages and help screens. A smaller number of products give libraries control over screen layout and design. No commercial system permits changes to command parsers, screen or window sequencing, or searching algorithms beyond setting rudimentary system-wide parameters. TRLN will prefer products that provide the most local control over interfaces with the least intervention or action by the vendor.

12.  *Advanced record validation and editing system:*   The BIS software provides edit validation and management facilities that rank among the most advanced in the field. TRLN will prefer products that provide the largest subset of these facilities, particularly security measures and control over when an edited record is released for application to the database.

## FUTURE OPAC CAPABILITIES

The feature sets of current state-of-the-art library systems do not include crucial functionality that TRLN libraries can project as technically and financially reasonable, and likely to be required by their chief constituencies, by the mid to late 1990s. Furthermore, the scope and rate of change shown by information systems technologies in the past is unlikely to abate, so that capabilities unenvisioned now or deemed unrealistic will become standard requirements for future systems. Commercial products appropriate for research libraries will accommodate future OPAC capabilities and requirements by demonstrating systems architecture and development planning along the following lines.

1.    *Extendable system architecture:*   The product architecture permits or will permit integration of locally developed modules for specialized tasks, particularly modules for connectivity or local data capabilities. Appropriate products will show modular designs with well-documented global environment requirements and interface parameters values. TRLN will seek vendor relationships that share goals towards future functionality, using a product whose design allows local development and enhancement with local software engineering expertise.

2.    *Interface flexibility:*   The product architecture distinguishes interface from search engine sufficiently for local extensions or development of interfaces to the catalog. Ideally, the product will permit customized interface design beyond that offered by most existing products. The product will have development tools and training to manipulate the interface as required.

3.    *Precise retrieval of data in terms of its relevance to a user-defined need:*   The OPAC architecture is open to exploring or implementing new searching techniques other than Boolean sets for managing retrieval, such as transferable retrieval sets and relevance weighing and vector retrieval. These capabilities would be added to state-of-the-art query functions available in commercial systems for constructing retrieval sets based on title, author, keyword, and so forth.

4.    *User-defined arrangements of retrieval sets:*   An increasingly difficult problem with centralized library information systems is the size of retrieval sets: as the scope of library information systems expands, retrieval sets grow to intimidating proportions. The OPAC feature set provides or will provide flexible, user-defined ways to segment or subset large retrieval sets, for example viewing only those portions of a retrieval set available locally or only those items within specified publication date ranges.

5. *Classification access for subject browsing:* Current products provide for limited use of classification schedules for subject retrieval. Research points to improvements in retrieval through expanded use of classification searching, particularly for browsing collections. Classification searching will form the basis for a "virtual stacks" system. Virtual stacks will permit users to browse through shelf ranges, pick items from shelves and "open" them to scan the title and tables of contents, and move through the shelves from subject area to subject area regardless of the location of items in the "real" library.

6. *Flexibility in search engine and database content:* Library information systems will become a major component of university-wide information systems. To do so, the architecture of the system must provide a rich set of access and manipulation tools for enhanced bibliographic data, such as the full text of journal articles, tables of contents, and graphical images. In addition, the system architecture must provide for integrating different record structures and sources, for instance indexing records, electronic journals, electronic documents (compound documents), and other non-bibliographic databases.

7. *Integrated support for access by and to other computers:* The product architecture must provide for standards-compliant communications with other computers. The product should look to such capabilities as compound document transfer, subset transfer, transaction exchange (for interlibrary loan, automatic exchange of bibliographic records, circulation transactions, accounting data related to acquisitions, etc.), and machine-driven sessions with client desktop computers. The product should also look to support of gateway functions to data on other computers through standards-compliant techniques, for instance to locally developed databases on other computers, CD-ROM databases, and the like. Support for standard windowing techniques, particularly X, and low-end terminals (VT-100) is important. This functionality encompasses data transfer, but not data analysis; data is transferred to user computers for refinement and analysis.

8. *Modular construction:* The product architecture allows for sizing from small to large implementations in a modular fashion. Modular architecture also applies to adding other databases or other libraries in a multi-library system.

9. *Standardized, user-manipulated reporting tools:*   Database design should be open to the use of general end-user database tools such as SQL and other report generators.

10. *Advanced tutorial and help subsystems:*   Product architecture ideally supports locally constructed subsystems that provide complete tutorial instruction on the use of the OPAC, with access from the subsystem to the OPAC for conducting tutorial searches, realistic retrievals, and the like. Tutorial subsystems provide complete instruction that would otherwise require a librarian. Librarians likewise control the content of succinct online help for reminders and guidelines in using software facilities.

TRLN recognizes that this description of current and future OPAC capabilities ignores important details and cannot serve as a reference guideline for evaluating system functionality. Nevertheless, it captures widespread professional consensus concerning the basic requirements for next-generation OPAC systems in research libraries. It should serve as the first-line assessment model to determine whether candidate systems should receive further evaluation.

## CONCLUSION

This document offers a different perspective to systems acquisitions than that in general use by staff at TRLN institutions. Instead of evaluating details of functionality and performance, TRLN has decided to emphasize the strategic nature of systems acquisitions. Consequently TRLN has, for the moment, passed by specifying checklists of feature sets, guidelines for acquisitions, and other materials normally amassed prior to issuing an RFP. Instead, this document is intended to serve as the principal guideline for assessing commercial products with an eye to their strategic value and their suitability not only to bringing about TRLN's vision of future library systems, but to developing, in cooperation with hardware and software vendors, a new and expanded vision of library information systems and their role in academic information exchange. Products will be regarded more favorably as they provide greater flexibility for local development, openness to connectivity with other computing communities, and particularly as their vendors are open to establishing a mutually beneficial relationship for development and refinement of systems.

## DISTRIBUTION OF CONCEPT PAPER TO VENDORS

The above *Concept Paper* was completed in late November, 1990, and submitted to the TRLN Executive Committee for approval in mid-December. On December 17, 1990, the TRLN Director distributed the *Concept Paper* to a list of some three dozen vendors who had been identified earlier in the year when TRLN had sent out a Request for Information to companies marketing turnkey library systems. Accompanying the paper was a memorandum explaining that the *Concept Paper* was being used as part of the next step in selecting the second generation online system for TRLN. Vendors were asked to respond to the *Concept Paper* by providing TRLN with information that demonstrated how their software met the expectations and needs of TRLN Libraries and how their company's relationships with customers exhibited the kind of codevelopment partnership desired by TRLN for the future. In order both to elicit comparable information from vendors and to forestall responses long on philosophy but short on specifics, the memorandum posed the following six questions derived from issues in the paper:

1. What partnership programs do you have in place? To what extent does your organization support independent development? Cooperative developments? Please provide examples of such partnerships.

2. Do your libraries mount other software applications in combinations with your applications software? For example, may they mount office automation packages, imaging software, and so forth on the same processor? What are some examples?

3. To what extent does your applications software comply with standards such as those mentioned on page four (4) of the concept paper? As mentioned, the standards listed on page four (4) do not include all standards but are merely representative of our interests. What are your plans to support these or other standards? Please cite examples of your work in complying with standards.

4. What is the process for adding new capabilities to your software application? Please use a specific example to describe the process.

5.    What elements in your system's design and implementation facilitate database growth and the change or addition of functionality? Please describe specifically why you believe your system provides a platform on which future system requirements can be implemented.

6.    What hardware platforms does your system use? Describe cooperative programs in which you participate with the hardware vendor.

Vendors were asked to respond in writing to these questions and to comment on other issues addressed in the paper by no later than January 14, 1991.

The December distribution of the *Concept Paper* was necessary in order for TRLN to meet internal deadlines for a proposal to a potential funding source. The timing proved fortuitous for the exchange of information as well since it gave many of the vendors an opportunity to discuss the paper with staff members of TRLN libraries during the American Library Association Midwinter Conference, which was held in early January.

By the mid-January deadline, 13 software vendors and two hardware vendors (in support of their software partners) had responded to the TRLN memorandum. One software vendor provided two responses, based on different hardware platforms. One software vendor stated that it had no interest in establishing a codevelopment partnership as envisioned in the *Concept Paper* and that it would not make its source code available. That vendor was, accordingly, eliminated from further consideration. The 13 responses from the remaining dozen software vendors were the basis of evaluation by staff from the three TRLN institutions.

The responses from the vendors varied in their depth of coverage from about four pages to over 30. Although the TRLN cover memorandum had invited additional comment on issues raised in the *Concept Paper* and on the paper itself as a mechanism for gathering information on which to make a system selection, few of the vendors chose to respond formally to more than the six "required" questions. Among the volunteered comments on the paper, roughly half were brief, laudatory statements such as one might expect in correspondence to a prospective client. Two, however, discussed the paper more substantively. The first of these vendors indicated that the paper provided a good overview of the course libraries should follow when acquiring new automated systems and then went on to say, "Too often libraries select the most popular or glitziest system without considering the long-term implications of the soundness of system design or the degree to which the system can be adapted to meet changing needs or changing technology." The second of the vendors commented at length on both the content of the paper itself and on the process it outlined for system acquisition. They indicated that "the usual RFP process has little to do with the long range success of a library automation system. Many local systems have failed in spite of carefully and thoroughly prepared RFPs and even performance bonds. An RFP looks at minutiae and seldom looks at broader, more global issues." They went on to say, "The TRLN efforts to select and operate a library automation system based on the solid foundation of technology and partnership is commendable and is the best way to guarantee success."

The *Concept Paper* was developed in a relatively short timeframe, which did not allow wide discussion of its content among staff in TRLN libraries prior to its distribution to vendors. During early January, 1991, however, library staff, selected faculty, and staff members from the computing centers on each campus were brought into the evaluation process, using the paper as the focus for discussion of future needs and expectations of the next generation online system. Those involved were asked to study the paper, and they were invited to attend meetings that month at which the philosophy embodied in the *Concept Paper* and evaluation process itself would be discussed. This initial phase of the process was aimed at involving a broad range of staff in assigning weights to a set of evaluation criteria derived from principles that had been articulated in the *Concept Paper*. The authors of the *Concept Paper* were asked to develop the set of evaluation criteria to be discussed by the staff and faculty, who were then asked to assign to each criterion a weight ranging from 1 (lowest) to 10 (highest). The same weight could be assigned to more than one criterion since respondents were not asked to prioritize the criteria.

Fourteen criteria were defined, and these were divided into three categories.

Vendor criteria comprised four elements:

1. financial security and stability of the vendor,
2. vendor's commitment to the library/education market,

3.  presence of the vendor's products and hardware platforms on TRLN campuses, and
4.  the vendor's response to codevelopment.

There were four technical criteria:

1.  standards compliance,
2.  the extent to which the vendor employs modern software engineering techniques,
3.  the degree to which the vendor's products provide for easy access to/by other devices, and
4.  the availability of an architecture and development tools that allow for creation of interfaces to a wide range of devices.

Finally, there were six functional criteria defined:

1.  the availability of standard library functions in the vendor's products,
2.  the extent to which the vendor's products provide for integrated access to information,
3.  the availability of advanced features for database maintenance and authority control,
4.  the comprehensiveness of the vendor's searching capabilities in the online public access catalog,
5.  the flexibility of the vendor's software to allow easy modification of user interfaces, and
6   the effectiveness and efficiency of the vendor's report/ management information tools.

While the process of determining weights for each of the criteria was underway with faculty and staff, a designated group from the three TRLN libraries was independently rating the vendors' responses on a scale of from -5 to +5, using the same 14 criteria. The standards to be used in this rating were arrived at by consensus among the raters and documented before the ratings were assigned. For example, in assessing the criterion related to presence of vendor hardware and software on campus, the evaluators agreed to assign a rating of +5 to a vendor whose hardware and related system software was commonly found on all Triangle University campuses, a zero to a vendor well established in the industry and higher education but whose products were not found on Triangle University campuses, and a -5 to a vendor whose products were unknown.

Once the raw scores from the rating process were determined, the weights assigned by the faculty and staff groups were applied as multipliers in order to arrive at a final score for each vendor. The scores resulted in clear groupings, with a significant difference between the top two vendors and the next highest scoring group of companies. These two vendors were then invited to demonstrate their systems on each of the campuses and to prepare cost proposals both for a centralized and for one or more decentralized implementations of their systems. The demonstrations scheduled for mid-February, and cost proposals were to be received by the end of that month.

The evaluation of the systems now took a somewhat different turn. Up to this point, the development of evaluation criteria and the assessment of vendor responses had been joint efforts, engaging representative groups from the three campuses working together or having staff of the three institutions work separately but utilizing identical evaluation criteria. After the initial field had been narrowed to the top two vendors, it was felt that more independent evaluations of the two candidate systems would provide for broader staff input and allow for a fuller assessment of each system's potential in the working environment of the separate campuses. While staff at the three universities continued to consult with each other and to share information, the process for arriving at a recommendation for purchase essentially proceeded along parallel lines, with staff at each campus making independent assessments of system strengths and weaknesses. Staff were invited to the vendor presentations and were asked to evaluate each system in terms of a checklist of functional criteria developed at each campus. The form and content of the checklists varied considerably among the three campuses, but they all tended to be quite detailed, with considerable focus on searching capabilities and functionality that would have significant impacts on staff workflow and end-user interaction with the system. Each vendor made day-long presentations to the staff at each university and provided a number of terminals during the presentations for the staff to use in testing specific functions. In addition to the hands-on portion of the formal presentations, vendors also provided staff with dial-in access to selected customer systems and to test files for a few days before and after their on-campus visits. Many staff took advantage of this access to the systems as well to gain a fuller sense of how each system performed various functions. Staff at two of the TRLN institutions also made site visits to university libraries running the candidate systems and then shared their experience with other staff at the three universities.

The cost proposals were received at the end of February, and in early March both the hardware and software vendors made formal presentations to the library directors and the TRLN Board. These presentations were followed by a series of technically oriented meetings to clarify points in the proposals and to answer questions of functionality arising from staff evaluations and observations of the two systems. During this time, library staff also prepared five-year cost projections for each vendor based on similar functionality and configurations. This five-year cost cycle projection was deemed an essential element of the evaluation since only through that means can the true cost of the system over a reasonable lifespan be estimated.

Using the information gathered throughout this process, staff at each institution then arrived at independent selection decisions. Staff assessments indicated that neither system provided superior functionality in all areas of importance; each system had some superior qualities over the other, and both failed to provide some of the advanced functionality present in TRLN's locally developed BIS system. Despite the lack of clear superiority of one system over the other, the decision from the three campuses was, to everyone's surprise, unanimous. The recommendation was conveyed to the TRLN Executive Board and, with their approval, a proposal to the funding agency was prepared and the TRLN Executive Committee entered into contract negotiations with the selected vendor.

## EVALUATION AND CONCLUSION

The purpose of the *Concept Paper* was to describe a vision of TRLN's next-generation online systems and the general qualities of systems and vendors that would match that vision. The paper provided a framework for vendors, library staff, and computer center personnel to evaluate current system characteristics as well as potential development opportunities. It also served to emphasize to library staff that this selection process represented a change in strategic direction for TRLN systems development.

The computing center and library staff of the three TRLN institutions are rich in system development and operation expertise. The paper attempted to communicate to vendors the relevant strengths of TRLN staff and the potential benefits of a partnership role in the future development of our network system. The vendors of the systems selected for evaluation shared TRLN's enthusiasm for the vision expressed in the *Concept Paper* and were interested in discussing potential codevelopment areas. Interactions among computing and library staff from the three institutions and the hardware and software vendors were of a different nature than those that usually occur during the traditional RFP process. Rather than point-by-point discussions of system functionality and performance, these discussions were aimed at exploring areas of common interest and exchanging information on projects with similar development partners. The *Concept Paper* helped all parties to be aware of the fact that the vendor/client relationship was one of the most crucial components of the selection decision.

The selection process used by TRLN did not provide library staff with as much involvement in detailed functional-level examination as found in the traditional procurement process. Therefore, it was of utmost importance for them to have a broad understanding of the principles expressed in the *Concept Paper*. A considerable amount of time was spent discussing the paper and the vision it presented with staff on all three campuses. As a result of these discussions the staff began to think differently about the process and to develop a more sophisticated view of system selection generally. The *Concept Paper* reenforced the premise that the system did not have to be perfect and the criteria in the paper set the priority areas for investigation at a general level rather than as parochial functional concerns. With the *Concept Paper* as a guide, the checklists of functions were developed on each campus so that the evaluation process sought to uncover fatal flaws rather than serve as a shopping list of requirements.

Those who managed the selection process and most of the staff involved in it believe that it worked well in this situation. TRLN arrived at a unanimous decision for a system and for hardware and software vendors that matched its vision. Quantitative measures and the evaluation process supported subjective selection factors. However, it is difficult to judge the immediate success of the system selected since TRLN was not choosing a solution for today, but a platform to provide successive iterations of online systems. The final proof of the success of this process will be in the value that the vendors place on the codevelopment relationship referred to in the *Concept Paper*. The details of this relationship will have to be agreed cooperatively with the vendors.

The *Concept Paper* authors drafted a second document, *Concept Paper on Strategic Partnership* which outlines a model program for codevelopment. This paper suggests goals and principles for a strategic partnership and describes three types of projects. Each project type requires different relationships between the codevelopment partners and a different mix of resources and responsibilities. TRLN suggested the following types of projects:

1. **Software improvement projects** which would enhance applications software by adding new functionality or improving existing functionality. These types of projects would require significant commitments from both the vendor and the TRLN institutions. The functions developed by such projects would share three characteristics: the targeted function has a wide appeal to an important segment of the library systems market as well as to TRLN libraries; codevelopment represents a cost-effective avenue to develop the targeted function; and the vendor desires to revise or improve the targeted function outside the normal development schedule.

2. **System integration projects** which would add features or capabilities to software that would permit its full integration into, and interaction with, local networking and applications environments. An example of such a project might be to develop X-based client-server relationships over TCP/IP networks. These projects would involve strong partnerships with the library staff, other technical staff on campus sites, and the software and hardware vendors.

3. **Advanced technology projects** which would implement information technologies well proven in laboratory or small-scale settings but not applied to research library environments. An example of such a project might be access to documents with complex architectures such as structured documents, multimedia documents, and user-enriched documents. These projects must rely on resources and experience from a wide array of sources which may include regional and national experts as well as outside funding.

The codevelopment relationship with the vendor is still unresolved. However, the discussions with hardware and software vendors that took place throughout the selection process were useful in setting the stage for an ongoing relationship with TRLN, and it is expected that productive discussion of codevelopment and strategic partnership will take place after the full implementation of the system.

While the TRLN *Concept Paper* may not apply to all libraries or institutions, the selection technique itself may be useful. The process forces the library to assess the situation in a very different way, and is a useful method for bringing others outside the library into the process. The idea of choosing a system on the basis of its promise for future development may not appeal to some institutions, but it could be argued that every system is selected based on future prospects since no system remains static. Several cautions, however, are in order with respect to this approach to system selection.

First, it may prove more difficult to provide written justification for a selection made through this process than for one made through the traditional route, although the inclusion of some quantitative measures and an evaluation phase will assist in preparing such a justification. Secondly, it may be more difficult to rationalize a wrong decision reached by this process. Finally, it was also found that contractual arrangements were not given as much attention in the evaluation discussions as is customary in the traditional procurement process. Therefore, the contract negotiation phase took longer than anticipated.

In spite of these problems, TRLN found the use of the *Concept Paper* to be a practical approach for quickly reducing the field of vendors to the few who were most compatible with its strategic vision, so that it was possible to proceed directly to the evaluation stage. As library automation progresses, selection procedures used in earlier stages may become irrelevant. With more and more systems maturing, the traditional checklist of functionality may loose the ability to distinguish among systems. Thus, the TRLN approach may be more useful for second-time buyers than for first-time buyers. Second-time buyers tend to be more educated about automated systems and more familiar with their drawbacks. In fact, institutions may require experience with another automated system to be able to use the *Concept Paper* approach effectively. In addition, smaller libraries and institutions may not be able to offer codevelopment as a consideration in the selection process. However, it may still be useful to focus on the potential relationship with a vendor as part of their selection criteria.

It must be emphasized that the most valuable step in a selection process of this kind is to produce a document that articulates a vision of the system in a narrative fashion. This exercise helps the procuring organization to look beyond the functional specifications to the future of its systems. Such a document becomes an instrument for sharing the organization's vision widely among staff, constituencies, and vendors and thus becomes a defining element of future systems and the relationships required to bring them into being.

# RESEARCH ON THE DISTRIBUTED ELECTRONIC LIBRARY

Denise A. Troll

## INTRODUCTION

In 1986, the Carnegie Mellon University Libraries released their first automated retrieval system providing access to the Library Catalog and several other commercial and campus information databases. The Library Information System (LIS) operated on an IBM 3083 mainframe computer, offered one user interface, which ran on any machine that could emulate a TN3270 terminal, and displayed information in one format, ASCII. Though LIS was popular, from the users' perspective it was cumbersome and unreliable and did not take advantage of the power of their personal computers. If many people were using the system at the same time, searching and sorting were discouragingly slow. Often, the system was unavailable for technical reasons. When it was available, the user interface could display only ASCII text—even on computers with the capability to display information in other formats. From the perspective of library and system administrators, LIS was expensive and tedious to

Advances in Library Automation and Networking, Volume 5, pages 203-277.
Copyright © 1994 by JAI Press Inc.
All rights of reproduction in any form reserved.
ISBN: 1-55938-510-3

maintain. The mainframe made it difficult to add space for additional databases and impossible to provide speedy retrieval of full text and graphics. A new architecture was required to meet the needs and expectations of system users and administrators.[1]

In 1989, the University Libraries received support to build an advanced retrieval system. The Mercury Electronic Library Project had two goals.[2] The first goal was to build an affordable, efficient infrastructure that could deliver bibliographic and full-text information to desktop computers. The second goal was to monitor usage of the system to discern what people did with it, and to determine how their behavior changed over time as well as across databases and academic disciplines. The infrastructure developed by the Mercury Project was released to the Carnegie Mellon campus and the Internet on January 1992 as Library Information System II (LIS II).

Using a distributed architecture, LIS II offers multiple user interfaces, displays information in multiple formats, increases the speed of information retrieval, and increases the number of simultaneous users that can be supported. The architecture also improves reliability—users can access some databases while others are down for maintenance. The differences between running information retrieval on a mainframe (LIS) and running it in a distributed environment (LIS II) challenge the user's conceptual model of the electronic library, and decrease the cost of operating such a library. This paper describes the architecture and electronic resources in LIS II, the functionality of LIS II, and the performance and user interface studies done prior to its release.

## THE ARCHITECTURE OF LIS II

The architecture of LIS II is a distributed system of networked clients and servers. The clients are the machines on people's desktops (e.g., UNIX workstations, Apple Macintoshes, IBM PCs or compatibles, and terminals). The servers are workstations where the databases and retrieval and system administration software reside. Databases are built on a VAX 6410, then moved to the servers, which are DECstation 5000s. LIS II currently has four servers, but more will be added in the future to provide access to new databases. There is also an additional server for testing new databases and software prior

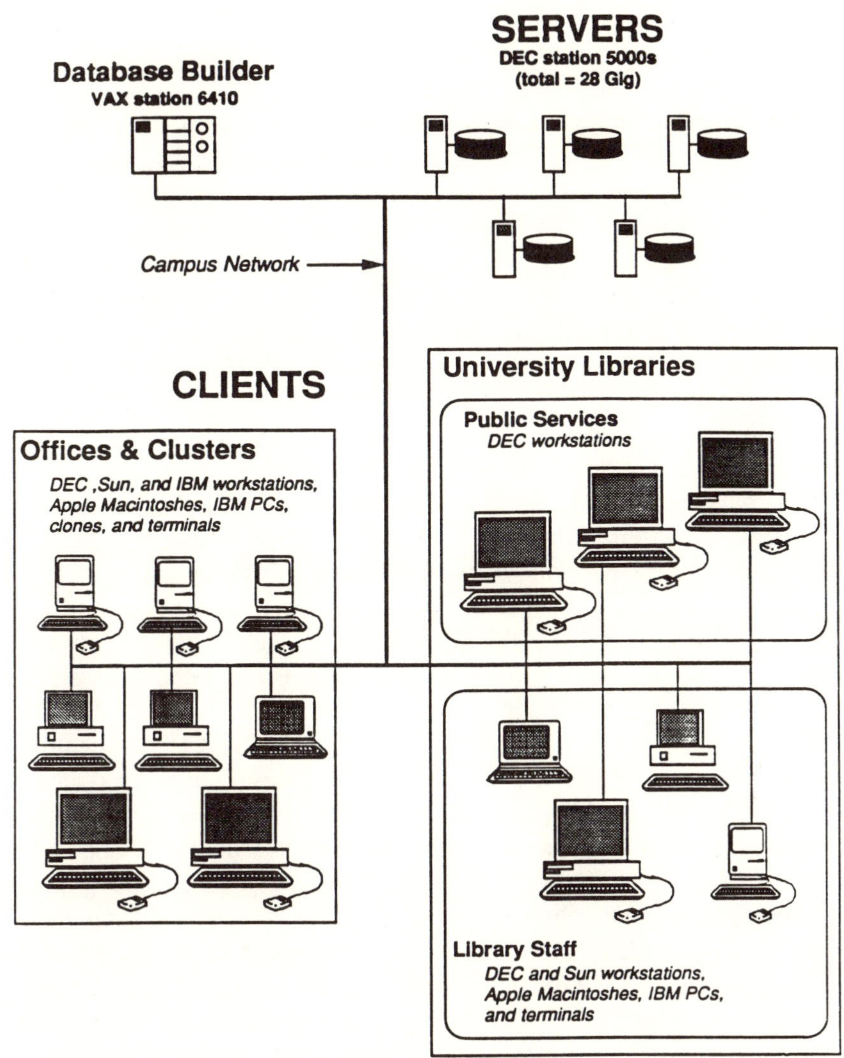


*Figure 1.* The Distributed Architecture of Clients and Servers in LIS II

to their release. (See Figure 1.) Though servers can reside at different locations on the network and be maintained by different groups, users perceive them as providing a unified information base. Clients and servers communicate with one another using the Z39.50 retrieval protocol layered on TCP/IP. The system is designed to be machine independent, and it incorporates existing or proposed standards.

Clients and servers share the work in LIS II. The division of labor improves performance and enables the provision of different user interfaces for different clients. Offering multiple user interfaces, LIS II can take advantage of the power of personal computers on campus and use the software conventions with which people are familiar. In the first release of LIS II, two client user interfaces support access to the servers and to network services like filing, mailing, and printing. An OSF (Open Software Foundation) Motif user interface is provided for UNIX workstations running X.11 windows, and a terminal interface is provided for other machines. A Macintosh user interface is being developed and will be available by the end of 1992. Some discussion has taken place about providing a user interface for DOS machines, but no commitment has been made. The Motif user interface is available on dedicated LIS II workstations in the three University Libraries and on workstations in offices and computer clusters across campus; it has been ported to DECstations and Sun Sparcstations. The VT100 user interface has been ported to DECstations, Sun Sparcstations, and IBM RTs; it can also run on a large number of similarly capable terminals. VT100 LIS II will be used by people at Carnegie Mellon who have an IBM PC or terminal; by all Internet and PREPnet (Pennsylvania Research and Economic Partnership Network) guests; and by users of the Oakland Library Consortium (OLC) Connection software that provides access to the library catalogs of Carnegie Mellon, University of Pittsburgh, and Carnegie Library of Pittsburgh. It will also be used by people who have a Macintosh until the Macintosh user interface is released. LIS II support is provided for machines connected to the campus network via synchronous or asynchronous connections (e.g., AppleTalk, Ethernet, Token Ring, Micom line, and Annex terminal server).

The work of LIS II may be described as a set of administrative and information retrieval services. Administrative services identify the user, determine what databases that user can see; locate those databases on the servers, and log what the user does. Information retrieval services search, retrieve, and display information. Different system components provide each of these services. Each software component is called a "server" because it provides a service. The term "server" therefore has two meanings in the context of distributed computing. One meaning refers to hardware: the workstations on which databases and retrieval software reside are called "servers." The other meaning refers to the software that provides a particular kind of service to a client; the kind of service provided is typically included in the name (e.g., authentication server, protection server, and retrieval server). Using these two meanings of the term "server," it is possible for several software "servers" to be running on one hardware "server." Throughout this paper, the word "server" alone refers to hardware; if software is meant, the server will be referenced by its name as in "authentication server." Delineating the services and the interactions between clients and servers in LIS II will explain how the distributed architecture works.

## Administrative Services

Because Carnegie Mellon is connected to the Internet, provisions must be made to ensure that site-licensed databases in LIS II can be accessed only by members of the Carnegie Mellon community. To do this, the information retrieval service needs to know the identity of each user. LIS II provides two interrelated administrative services that determine who the user is and what databases that user may see. The services are called authentication and protection, and both of them run on the server side of the distributed architecture. Two additional administrative services are also provided: name service, which enables clients to locate databases in the distributed system, and usage monitoring service, which logs transactions for later analysis.

### Authentication Service

LIS II authentication service is based on Kerberos, which was developed at MIT. The purpose of the authentication service is to get trustworthy information about the identity of each user. When users login to LIS II, the client prompts them for a user ID and password and then passes this information to the authentication server. Only the user and the authentication server know this unique combination of user ID and password. If the combination of user

ID and password is correct, then the authentication server issues the client an electronic ticket. The client passes this ticket to the servers when it requests services. The ticket contains the identity of the user encrypted in a way that only server software can read.

To facilitate usage, LIS II authentication has been merged with the authentication of two computing systems at Carnegie Mellon: the Andrew System, which is the central computing system on campus, and the system operated by the School of Computer Science (SCS). If users are already logged into one of these systems, they are not required to supply their user ID and password again when they run LIS II. LIS II picks up the authentication ticket that has already been issued to them.[3]

*Protection Service*

LIS II protection service is provided by the Andrew System. Its purpose is to control access to the databases. The protection server trusts the authentication server. When it receives a ticket from Kerberos, it knows who the user is and, based on its own database of information, which databases that user may see. To simplify maintenance, users are divided into groups and protections are set on the groups. LIS II currently has the following protection groups:

- *Public users.* Users who do not have or choose not to use a Carnegie Mellon user ID and password can see all released databases except those that are site licensed. For example, Internet guests can see the Carnegie Mellon Library Catalog and Journal List, but not the *American Heritage Dictionary* or *Academic American Encyclopedia* databases.

- *Authenticated users.* Those who use a Carnegie Mellon user ID and password (i.e., those who authenticate with Kerberos) can see all of the released databases, including the site-licensed ones.

- *Librarians.* Authenticated librarians can see all of the released databases and the databases that are in the final stages of testing prior to release.

- *Database testers.* Authenticated database testers can see all of the databases that have been built: all released databases

> and all test databases—whether or not they are ready for testing by the librarians.

More protection groups will be added in the future as different kinds of databases become available. For example, long-term plans include enabling departments to mount databases of working papers that will be accessible only by members of that department. Gateways to commercial information systems like DIALOG will be made available to people who have accounts with the University Libraries to pay for this service. In addition to being able to create new groups, the protection service enables system administrators to add or delete users from groups, and it allows them to specify or modify the database list associated with a group.

## Name Service

At this point in the login procedure, LIS II knows who the user is and what databases that user may see, but not where those databases are. In the distributed environment of LIS II, clients must know on which server a particular database resides. The name service functions to map database names to network addresses. The LIS II name service currently uses a text file that contains the names and addresses of the databases. The file is stored on the client side of the distributed architecture. When users login, the authentication service verifies who they are, the protection service returns a list of the databases they may see, the name service supplies the network addresses for those databases, and the client connects them to the four LIS II servers.

Because workstations are less expensive than a mainframe, important or heavily used databases may be replicated in a distributed computing environment to improve reliability and performance. If a database has been replicated, name service translates the database name into multiple network addresses. For example, there are two copies of the Library Catalog in LIS II because six years of transaction logs from LIS show that approximately 50% of the searches are done in the Library Catalog. The copies of the Catalog reside on different servers, so that, if one server is unavailable, the Library Catalog is still available on the other server. LIS II clients currently split the load between the copies of the Catalog using the time of day as a random number. Splitting the load between replicated databases improves performance.

In June 1992, a version of LIS II will be released that connects users to only one server at start up, rather than all four. The server will be the one with the least busy copy of the Library Catalog. When users select a different database, the name service will supply the network address of the server where that database resides and enable the client to connect to that server. Connecting to servers upon request will improve performance because idle connections use memory. This version of the software is being tested now. Also being tested for the same release is a Database Meta-Information (DMI) server that moves name service from the client to the server side of the distributed architecture. The DMI server software replaces the text file that currently provides LIS II name service. In the future, LIS II may use the OSF Cell Directory Service or something similar.

Usage Monitoring Service

LIS II provides an additional administrative service to monitor what users do. System administrators and designers need this information to improve service. To date, usage monitoring service has been implemented on the server side of the distributed architecture. The following transactions are being logged:

- Start up (login) and exit (logout or timeout).[4]

- Search and browse queries (terms, operators, truncation characters, and limits). To maintain the users' privacy, search terms are processed to remove all subject information but keep restrictors. For example, the query *ong/au and litera?/ti* is converted into *xxx/au and xxxxxx?/ti* in the transaction logs.

- The number of titles located in each search.

- The number of searches submitted and the number of searches completed. (Users may cancel searches in progress or resource control within the system may halt searches.)

The time, date, database, and encrypted user ID are logged with each transaction. The June release will also log the type of sort used to organize the titles retrieved in a search and the number of ASCII bibliographic records or full-text documents displayed. Scripts have been written that automatically generate weekly reports from the logs for each database; the reports contain simple counts for the numeric items noted above. The next step is to generate weekly reports of search complexity per database using the data logged from each query. Plans also include post-processing of the logs to associate each encrypted user ID with a college or department in the university.[5]

Data gathered in the transaction logs will be used to create different usage models. One model will establish usage per database, to determine if people use different search strategies with different databases. This information will enable the development group to pinpoint problematic searches and provide features dovetailed to each database. For example, perhaps a special tool or template needs to be provided to search chemical formulas in INSPEC or to do range searches of call numbers in the Library Catalog. Another model will establish usage per college or department, to determine whether, for example, humanists search databases differently from scientists. In conjunction with the per database usage model, this information will enable the development group to add support features for different demographic groups on campus.

As new features are added to LIS II, additional transactions will be logged at the servers. For example, LIS II will deliver full-text documents in bitmapped "page-image" format by the start of the fall semester; when this feature is released, the retrieval servers will monitor usage of the images. In the future, several transactions may be monitored at the client because they cannot be monitored at the server. For example, requests to save, mail, or print information must be monitored at the client because these requests are not sent to LIS II servers but to other service points on the network. Similarly, tracking whether users compose new searches by copying controlled vocabulary terms from bibliographic records or browsing the database indexes requires monitoring usage at the client. The data will shed light on what people do with electronic information and how they use the interactive context provided by LIS II clients. Building a comprehensive model of distributed retrieval requires logging transactions at both the client and the server.

In addition to building usage models based on data in LIS II transaction logs, a proposal has been submitted to the Department of Education and the National Science Foundation to receive funding for a longitudinal study of user attitudes and behaviors. The goal of the proposed study is to determine how acceptance of electronic library services is influenced by characteristics of the users and characteristics of the system. For example, how do gender, social group (e.g., student, faculty, staff, and alumni), and discipline (e.g., computer science, social science, and philosophy) influence how people feel about and what they do with LIS II? How do different features of the system itself (e.g., multiple windows, databases, and indexes) influence people's response to and usage of LIS II? Understanding the dynamics of how people use and adapt to electronic library services will help the Carnegie Mellon University Libraries choose the best services to provide and appropriate ways to promote them.[6]

## Information Retrieval Services

People use LIS II to retrieve information. What they do at their computer initiates exchanges between LIS II clients and servers. Information retrieval in a distributed environment is a series of interactions between clients and servers using retrieval software and a retrieval protocol. The database-building and retrieval software currently used in LIS II is Newton, developed by the Online Computer Library Center (OCLC).[7] Newton is optimized for large databases and Boolean retrieval. It has its own syntax for querying the databases it has built. The retrieval protocol is version one of NISO's (National Information Standards Organization) Z39.50 standard, which specifies a Boolean search language, the format for retrieved records, and standard errors. Using this implementation of the standard prepares LIS II to send queries to retrieval systems using the same protocol at other sites. However, Z39.50 syntax is different from Newton syntax, so translations are made on the server side of the distributed architecture every time client and server communicate.

In communication with a client, LIS II information retrieval servers perform the following functions:

- Translate queries sent from the client user interface in Z39.50 syntax into Newton syntax.

- Search the specified database for information that matches the search criteria.

- Create a set of record identifiers or pointers—called a "result set"—to the information found.

- Translate Newton syntax into Z39.50 syntax for return to the client.

- Send unformatted information to the client upon request and in a sequence marked by increasing detail (e.g., result set, list of titles in a result set, full bibliographic records for the titles in the list, then the full text of the articles indexed in the bibliographic records).

- Sort a list of titles in a result set.

In communication with an information retrieval server, LIS II clients perform the following functions:

- Accept input from the user, construct queries in Z39.50 syntax, and send them to the server.

- Format and display the information retrieved—in the sequence of increasing detail requested by the user and sent from the server.

- Maintain a context or interactive session log of the user's activities (e.g., result sets and index terms can be used to create new queries or modify previous ones).

- In the near future, LIS II clients will also request non-electronic services (e.g., interlibrary loan, book orders, book reserve, and courier service).

The information that users can search and retrieve in LIS II is stored on the servers in a growing collection of campus and commercial databases. The January release provides access to information in ASCII format. By fall 1992, LIS II will also provide access to information in page-image format. Databases were selected for inclusion in LIS II based on what information would be the most beneficial to students and researchers at Carnegie Mellon. The University Libraries wanted to provide different types of reference databases that offered subject coverage of all disciplines.

LIS II provides access to the following ASCII databases. Unless otherwise indicated, the database is available now:

*Table 1.*    LIS II Databases

---

**Bibliographic Databases**

*Local Campus Information*

Library Catalog
Journal List
ArchPics[8]

*Commercial Information*

ABI/Inform (UMI)
Computer Database (IAC)
INSPEC (IEEE)
Newspaper Abstracts (UMI)
Periodical Abstracts (UMI)
Social Sciences Index (UMI—available fall 1992)

**Full-Text Databases**

*Commercial Information*

*Academic American Encyclopedia* (Grolier)
*American Heritage Dictionary* (Houghton-Mifflin)
Business Dateline (UMI—available summer 1992)

**Other Databases**
*Local Campus Information*

Who's Who at Carnegie Mellon[9]
*Tartan* and *Focus* Index (available fall 1992)[10]

*Commercial Information*

Current Reviews for College Libraries (Choice)
ICPSR (*Guide to Resources and Services*—available winter 1992)[11]

---

Throughout 1992, LIS II will enhance information retrieval and document delivery service by linking databases. Databases may be linked in the sense that information in one database provides unique keys for retrieving information from another database. For example, ISBN numbers in the Library Catalog can be used to retrieve book reviews from the *Choice* database. Several kinds of links are planned and were considered when commercial databases were selected.

By fall 1992, ASCII databases will be linked to full-text page-image databases. Links are required to retrieve page images because page images cannot be indexed and searched directly. Image documents will be retrieved using keys in ASCII bibliographic databases. Users will search a bibliographic database, learn whether the full text of a particular item is available, and, if so, submit an electronic request for the image document. The Z39.50 retrieval protocol, originally designed to deliver bibliographic information in ASCII format, had to be modified to deliver full-text documents in page-image format.[12] Two LIS II image projects are currently underway:

- In a project with University Microfilms Incorporated (UMI), three bibliographic databases are being linked to full-text page-image databases on CD-ROM. Bibliographic records in ABI/Inform, Periodical Abstracts, and Social Sciences Index contain Article Reference Numbers (ARNs) that identify where the page images of the articles reside in Business Periodicals Ondisc, General Periodicals Ondisc, and Social Sciences Ondisc respectively. In the first phase of the project, the images will be used to provide print service; users will submit electronic requests to print the articles. In a later phase of the project, the images will be delivered over the network for online viewing.

- In a research project with Elsevier and IEEE (Institute of Electrical and Electronics Engineers), articles in selected computer science and artificial intelligence journals are being scanned, compressed, and stored on LIS II servers in hierarchical directories by journal name, volume, issue, and page. By fall 1992, the page images will be available for online viewing. The images are linked to bibliographic records in INSPEC and are also available using an Image Browser. Test implementations of both features are available now. People can search INSPEC, retrieve a bibliographic record, and then retrieve the full-text page images for the article indexed in that record. Using the Image Browser, people can select an issue of a journal and use it the way they would use a printed journal (e.g., beginning with the table of contents). Print service for these images will be added by the end of 1992.

Details of the image projects are provided later in this paper. When the image databases are released to campus, their use will be monitored. Usage (printing) of the UMI page images will be monitored at the UMI print server. Usage of the Elsevier and IEEE page images will be monitored at the LIS II retrieval server. Plans include monitoring how frequently page images are viewed, how many different people view them, which pages of an article are viewed, and the sequence in which the pages are viewed. When print service is provided for the Elsevier and IEEE image collection, printing will also be monitored. The data will be used to build a model of usage per unidentified user. This information will enable publishers to determine the size and interest of the market and a reasonable pricing structure for delivering full-text documents to the desktop.[13] This same information will enable the development group to establish effective caching and printing procedures.

By the end of 1992, several databases will be linked to provide users with information about the University Libraries' holdings. The Library Catalog will be linked to the circulation system so that users viewing a Catalog record will be able to find out whether the item is available or when it is due back in the library. Site-licensed bibliographic databases will be linked to the Library Catalog and Journal List. For example, INSPEC will be linked to the Journal List so that users viewing an INSPEC record can easily find out whether the University Libraries own the journal. As part of an enhancement project supported by Pew Charitable Trusts, bibliographic records in the Library Catalog may be linked to book review records in the *Choice* database.[14] With this link in place, LIS II will also search the *Choice* database when users search the Catalog, and it will return only those records for which there is a matching Catalog record. Because book reviews provide additional keywords for searching, linking these databases will enable users to retrieve Catalog records that they would not otherwise retrieve.[15]

The University Libraries also have plans to add electronic resources and increase document delivery service:

- Negotiations are underway with the Carnegie Mellon School of Computer Science (SCS) to create a page-image database of SCS technical reports and link it to the Library Catalog. Long-term plans include delivering the images over the Internet to other institutions.

- A proposal was submitted to DARPA (Defense Advanced Research Projects Agency) to support the development of technical report databases at several universities. Each university will create an image database of its technical reports and provide bibliographic indexing in ASCII format. The bibliographic information will provide keys for linking to the image databases. The ASCII indexing will be replicated at each university, but the page images will be retrieved over the Internet.

- Carnegie Mellon is one of the sites being considered for Elsevier's University Licensing Program (TULIP). TULIP would provide the full text of 25 to 35 materials science journals in either page-image, ASCII, or SGML format. The format of the information will constrain the retrieval mechanism. For example, page images could be linked to INSPEC and provided through the Image Browser. ASCII could be indexed and searched directly, but would require additional usability testing to assure that users could search and navigate the journals the way they wanted.

- To improve access to campus information, the full text of the Carnegie Mellon staff handbook and the documentation produced by Academic Computing and Media, Carnegie Mellon's academic computing organization, will be added to LIS II. Long-term plans are to convert all of the online and printed documentation produced by the libraries and the computing organizations at Carnegie Mellon to a format that can easily be used to build and maintain LIS II databases. SGML (Standard Generalized Markup Language) will probably be the first format investigated.

In addition to linked databases and document delivery services, LIS II will also improve retrieval using logical databases and natural language processing. A "logical database" is a group of databases that can be searched as if they were one database. With logical databases, users would be able to specify, for example, that a search be run in the Library Catalog and Periodical Abstracts, rather than having to do the same search twice. In addition to the technical difficulties involved, implementing logical databases raises design issues that will require user interface tests. For example, how do you provide field limits when the databases have different fields? How do you browse the indexes when the databases have different indexes? How do you identify the group of databases that are active without cluttering the user interface?

As databases grow in size and complexity, keyword and Boolean searching become inefficient retrieval strategies. The successful electronic library must eventually process actual English phrases, not keywords. To this end, a proposal has been submitted to the Markle Foundation for support to incorporate the work of the CLARIT project (Computational Linguistic Approaches to the Retrieval and Indexing of Text) into LIS II. CLARIT has developed techniques for indexing, retrieval, and browsing that are based on noun phrases. Integrating CLARIT into LIS II means developing and evaluating the effectiveness of a user interface that provides natural language tools instead of the customary keyword and Boolean tools for information retrieval.[16]

## THE USABILITY OF LIS II

Given the electronic resources, retrieval enhancements, and document delivery services in LIS II, how easy and convenient is it to use? How well does it meet user expectations? How well does it meet the goals of affordability and efficiency? The University Libraries conducted a variety of usability studies over a two-year period prior to its release to determine whether LIS II enables library users, staff, and administrators to do what they want to do the way they want to do it. For LIS II to be successful, the personal and financial costs of using it must be small and the reward great. The system must be easy to use, and it must provide better service than its predecessor, LIS. Usability is discussed here in terms of functionality, performance, and user interface design.

### Functionality

Years of experience with LIS provided the libraries with substantial information about how people use databases and what they expect in a retrieval system. This information, gathered from transaction logs, reports from librarians, and comments from library users, was compiled to produce design specifications for LIS II in 1989.

Additional methods were used to gather information in 1990 and 1991 to ensure that the first release of LIS II provided the essential features and functionality that library users and staff wanted. In addition to providing electronic bulletin boards where staff and users could post suggestions for LIS II, the University Libraries hosted focus group luncheons in October 1990 with 19 graduate and undergraduate students, faculty members, and staff members from different departments in the university.[17] A librarian and the senior researcher in the LIS II development group attended the luncheons. The meetings had two goals. First, the libraries wanted to understand the perceptions people had of LIS, the mainframe-based system that LIS II would replace. Second, they wanted to determine what changes and enhancements would provide sufficient incentive for people to make the transition to LIS II. Users would have to learn a new system that challenged their previous model of information retrieval. The question was: What would make it worth their effort?

The focus group participants explained behavior that had been observed in transaction logs from LIS, for example:

- People did simple keyword searches more frequently than Boolean searches in part because LIS required an extra keystroke to move from "simple search mode" to "command search mode." Users thought that the extra keystroke was annoying and refused to do it. They wanted a modeless user interface.

- Users did not use the "Scan index" function to choose search terms because the display could not be used interactively to compose a query and it did not provide location information (e.g., the term is in the Title or Author field of the bibliographic records). They wanted an interactive display of index terms that contained location information.

- Users seldom sorted the results of a search because sorting was too slow. They wanted a faster search algorithm, and they wanted to be able to search longer lists of titles.

Participants in the focus groups cited several problems with LIS, some of them pertaining to how the system worked, others to the user interface design. Users were annoyed that the system timed out after a short period of inactivity and that doing a new search meant losing the results of previous searches. They complained that the system was too slow. They didn't like that they could see a list of only 10 titles at a time, and that the wording and placement of instructions in the user interface were ambiguous and inconsistent. In particular, they stressed that the hierarchical design of the interface was tedious to maneuver. They wanted to be able to cancel searches in progress as well as to quit, choose a new database, or start a new search from anywhere in the system. Though they understood the need for authentication to see site-licensed databases, they did not like having to authenticate to search the non-licensed databases like the Library Catalog, and they did not want to have to authenticate twice (i.e., if they were already logged into a Carnegie Mellon computer system, they did not want to have to enter their user ID and password again when they ran LIS II). When asked what changes or additional features would provide sufficient incentive for them to make the transition to LIS II, participants eagerly composed a list of basic requirements and a wish list for future enhancements.

Based on this information, the development group compiled the following list of goals for the first release of LIS II:

- Merge library authentication procedures with Andrew and other campus computing authentication so that users only have to login once.

- Provide a way to access the campus information databases (e.g., the Library Catalog and Journal List) without having to authenticate.

- Lengthen the amount of time before the system times out.

- Provide faster searching, sorting, and retrieving of records.

- Provide intelligible, consistent instructions and commands that enable users to quit, change databases, and start a new search from anywhere in the system.

- Enable users to do simple keyword or command (Boolean) searches without having to specify a search mode.

- Provide an interactive log of previous queries so that search results can be viewed again or used as the basis of a new search.[18]

- Provide an interactive display of index terms that includes location information.

- Display more than 10 titles at a time.

- Reorganize the fields in full bibliographic records so that the more useful fields are displayed at the top. Rename the fields to be more intelligible.

- Enable users to save information to a file and print information on networked printers.[19]

- Enable users to cancel searches.

- Link circulation information to the Library Catalog so that users know if an item is available now or when it is due back in the library.

- Link local holdings and circulation information to commercial databases so that users know whether the Carnegie Mellon University Libraries own an item, where it is located in the libraries, and whether it is available now (or when it is due back in the library).

- Enable users to submit electronic requests for library services such as book check-out, book reserve, journal article delivery (courier service), and interlibrary loan.

Meeting these goals occupied the development team for much of 1991. All of the items on the list except the last three were provided in the first release of LIS II. These three—linking circulation to the Catalog, linking local holdings and circulation to commercial databases, and enabling the electronic submission of requests for non-electronic services—will be completed by the end of 1992. In addition, the January release of LIS II also provides several of the features that were on the focus group participants' wish list. For example, LIS II enables users to mark titles in a list so that they can act on them as a group (e.g., for saving, mailing, and printing) and it enables users to view only citation information or full bibliographic records for titles retrieved in a search.

## Performance

Years of feedback from users made it clear that LIS was too slow. Focus group participants reiterated the sentiment. Users expect to search, retrieve, and sort information quickly, regardless of how many people are using the system at the same time. One of the drawbacks of stand-alone CD-ROM databases is that they support only one user at a time. The viable electronic library must support many users simultaneously. The goal for LIS II was to increase the speed of the retrieval system and support more simultaneous users than its mainframe predecessor, LIS, did.

Automated and manual tests were done in the spring and summer of 1990 to assess the performance of LIS II. The automated tests were based on a model of searching behavior derived from LIS transaction logs. Approximately 1,800 INSPEC searches from February 1990 were used to build the model.[20] According to the model:

- Over 70% of the searches use one to four keywords and the "AND"(LIS default) operator. Most of these "simple" searches use only two keywords, and 23% of them use truncation.

- Less than 10% of the searches use operators other than "AND."[21] Most of these "command" searches use two to four keywords, and 41% of them use truncation. Apparently, as users compose more logically complex searches, they take alternative spellings or word variations into account.

- Over 10% of the searches restrict retrieval to records where the keywords appear in a particular field. Most of these "field-specific" searches use the LIS "author search" feature, which does not require users to know the syntax for field limits, and 7% of them use truncation.

- Less than 10% of the searches are limits on the previous search, where users added criteria—such as keywords or date or location specifications—to reduce the number of records retrieved. Most of the limits are keyword limits, and 20% of them use truncation (i.e., most limits resemble simple keyword searches).

Using this model of search behavior, a script was written using real user searches in the ratio of complexity that appeared in the logs.[22] "Complexity" here means the number of terms in the query, the total number of operators and the number of different operators, the number of truncated terms, and the application of field restrictors. This script of searches was then sent to a retrieval server in a way that simulated the behavior of concurrent users. The number of simulated users was increased until system degradation was detected. Manual performance tests were also done. In these tests, the development group simultaneously generated complex searches of the same database. Together these experiments determined that LIS II supports twice as many simultaneous users per database as LIS did. Overall, LIS II supports many more users than LIS because of the multi-server architecture.

To assess the speed of LIS II, the same searches were issued manually in both LIS and LIS II at different times of the day. Though the number of concurrent users at the time affected performance, these tests indicated that LIS II provides (on the average) a 50% improvement in the speed of searching, sorting, and retrieving information.

When compared with mainframe-based LIS, the performance gains in LIS II are due to the better file system and faster CPU of the servers as well as the division of labor between clients and servers. To further improve performance, a version of LIS II will be released by summer 1992 that connects to servers on demand and automatically splits and balances the load between replicated databases. Because sorting is CPU-intensive, it may be moved from the server to the client side of the architecture in the future to enable users to sort longer lists of titles.

LIS II certainly performs for the users, but does it perform for library administrators? Is it cost effective? The answer is emphatically "yes." A rough estimate of the cost differences between running information retrieval on a mainframe and on workstations is twenty to one. It cost the University Libraries approximately $1 million to do on the LIS IBM 3083 mainframe what the distributed architecture of LIS II can do for $50,000. Without a doubt, distributed computing enables the libraries to provide better service to more users for fewer dollars.

## User Interface Design

Operating on a mainframe, LIS provided only one user interface, which ran on any machine that could emulate a TN3270 terminal.

Users with UNIX workstations, Apple Macintoshes, and IBM PCs complained that this user interface did not use the software conventions that they preferred or take advantage of the power of their personal computers. The distributed architecture of clients and servers in LIS II enables the provision of different user interfaces that can use the conventions and harness the power of different machines. Using the conventions with which people are familiar facilitates learning and thus the transition to LIS II. Using the power of the personal computer improves service. For example, harnessing the power of the Macintosh and UNIX workstation enables LIS II to provide document delivery service in page-image format; if the only user interface available emulated a terminal, LIS II could only deliver ASCII text. Harnessing the power of personal computers on campus also improves performance by having the user's machine do some of the work of information retrieval, rather than having it all done on the servers.

The first release of LIS II provides a Motif user interface for UNIX workstations running X.11 windows and a VT100 (terminal emulation) user interface for other machines. A Macintosh user interface is being developed and will be released by the end of 1992.[23] A few points about the history and chronology of the Motif and VT100 user interfaces will serve as an introduction to their overall characters. The prototype LIS II user interface was developed for UNIX workstations running X.11 and DECwindows. It had five primary windows, could deliver information in ASCII and page-image format, and was demonstrated at EDUCOM '89. In early 1990, the workstation user interface was implemented in Motif because Motif uses a widely accepted UNIX window manager and can run on multiple platforms. Centrally supported workstations at Carnegie Mellon run X.11 windows, the Motif Window Manager (MWM), and applications with graphic user interfaces. The first version of the Motif user interface replicated the DECwindows version with one significant change: the Motif user interface was "modeless," meaning that users did not have to specify whether they wanted to do keyword or Boolean searches. Keywords and operators could simply be entered at the search prompt. Focus group participants (October 1990) confirmed that this was the right decision.

The initial Motif user interface had five windows, each of which provided particular functions and displayed a particular kind of information:

- The *Search window* enabled users to create and modify database queries, and it allowed them to sort or request the display of items that matched the search criteria. It provided two information displays: a list of queries (the search criteria sent to the servers from the client) and a list of result sets (a symbolic display of the record identifiers sent to the client from the servers).

- The *Browse window* enabled users to examine and interactively use database indexes. Like the Search window, it provided two information displays: a list of queries (the browse criteria sent to the servers from the client) and a list of index terms (the terms sent to the client from the server).

- The *List of Records window* enabled users to examine a list of author, title, and date information (one-line records) for each item retrieved in a query, and it allowed them to request the display of more information on one item in the list.

- The *Full Record window* enabled users to examine one complete bibliographic record or full-text document in ASCII format.

- The *Image window* enabled users to examine one page at a time from a full-text document in page-image format.

Following the *Motif Style Guide*, the Motif user interface provided access to basic features on buttons and menus. Additional information was provided in dialog boxes. Users interacted with the LIS II client using the keyboard and the mouse.

The first VT100 user interface was implemented in early 1991. With few exceptions, it provided the same windows, functionality, and information displays as the Motif user interface. There is no VT100 Image window because terminals can not display page images, but there are Search, Browse, List of Records, and Full Record windows. There is no mouse, so commands are issued using only the keyboard. The limited functionality and screen space of the VT100 restrict each window to one ASCII information display. The Search window displays a list of result sets; the Browse window a list of index terms; the List of Records window a list of author, title and date information; and the Full Record window a bibliographic record or full-text document. The displays are identical to those provided in the Motif user interface. Limited resources mandate using the same information displays in both user interfaces, therefore the default line length in LIS II does not exceed 80 characters.

Several studies were done in 1990-1991 to assess the usability of the Motif and VT100 versions of LIS II. Table 2 provides an overview of the research and development agenda. Most of the studies were

*Table 2.* LIS II Research and Demonstration Agenda (1990-1991)

| | |
|---|---|
| Fall 1989 | DECwindows (workstation) user interface demonstrated at EDU-COM '89. |
| Spring 1990 | Motif (workstation) user interface implemented. |
| Spring 1990 | Study to build usage model of the INSPEC database in LIS. |
| Summer 1990 | Studies to assess the performance of LIS II. |
| September 1990 | Study to determine the appropriate number and configuration of windows in the Motif user interface. |
| September 1990 | Study to determine the best sequence and names for fields in bibliographic records. |
| October 1990 | Study to determine the functionality required to facilitate the transition from LIS to LIS II. |
| January 1991 | Study to determine the overall usability of Motif user interface. |
| March 1991 | Study to determine the overall usability of the Motif user interface. |
| Spring 1991 | VT100 user interface implemented. |
| April 1991 | Study to determine the overall usability of the VT100 user interface. |
| June 1991 | Study to determine the overall usability of the VT100 user interface. |
| May 1991 | Study to determine the appropriate vocabulary for LIS II error messages, user interfaces, and documentation. |
| October 1991 | Motif and VT100 LIS II demonstrated at EDUCOM '91. |
| October 1991 | Motif user interface released on dedicated LIS II workstations in the Carnegie Mellon University Libraries. (LIS II still not available outside of the libraries.) |
| January 1992 | Motif and VT100 LIS II released to the Carnegie Mellon campus as the default library information system, both inside and outside of the libraries. |

"think aloud protocols" where subjects worked individually with LIS II following a script that required them to use all of the basic features. They also had time to use the system freely, the way they normally would, without following a script. Their comments were tape recorded and later analyzed. Additional research methods were used to ascertain the effectiveness of different information displays. For example, what is the best sequence for presenting information in a bibliographic record, or what is the best way to display error messages and help users solve the problems they pinpoint? At least six subjects participated in each research study. Subjects were representative of the following user groups: undergraduate students, graduate students, librarians and library staff, and (less frequently) faculty.

Early studies indicated serious problems with the way the Motif and VT100 windows were designed and the way some of the features worked. The appearance and functionality of both user interfaces were changed based on the results of the research and the addition of new features. Later studies showed significant improvement. Motif LIS II was released on dedicated workstations in the University Libraries during the fall semester 1991. Both the VT100 and Motif user interfaces were demonstrated at EDUCOM '91. Feedback from users led to a few more changes after EDUCOM, and the user interfaces were released for use outside of the libraries in January 1992. LIS II is now the default Library Information System on campus.[24] Describing the functionality and appearance of the Motif and VT100 user interfaces will convey the "look and feel" of distributed retrieval.

## The Number and Overall Design of the Windows

*Motif.* Feedback from users on the DECwindows and early Motif user interfaces indicated that five windows were too many. Users with little or no experience with workstations and information retrieval software were overwhelmed by the number of windows and by the location of information on the computer monitor (the screen real estate of the workstation enabled all of the windows to be open at once). Experienced users were uncomfortable with having to open and close so many different windows. Based on this information, a study was designed to ascertain a better configuration of windows, specifically to determine whether some of the windows could be combined to make a more friendly, usable system.

Using the SmethersBarnes Prototyper software, two alternate window configurations were created for testing purposes. The windows were interactive, but they were not connected to a fully functioning retrieval system; specific searches were programmed into the prototypes. Both of the prototype configurations combined: (1) the Search and Browse windows, and (2) the List of Records and Full Record windows. This reduced the four windows to two windows. These window combinations were selected because of the similarity of the information they displayed and the function used to retrieve that display.[25] The Image window was not considered for combination with any of the other windows because of the technical and human factors problems entailed in displaying information in different formats (ASCII and bitmapped page images) in the same window. The Image window was not included in the study.

In September 1990, each of four subjects worked with two different window configurations: the implemented four-window version and one of the two-window prototypes. Based on the results of this study, the List of Records and Full Record windows were combined into one window called the Records window. The window contains both information displays and a divider bar that can be dragged using the mouse to reallocate space between the list and the full record, which may be either a bibliographic record or a full-text (ASCII) document. Now users need to open or close only one window to examine or dispense with the (ASCII) results of a search. Both of the prototypes combining the Search and Browse windows tested poorly, so these windows were not combined. The reasons why the combinations tested poorly are presented later in this paper in the discussion of "Browsing Database Indexes." The Motif user interface now has three windows that display ASCII information (Search, Browse, and Records) and one window that displays bitmapped information, the Image window. Illustrations of all of the windows are provided later in this paper.

The current Motif window configuration may still prove to have too many windows. User interface tests scheduled for spring 1992 will include the Image window and a reassessment of the number of windows. The University Libraries are still learning how to use the screen real estate of the workstation effectively. The process is one of negotiation between building a user interface to run on dedicated LIS II workstations in the libraries, which can run no other software and therefore can use all of the screen space for LIS II, and building a user interface to run on UNIX workstations outside of the libraries, which can simultaneously run other software like electronic mail and a word processor—each of which requires screen space for its own window. The problems are complicated. Some users are experienced with both retrieval software and managing windows; other users have little or no experience with online retrieval or window management. Some users want their windows to be tiled, not overlapped; other users want overlapping windows. The solution may be to provide an initial configuration for novice users and a way for experienced users to customize the windows. Providing one configuration for dedicated workstations in the libraries and another for workstations outside of the libraries would multiply design and maintenance problems for the development team and create training problems for public services staff who must answer user questions about all of the user interfaces.

*VT100.* The default configuration for the VT100 user interface is limited to displaying 80 characters by 24 lines of ASCII text. The limited screen space means that only one window can be viewed at a time and the space is too small to combine the list of records and full record displays. The VT100 user interface therefore has four primary windows: Search, Browse, List of Titles, and Full Record. There is no Image window because VT100 cannot display images. The name of the List of Records window was changed to "List of Titles" based on the research. Illustrations of the windows are provided later in this paper. For users with large-screen Macintosh or workstation monitors, the ability to resize the VT100 windows has been added to LIS II. If users widen the windows, the text wraps around to create paragraphs with longer lines; if users lengthen the windows, they can see more of a list of titles or a full record.

The first implementation of the VT100 user interface attempted to replicate not only the window configuration but the menu structure of the early Motif user interface. The VT100 windows were built with menus across the top that contained all of the features that were on the Motif menus plus the features that were provided on the Motif buttons. Additional menus were created for functions that were required in VT100, but not in Motif. For example, since VT100 windows must be viewed one at a time, a Go To menu was created to enable users to move among the windows. The result was a large collection of menus and options and an overwhelming sense of hierarchy. Commands to maneuver the information in the windows were displayed at the bottom of each window, much like in the LIS TN3270 user interface.

"Think aloud protocol" studies done in April 1991 indicated that users had tremendous difficulty maneuvering the VT100 menus. They were annoyed by the number of keystrokes required to move the cursor from the search prompt to the menu bar, then to the proper menu, then to the menu option. If they made a mistake and moved the cursor into the wrong menu, they had no idea how to undo what they had done. They often lost track of whether the cursor was at the prompt or in the menus. For these reasons, the VT100 user interface was rebuilt in May 1991 without menus.

In the revised user interface, two groups of commands are displayed at the bottom of each VT100 window. Both groups are consistently placed and labeled. One group provides CTRL commands to navigate the information displayed in the window.[26] The commands are consistent and window specific. For example, CTRL-V shows the next "page" of a display, but the on-screen instructions describe the display in that window (e.g., "Show next page of sets," "Show next page of list," or "Show next page of record"). The other group provides ESC commands to do the things that subjects in the protocols complained vehemently about doing with menus—even if the menus could be made user friendly. Much like the focus group participants' complaints about LIS, protocol subjects complained that menu-driven VT100 LIS II forced them to move up and down a hierarchy of screens to do certain functions. For example, it forced them to move to the top of the hierarchy, the Search window, to change databases. Users wanted to be able to start a search, change databases, browse indexes, get help, and quit the program from anywhere in the system. In the revised user interface, the ESC commands remove the hierarchy and enable users to do what they want where they want. The ESC commands are mapped to the function keys on a VT100 terminal. For example, ESC 3 is mapped to F3, ESC 2 to F2, and so forth. Less frequently used features like sorting, limiting, and printing are provided in an Options dialog box displayed when users press ESC 3. The Options are specific to that window (e.g., limit options are provided in the Search window; marking titles options are provided in the List of Titles window).

A second set of VT100 protocol studies was done in June 1991 to assess whether replacing menus with groups of on-screen commands improved usability. The results of the tests were very good. Still, small changes were made to the vocabulary and system functionality based on the test results. For example, arrow keys were enabled to move the highlight up and down in a list because protocol subjects inevitably tried to use the arrow keys to maneuver the information displayed in windows or dialog boxes.

The remainder of this paper discusses the Motif and VT100 user interfaces in detail. The discussion is organized around important tasks in LIS II: authenticating, selecting a database, searching a database, displaying the results of a search, and so forth. The discussion includes an overview of LIS II documentation because documentation is an important component in the interface between users and computers. The paper ends with a brief statement of conclusions about distributed computing and usability testing.

## Authenticating

Focus group participants were emphatic about wanting to authenticate only once or not at all. If they were already logged into a Carnegie Mellon computing system, they did not want to have to enter their user ID and password again when they ran LIS II. If they only wanted to search non-licensed databases like the Library Catalog, they did not want to have to authenticate at all. The architecture of authentication and protection services in LIS II has already been discussed. The implication of this architecture for the user interface is that a Login window is required in some instances and not others. If a user is authenticated in the Andrew System or SCS, no Login window is required. In all other cases, a Login window is required. Though LIS II supports unauthenticated access to non-licensed databases, a window is still required to enable users to specify that they want this kind of access.

*Motif.*   When authentication was added to LIS II in 1990, a Motif Login window was designed and tested. There were two problems with the initial design of the window. Users had problems with the labels on the buttons ("Authenticate" and "Reset"), and they were annoyed that the window would not let them search the non-licensed databases unless they entered a valid user ID and password. The window was not functional for the public LIS II workstations in the University Libraries, where providing a way for people to search the Library Catalog and Journal List without having to authenticate was a high priority. A new Login window was designed in early 1991 to solve the functionality and design problems in the first implementation. Though the new window provided unauthenticated access and did not use the problematic vocabulary of its predecessor, users were still confused by the window. It offered: (1) a Catalog button that they could click to access only the non-licensed databases in LIS II, (2) prompts for entering a user ID and password to access all of the databases in LIS II, and (3) a Help button that when clicked displayed an explanation of what was available with and without a user ID and password and why. Users didn't read the on-screen instructions carefully and thought that they had to both enter a user ID and password and click the Catalog button. The "public" Login window was redesigned and enlarged to clarify the alternatives. The new window has solved the login problems in the libraries.

For users of UNIX workstations outside of the University Libraries who have not authenticated in Andrew or SCS, a small Login window appears on the screen when they start LIS II. No unauthenticated access is provided for the Motif user interface outside of the University Libraries, so users must enter an Andrew or SCS user ID and password. The design of this "private" Login window was influenced by feedback on the Login windows described above. It underwent several revisions to reach its current state. When users have authenticated or, in the University Libraries, specified unauthenticated access, the Motif Search window appears in the upper left quadrant of the workstation screen.

*VT100.* The VT100 user interface is only available in the University Libraries on the Macintoshes that run the OLC Connection software. Therefore almost all users who run VT100 LIS II do so from outside of the libraries (e.g., over the campus network, the Internet, or PREPnet). Since LIS II authentication has been merged with Andrew System and SCS authentication, users who have logged into one of these systems do not need to provide their user ID and password again, so no VT100 Login window is needed. These people simply type the appropriate command at the system prompt and the VT100 Search window appears on their computer screen. Users who have not authenticated in Andrew or SCS, however, need a Login window. To access LIS II, these users TELNET to a server called library.andrew.cmu.edu.[27] The server automatically displays the VT100 Login window. Internet and PREPnet guests enter "library" at the Login prompt, and the VT100 Search window appears on the screen; they have access to only the Library Catalog, Journal List, and ArchPics, not the site-licensed databases. Carnegie Mellon students, faculty, and staff can Telnet to library.andrew.cmu.edu, enter their user ID and password at the appropriate prompts, and have access to all of the databases in LIS II, including the site-licensed ones. Because there are many Macintosh users at Carnegie Mellon, a desktop icon has been prepared that automatically connects them to library.andrew.cmu.edu and prompts them for a user ID and password. The icon enables Macintosh users to run LIS II without knowing the name of the server or how to Telnet.

### Selecting a Database

*Motif.* The default database in LIS II is the Library Catalog. When Motif users want to change databases, they open the Select menu in the Search window and choose the Databases option. The name of the menu—"Select"—complies with the *Motif Style Guide*. Choosing Databases from the Select menu opens a dialog box that displays the names of the databases to which a user has access. This method of providing access to databases, rather than using a "Databases" menu with options for each database, was selected for technical and practical reasons. The technical concern was to provide a list of databases that was not hard coded into the system. The list of databases has to be created dynamically at run time because it is different for different users. Furthermore, if the list of database names is created dynamically, the user interface does not have to be rebuilt every time a database is added. Another practical consideration was the number of database names in the list. The first release of LIS II has twelve databases, with more to be added in the near future. Twelve or more options makes a long menu that could cause navigation problems. To ensure that meeting these technical and practical demands did not frustrate users, transaction logs for LIS were examined to determine how often users change databases. Since users typically change databases only once or twice per session, the feature was implemented using a dialog box to display database names rather than a menu.[28]

Motif users had several problems with the initial design of the Database Selection dialog box. It displayed no instructions and further confused users by providing two ways to select a database. They could use the mouse to select a database name from a list or they could type the name of a database at the prompt; both a list and a prompt were displayed in the dialog box. However, if they did not type the name exactly as it appeared in the list, they got an error message. Users also complained that the system did not offer online help on the individual databases. They wanted to know the subject coverage, date range, and update schedule for each database. The Database Selection dialog box was revised based on the results of the study. (See Figure 2.) The new dialog box has instructions, no prompt, and a way to display help on each database. The help text is stored on the client side of the distributed architecture in the same text file that provides LIS II name service; it can be edited without changing the software. In the future, this information will be passed by the Database Meta-Information (DMI) server.

To change databases in Motif LIS II, people use the mouse to highlight the name of the database that they want, then click the OK button or press Return; they can also simply double-click on a name in the list to change to that database. To display help on a database,

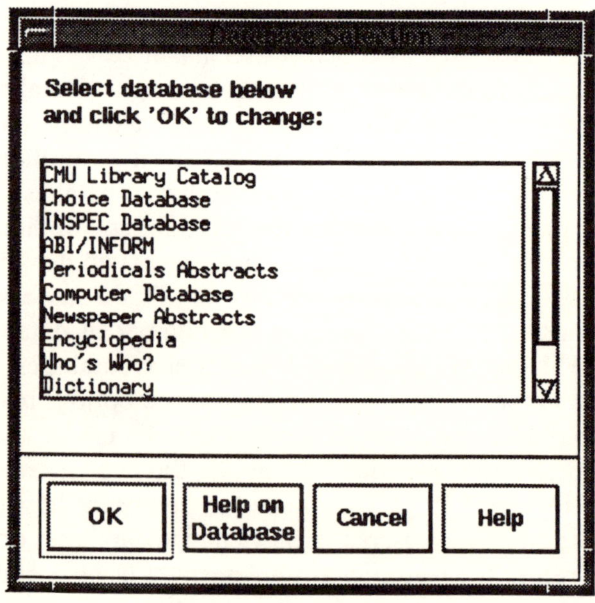


*Figure 2.*    The Motif Database Selection Dialog Box

it was removed because users accidentally clicked it and exited the program. Buttons now enable users to do a search (Search), use a result set in a new search (Use Set), delete the text at the prompt (Clear), browse the database indexes (Browse), or display the records retrieved in a search (Display).

- Menus were added and rearranged. For example, a Help menu and Edit menu were added to provide access to new features. A Limit menu was added to foreground this feature. (Limits are discussed later in this paper.)

- The banner displaying the name of the current database and the name of the server on which that database resides was moved to the top of the window and made easier to read.

- The instructions above the search prompt were revised to include the default operator.

The current Motif Search window is shown in Figure 4. There are two known problems with the window. Users are confused by the Display and Browse buttons. New users often click the Browse button because they want to browse the titles retrieved in their search. In the initial implementation of the window, the button labels were more descriptive: "Display Records" and "Browse Indexes." When the buttons were moved to the middle of the window, space constraints forced the labels to be shortened. Apparently the confusion is a "first encounter" phenomenon that quickly disappears with usage. Users are also confused by the instructions above the search prompt. They do not understand what "default" or "ADJ" mean. Though the instructions may be revised, space does not allow for a detailed explanation. To compensate for the confusion and frustration engendered by changing the default operator, an error message was added to LIS II. Now, when users do a search using the default operator and retrieve 0 records, LIS II displays a message explaining that no records were retrieved using adjacency, and it offers to do the search again using the "AND" operator. Users can click a button to do the search or cancel it. This error message will be removed when users are accustomed to adjacency as the default.

In addition to the changes to the window described above, the information displayed in the window was made easier to read. The initial result sets display was cluttered and confusing. Database

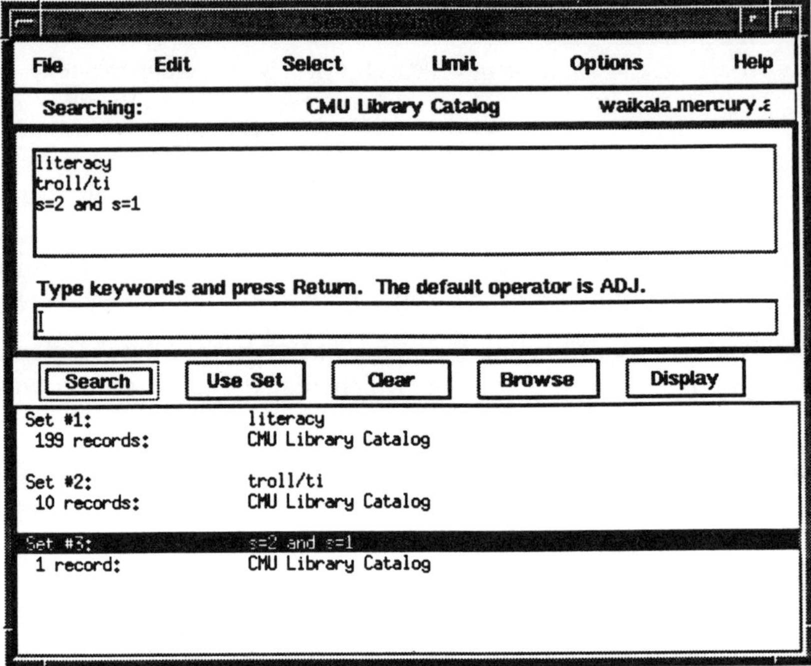


*Figure 4.*   The Motif Search Window

names were displayed using the four character abbreviation by which
the system knows them, not the names by which users know them.
The new design removes at least ten characters from each line in the
result sets display. The revised display is more intelligible and easier
for users to skim.

In the future, the display will include the number of occurrences
of each search term in the database rather than just the results of
the entire search. Adding this information will require amending the
Z39.50 protocol and testing to ensure that the display remains easy
to read and understand. Based on the results of the protocols, features
will also be provided to enable users to delete result sets individually
or as a group.

*VT100.*   The significant changes to the VT100 windows have
already been discussed. Based on protocol studies, menus were
replaced with dialog boxes and distinct groups of commands at the
bottom of the primary windows. The current version of the VT100

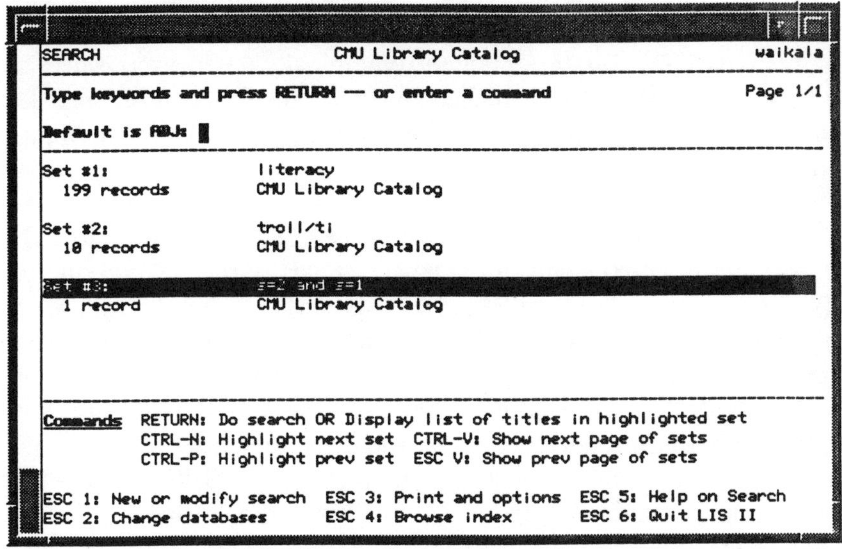



*Figure 5.* The VT100 Search Window

Search window is shown in Figure 5. The VT100 and Motif result sets displays are identical.

## Limiting a Search

Limits are ways to narrow or reduce the number of records retrieved in a search by making the query more specific. They can be applied at the time the original search is composed or added later if the number of records retrieved is too large to peruse comfortably. LIS II provides three types of limits:

- *Keyword limits*: the provision of additional search terms.

- *Field limits*: the provision of restrictors that indicate where in the database record the user wants a search term to be found (e.g., in the Title or Author field).

- *Other limits*: the provision of restrictors that require a special format (e.g., dates) or that will be successful with only a small number of terms (e.g., media or record type).

The Field and Other limits for each database are specified in the text file that provides LIS II name service. Users select from a list of what is available. The lists are created dynamically when users select a database, and they are displayed in dialog boxes upon request. In the future, this information will be passed by the Database Meta-Information (DMI) server.

*Motif.*   To do a keyword limit on a new search in Motif LIS II, users simply type the additional terms as part of the original query. To do a keyword limit on a previous search, they use the mouse to highlight that result set in the Search window, click the Use Set button (see Figure 4), and then type the additional terms and operators at the prompt. Protocols indicate that users are initially unaware that this is how to do a keyword limit, but, once they discover what the Use Set button does, they like it very much. LIS users were accustomed to choosing from a list of limits that included "Date," "Media Type," and "Keyword"; most limits in LIS were keyword limits. The term "keyword limit" could not be used in the Motif user interface in part because it would not fit on the button, but, more importantly, it could not be used because the button provides additional functionality. Besides enabling keyword limits on previous searches, the Use Set button can also be used to compose searches that combine result sets using different Boolean operations. For example, users can issue a search to find all of the records that are in both result set number 3 and result set number 4 by highlighting result set number 3 and clicking the Use Set button, and then highlighting result set number 4 and clicking the Use Set button. Alternatively they can type *s=3 and s=4* at the search prompt.

Designing user-friendly field limits was more difficult. In the initial implementation, this feature was accessed by choosing "Index" from the Select menu in the Search window. This opened a dialog box that displayed a list of fields and indexes. Users had several problems with this feature and the design of the dialog box. They were confused by the vocabulary and concept of an index limit as well as by how the limit worked. Even if they understood these things, they had trouble remembering that the feature was provided on the Select menu.

Though it was possible to do field limits in LIS, transaction logs and anecdotal evidence from librarians indicated that few people used the feature—probably because the instructions were buried several screens deep in the online help for "command mode" (Boolean) searches. LIS provided only one index per database, so there was no way to do an index limit. To complicate matters, some databases are called indexes (e.g., Social Science Index). What to call this limit in LIS II—a "Field limit" or an "Index limit"—was a complicated problem. Both "index" and "field" were unintelligible jargon to many users, and regardless of what the limit was called, some of the items displayed in the list were indexes and some of them were fields. LIS II does not have a one-to-one relationship between fields and indexes. Newton, the database-building and retrieval software, provides two features. One feature enables the provision of multiple indexes for each database. The indexes are built when the database is built. Several fields can be indexed in one index. For example, bibliographic records contain author information in several fields, so an author index can be built using terms from all of the fields that contain author information. Newton indexes can be viewed as well as searched. That is, users can display a list of terms in the indexes, not just search the indexes and retrieve records that match the search criteria. LIS II provides this feature in the Browse window, which is discussed later in this paper. In contrast, fields in Newton databases can be searched, but not viewed separately. Searches can be restricted to fields or indexes, but only indexes can be displayed in a list. With few exceptions, every field is indexed in at least one index. The exceptions are instances where information included in the database is not displayed in the user interface and therefore not indexed (e.g., control numbers in UMI databases).

Users were also confused by the labels on the buttons in the initial dialog box and by the way the feature worked. Apply to Keyword and Apply to All buttons enabled them to apply a field limit to a particular search term or to all terms in the query. Though the design provided maximum flexibility, users could not understand why the dialog box did not close and the search was not run when they selected an index name from the list and clicked an Apply button. More than anything, users were annoyed that the system did not allow them to apply field limits to result sets. Newton does not allow field limits on result sets, but subjects in the protocols inevitably tried to do this by clicking the Use Set button and then applying a field limit. They confused the result set, technically a set of pointers to database records, with the query used to retrieve that result set. The queries were displayed separately in the Motif Search window in the space above the prompt (see Figure 4), but users were confused by the distinction between queries and result sets. If people continue to be confused after using LIS II for a while, the concept of a "result set" may be removed from LIS II.

Users also had problems finding the field limit feature. LIS users rarely did field limits per se, but LIS did provide a separate, conspicuous Author search feature that restricted a query to fields in the database records that contained author information. Not surprisingly, protocol subjects did not connect choosing "Index" from the Select menu and the long list of field and index names displayed in the dialog box with doing an Author search.

Based on the results of the protocols, the Field Limit feature was revised to meet user expectations:

- The vocabulary was changed. The word "index" was reserved for the Browse window, where index terms can be viewed separately, and the word "field" was reserved for the Search window.

- The access point was changed. A Limit menu was added to make the feature more prominent in the user interface. Now users do a field limit by choosing "Fields" from the Limit menu instead of "Index" from the Select menu.

- The functionality was changed:

  - When users select a field name from the list and click OK, the dialog box closes, the search is executed with the field limit applied to all terms in the query, and the result set is displayed in the Search window. If users want to apply different field limits to different terms in the search, they must know the syntax to type the limits (e.g., *literacy/ti, smith/au*). Instructions are provided in the online help and the printed documentation. To facilitate learning, the two-character field name abbreviations are displayed in the revised dialog box (e.g., "TI" for Title field and "AU" for Author field). The two-character abbreviations for field and index names are in the spirit of the Z39.50 retrieval protocol standard.[29]

  - By popular demand, the ability to apply field limits to result sets was added to LIS II. Technically, Newton does not allow field limits on result sets, but code was written to compensate for this and give the users what they want. In the current implementation, if text is typed at the prompt, the field limit is applied to the new search being composed. If no text is typed at the prompt, the field limit is applied to the highlighted result set. Users can also click the Use Set button and then select a Field limit to limit a result set. The revised Motif Field Limit dialog box is shown in Figure 6.

How to distinguish fields from indexes in the user interface is still a point of contention. In the future, LIS II may provide online help on each field and index in the list, similar to the way online help is provided on the databases in the Database Selection dialog box. Another possibility is to provide templates to help people search authors and titles. Problems with author and title searches are discussed further in the section below on "Browsing Database Indexes."

LIS II also provides some limits that require special handling. For example, Date, Language, Media Type, and Location limits require the limit to be applied to only part of the query, rather than to all of the terms in the query. In addition, Date limits require the date to be entered in a specific format. Language, Media Type, and

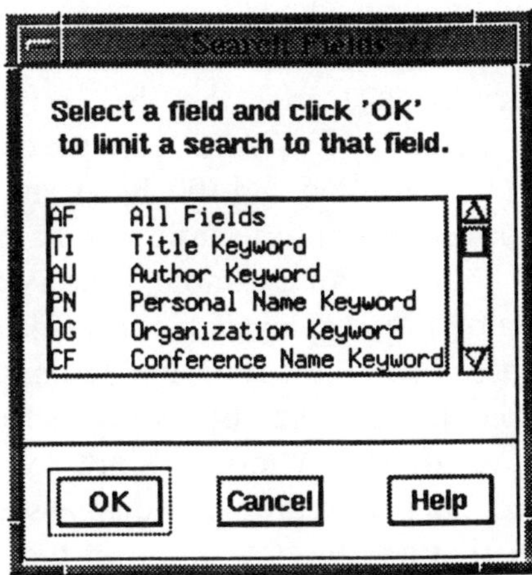


*Figure 6.*　　The Motif Field Limit Dialog Box

Location limits require users to know the available languages, media types, and locations. Technically, these limits are field limits, but the limited number of terms that will retrieve records and the required format for data mandate that LIS II provide a separate feature to handle these special cases. Users choose "Others" from the Limit menu, and the system displays a dialog box with all of the special cases for the current database; the Other limits are different for each database. If keywords have been typed at the prompt in the Search window, the limit is applied to this new search. If no search has been typed at the prompt, the limit is applied to the highlighted result set. Users can also click the Use Set button and then select an Other limit to limit a result set.

Protocols showed that users were confused by the original design of the Other Limit dialog box, specifically by the fact that the user interface did not indicate clearly what was a prompt where they would enter text (e.g., a date range) and what was a pop-up menu where they would select from a list of choices (e.g., media types). When users touched a space with the mouse, they were startled if a menu appeared. Based on this information, the dialog box was revised to clearly distinguish prompts from menus.

*VT100.* The VT100 user interface provides access to all limits from the Options dialog box displayed when users press ESC 3 in the Search window. The relevant options are "Use Set (Limit by Keywords)," "Limit by Field," and "Limit by Other." (See Figure 7.) Since the list displayed in the dialog box offers more space than a Motif button, librarians felt strongly that the "Use Set" option should be listed as "Use Set (Limit by Keywords)," so the development group implemented what they wanted. VT100 Field and Other limits are nested. If users choose these options, another dialog box opens and displays the list of choices. For example, if users choose "Limit by Field," the next dialog box displays a list of fields (and indexes) for the current database. Like the Motif Field Limit dialog box, the VT100 user interface displays the abbreviations for the field names to facilitate learning. If users choose "Limit by Other" from the Options dialog box, the next dialog box displays a list of the Other limits available for that database. Because of the limitations of the VT100 user interface, only one Other Limit can be applied at a time, though several can be applied to the same result set in succession.

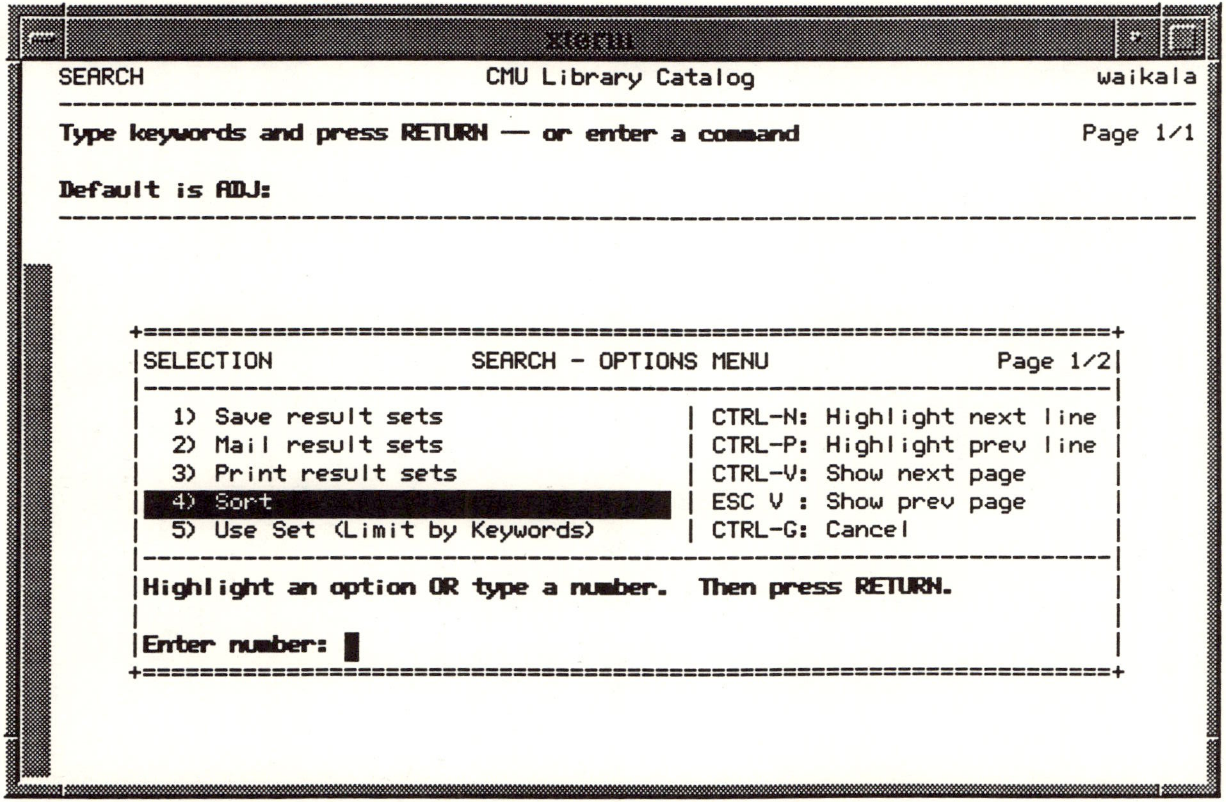

```
xterm

SEARCH                    CMU Library Catalog                    waikala
------------------------------------------------------------------------
Type keywords and press RETURN — or enter a command           Page 1/1

Default is ADJ:
------------------------------------------------------------------------



   +==================================================================+
   |SELECTION           SEARCH - OPTIONS MENU            Page 1/2|
   |------------------------------------------------------------------|
   |  1) Save result sets           | CTRL-N: Highlight next line |
   |  2) Mail result sets           | CTRL-P: Highlight prev line |
   |  3) Print result sets          | CTRL-V: Show next page      |
   |  4) Sort                       | ESC V : Show prev page      |
   |  5) Use Set (Limit by Keywords)| CTRL-G: Cancel              |
   |------------------------------------------------------------------|
   |Highlight an option OR type a number.  Then press RETURN.         |
   |                                                                  |
   |Enter number:                                                    |
   +==================================================================+
```

*Figure 7.*   The VT100 Options Dialog Box for the Search Window

*Browsing Database Indexes*

As databases grow in size, number, and specificity, users need new and better tools for composing queries. Selecting search terms is or should be a database-specific task. While retrieval systems lack artificial intelligence and rely on Boolean logic, viewing the actual terms indexed in a database is a powerful strategy. Focus group participants, particularly faculty and graduate students, considered the ability to view and manipulate database indexes a high priority for the new system, and they had a very clear picture of what they wanted. LIS II was designed to meet their expectations. Newton enables the provision of multiple indexes for each database. Librarians and members of the development group decide which indexes will be built for each database based on how users typically search the database, how much disk space those indexes will require, and how heavy the usage of that database is. Though the indexes for each database are different, the information included in the display of index terms is the same for all databases. The display includes location information (e.g., the term is in the Title field), and it can be used interactively to create new searches. Users can examine all of the indexes for a given database at once or look at one index at a time. The way to limit browsing to a particular index is identical to limiting a search to a particular field.

Users browse database indexes in the Browse window, not the Search window. Two prototypes that combined the windows were built and tested in September 1990. One prototype toggled between Search and Browse functions, providing only one prompt for users to enter queries. The other prototype provided two prompts: one for entering a search query and one for entering a browse query. In both prototypes, the window displayed a list of index terms when users were browsing; when they were searching, the window displayed a list of result sets. Both of the prototypes tested poorly, primarily because subjects in the study did not understand the function and value of browsing database indexes. In LIS, there was only one large index per database, and the display of index terms retrieved using the Scan Index function was not very helpful because it was not interactive and did not provide location information. Consequently, LIS users seldom used the Scan Index function—a fact easily derived from LIS transaction logs and confirmed by focus group participants. Though faculty and graduate students who participated in the focus groups wanted to be able to browse database indexes interactively, the undergraduate students who participated in the prototype study were confused by the feature. Until the user community is comfortable with the ability to examine multiple interactive indexes to a database, the LIS II development group decided that the Browse function should have its own window.

*Motif.* When users click the Browse button in the Search window, the Browse window opens in the lower left quadrant of the workstation monitor, below the Search window. The first implementation of the Browse window had the index names hard coded into the window. As more databases with different indexes were built, the index names were moved to the text file that provides LIS II name service. The list of index names is now displayed in a dialog box upon request. In the initial implementation, users chose "Index" from the Select menu in the Browse window. Protocols revealed that, like the Search window, users overlooked the feature that enabled them to limit browsing to a particular index and they were confused by the placement of buttons along the side and bottom of the window. The following changes were made to the architecture of the Browse window based on the results of the testing and the addition of new features:

- Buttons were moved, added, and renamed. Now, all of the buttons appear in the middle of the window in a sequence similar to the Search window. A Build Search button was added to enable users to interactively compose searches from index terms in the display; the label on the button tested poorly, so the button was renamed "Use Term" to be consistent with the Use Set button in the Search window. When users click the Use Term button, the index term highlighted in the Browse window is appended at the prompt in the Search window, which appears directly above it. Buttons also enable users to browse the indexes (Browse), delete the text at the prompt (Clear), and close the Browse window (Close). The June 1992 release of LIS II will save "state" between Browse sessions, meaning that the system will "remember" what users were browsing previously and open the Browse window with that display.

- Menus were added and rearranged, just like in the Search window. Help and Edit menus were added to provide access to new features. A Limit menu was added to foreground the ability to limit browsing to a particular index. Now users choose "Index" from the Limit menu rather than from the Select menu.

- The banner was moved to the top and revised, just like in the Search window.

- The functionality was changed. In the initial implementation, if people used multiple index terms in a new search (clicked the Use Term button multiple times), LIS II inserted the operator "AND" between them at the search prompt. Protocols indicated that the operator should be "OR" because users browsed indexes to select synonyms or avoid foolish truncation.

The current Browse window is shown in Figure 8. Users are requesting two changes to the display of index terms in the window. First, they want the columns of information to be labeled. They are confused by the abbreviations in capital letters and do not understand that the number is the number of records in the database that contain that term in that index. Users can display online help that explains the information in the list as well as a list of full index names and abbreviations. However, they are reluctant to use the online help and seem unaware that they can display a list of index names and abbreviations. Adding labels to the columns is not difficult technically, but coding that information into the user interface creates problems if anything other than database indexes is to be displayed in the Browse window. LIS enabled users to browse alphabetically arranged lists of entries in the Dictionary, the Journal List, and Who's Who at CMU. Long-term plans for LIS II include adding a similar capability. Users also want the full name of the index to be displayed with each line of information, rather than the abbreviated name (e.g., "All Fields" instead of "AF," "Author Complete" instead of "AC," and "Title Complete" instead of "TC"). Adding the full index name will reduce the number of characters that can be displayed in complete (phrase) indexes because of the 80-character restriction on line length. The ability to browse and interactively use multiple indexes is new in LIS II, therefore the development group is cautious about changing the display. The problems reported may be a "first encounter"

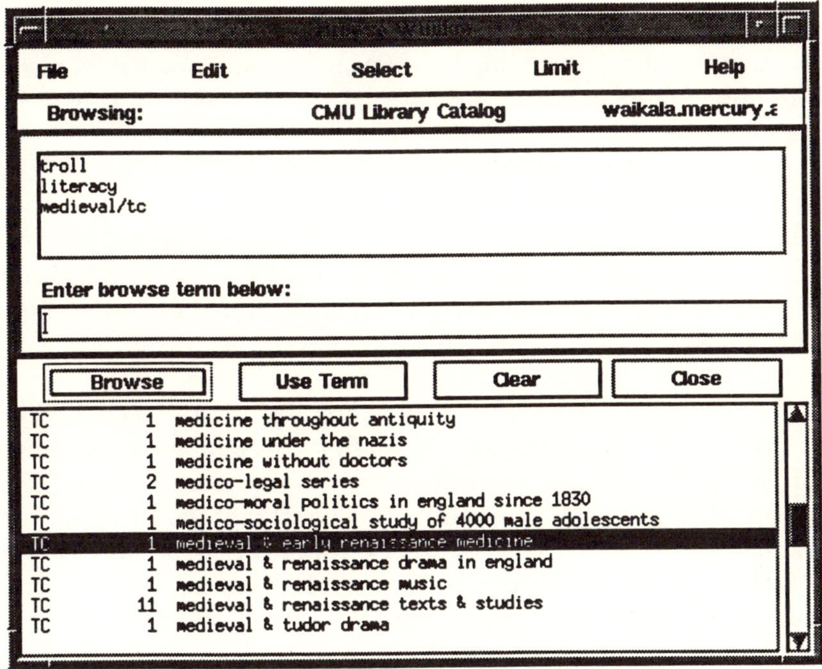


*Figure 8.*　　The Motif Browse Window

phenomenon that goes away as library users become familiar with the feature.

Though the display of index terms was not changed based on user feedback, the indexing itself was. For example, in the enhancements project supported by Pew Charitable Trusts, tables of contents have been added to Library Catalog records for collections of plays and books with individually authored chapters. The table of contents information appears in the Catalog records in the Contents field. The way this field was initially indexed caused problems for users searching authors and titles.[30] LIS II does not differentiate between author and title information in the Contents field, so contents were indexed in the author, title, and notes indexes. The redundancy confused people. Based on user feedback, the Library Catalog was rebuilt and reindexed prior to the campus release. The new version has an author index and a personal name index. The author index includes information from several MARC record fields that contain author information (e.g., Main Entry Personal Name, Variant

Personal Name, and Added Entry Personal Name). The personal
name index includes information from these fields, the Contents field
and several others, including Series Authors and Personal Names as
Subjects. This change seems to have solved the problems with author
searching, but the Catalog may have to be rebuilt and reindexed again
to provide the title indexing that users want. The problem of how
to index author and title information is complicated by inconsisten-
cies in cataloging procedures and by the fact that the names of artists,
illustrators, translators, performers, and editors may or may not be
considered "authors" by the people who catalog a book or the people
who search for it.

*VT100.*   The VT100 Browse window has the same capabilities
as the Motif Browse window, although the mechanisms are slightly
different. For example, instead of clicking a Use Term button to
use an index term in a new search, users highlight the term that they
want in the VT100 Browse window using the arrow keys or the
CTRL keys displayed at the bottom of the window, then press
Return. The limited screen space of the VT100 means that the Search
and Browse windows are not visible at the same time. In the initial
VT100 implementation, the Browse window displayed a message
indicating that the highlighted term was appended at the prompt
in the Search window when users highlighted a term and pressed
Return. Protocols revealed that users often did not see the message,
which was displayed above the browse prompt, and therefore did
not know if anything happened when they pressed Return.
Furthermore, they were annoyed by having to press ESC 1 to display
the Search window after they selected a term to use in a search
because they typically chose only one index term. Based on the
results of the testing, the functionality was changed to display the
Search window when users press Return so that they can see the
index term at the Search prompt. If they want to go back to the
Browse window and select another term to append at the prompt,
they can display the Browse window by pressing ESC 4. The VT100
Browse window is shown in Figure 9.

*Displaying the Results of a Search*

LIS II provides two primary displays of the records retrieved in
a search: "one-line records" and "full records." One-line records are

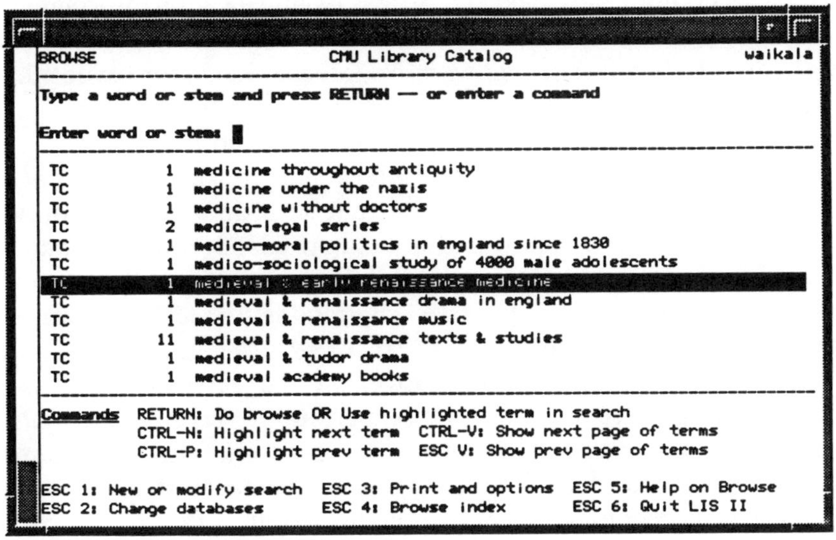

*Figure 9.* The VT100 Browse Window

displayed in a list—one line of information per item retrieved in a search. The one-line record display is called the "list of titles" because, though the display is database specific, it always includes the date and some of the title of each item. The 80-character restriction on line length often forces the information to be truncated. The information included in the list is very important because it is the first view that enables users to make relevance judgments about what they retrieved. It also determines what sort types can be provided for a database; for example, sorting by date can only be provided if date information is included in the list. Furthermore, since the one-line records are created when the database is built, changing the information in the list means rebuilding the database. Because of its importance, the information in the list is carefully selected by the LIS II development group in collaboration with the librarians.

User feedback indicated a problem with the list of titles display for only one database: the Library Catalog. The list of titles in LIS included location and call number information for one copy of an item, but the display was misleading when there were multiple copies in different locations. For this reason, librarians urged the development group not to include this information in the list of titles in LIS II, so the Catalog display was initially implemented without it. However, librarians and users missed having location information in the list and the ability to sort the list by call number. The Library Catalog was therefore rebuilt with this information in the list of titles prior to the campus release.[31]

When users find a title in the list about which they want more information, they can display the full or short record for that title. Full and short records are displayed one at a time. "Full records" may be bibliographic records or full-text (ASCII) documents. "Short records" contain only citation information. The citation display is called the "short record" because "citation" is unintelligible jargon to many undergraduate students.[32] In LIS II, one-line records and full records are stored unformatted on the server side of the distributed architecture. They are sent from the server to the client upon request. The client formats and displays them. The short record is created on the client by displaying only certain fields of information from the full record. The fields to be displayed in the short record are specified in the text file that provides name service and the lists of field and index limits for the Search and Browse windows. In the future, this information will be passed by the Database Meta-Information (DMI) server.

Over half of the databases in LIS II are bibliographic databases. LIS users complained that the display of bibliographic records in LIS was confusing. Rather than beginning with author, title, subject, or publisher information, it began with what users saw as esoteric library information (e.g., "Copyone," "008codes," "Acqnum," and "Docnum"). Furthermore, the names for some of the fields, particularly those dealing with title changes for journals ("Formerly" and "Continued") were meaningless to many users.

In September 1990, a study was done of the names and sequence of fields in bibliographic records. Eleven subjects examined three versions (different sequences of fields) of ten different types of Library Catalog records (e.g., book, journal, monograph, and technical report).[33] Based on the results of this study, the sequence of fields in bibliographic records in LIS II is significantly different from the sequence in LIS. Though the study focused on bibliographic records in the Library Catalog, the recommended sequence was promulgated to all bibliographic databases in LIS II because the information is similar across databases. Figures 10 and 12 show the LIS II sequence of fields for enhanced bibliographic records in the Library Catalog.

In addition to examining the sequence of fields in Library Catalog records, the study garnered information on the usefulness and intelligibility of the field names. Prior to beginning the study, each subject rated the 32 possible field names in Library Catalog records on a scale of one to four, where:

1. was very useful.
2. was somewhat useful.
3. was not useful.
4. was unintelligible—"I don't now what the information in this field means."

They rated the field names without the benefit of having a sample record to examine. Their responses to the sequences of fields in the Catalog records indicate that when confronted with a record, the content of the field in some cases helps them clarify the meaning of the name of the field.

Only one field was rated as very useful by all subjects: the Title field. The Author, Holdings, and Subject fields were rated as either very useful or somewhat useful by all subjects. The Organization, Conference, Abstract and Media fields were rated as very useful or somewhat useful by all but one subject, who rated them not useful. The Language field was rated as very or somewhat useful by most subjects. All of the other fields—22 of the total 32—were rated unintelligible by one to nine subjects. The field names were sufficiently problematic for both librarians and library users to warrant further study. Though the follow up study has not yet been done, some of the field names that scored poorly in this test were changed in LIS II. For example, the Citation field was changed to the Publisher field. The Formerly field and the Continued field were subsumed under a new field name, "Title Change."

*Motif.* The first implementation of the Motif user interface had a List of Records window for viewing a list of titles and a Full Record window for viewing (ASCII) bibliographic records or full-text documents like encyclopedia articles. For reasons discussed earlier in this paper, these two windows were combined into one Records window. (See Figure 10.) When users click the Display button in the Search window, the Records window appears to the right of the Search window. When the window opens, the list of titles (for the result set highlighted in the Search window) appears at the top, but the bottom of the window is empty. Users highlight a title in the list and click the Full Record button, or double-click on a title in the list, to display a full record in the bottom of the window. Search terms appear in capital letters in the full records; an upgrade to the next version of Motif (currently underway) will enable search terms to be displayed in a different font. Users can display the full record for the next or previous title in the list by clicking the appropriate button at the bottom of the window or by double-clicking on the title. They can reallocate space between the list of titles and full record displays by dragging the divider bar. LIS users complained about being able to see only 10 titles at a time. Motif LIS II enables them to see up to 45 titles at a time or a volume of text in a full record comparable to a printed page. Using a menu or only mouse buttons, users can mark titles in the list so that they can act on them as a group (e.g., for saving, mailing, and printing).

The Records window tested well and has undergone very little change since it was first implemented. The following changes were made based on the protocols and the addition of new features:

- Menus were added, renamed, and removed. Edit and Help menus were added to provide access to new features. An Options menu was added to enable users to toggle between displaying full and short records (citations). The first implementation of the window did not allow users to display short records, only save, mail, or print them. Users were annoyed that they could not display them, so the capability was provided. The Mark Records menu was renamed "Mark Titles." The Select menu was removed for the campus release because the features to be provided there (e.g., sorting the list of titles) have not been implemented yet in the Records window; these features are provided in the Search window. Protocols revealed that users are annoyed by menu options that are always grayed out as unavailable.

- A Print button was added by popular demand, though "Print" is also an option on the File menu in all of the Motif windows. Printing is discussed later in this paper.

The one known problem with the design of the Records window is the location of the buttons: they are too far away from the menus

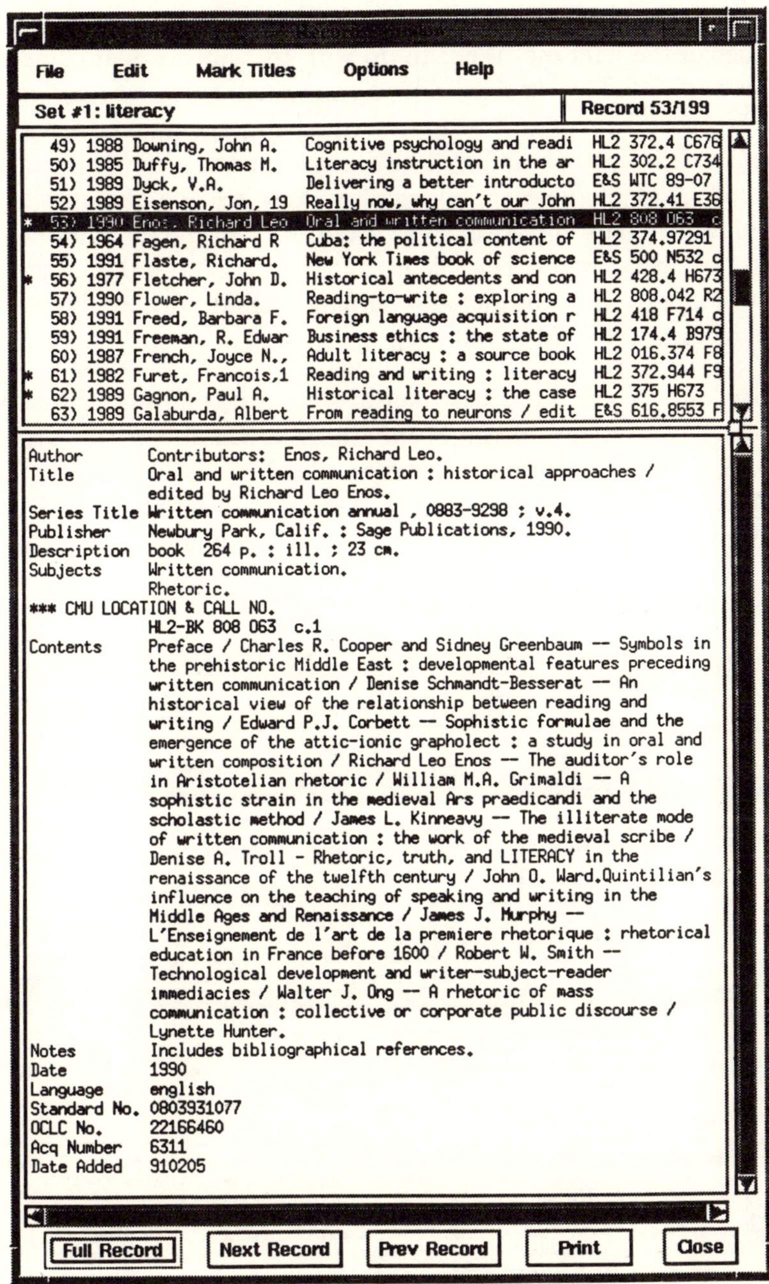



*Figure 10.*   The Motif Records Window

and the list of titles, which is where users typically position the mouse cursor in the window. In the future, these buttons may be repositioned higher in the window. What to do with the buttons will be decided after additional features are added and tested in the spring. Features like the delivery of full-text documents in page-image format will require the provision of additional buttons or menus. The functionality of the Records window may also be changed to: (1) display the first full record in the list of titles automatically when the window opens, and (2) enable users to display more than one short record at a time. Plans include enabling users to sort and limit result sets from the Records window.

*VT100.*   The VT100 user interface has two windows that provide all the functionality of the Motif Records window: a List of Titles window and a Full Record window. (See Figures 11 and 12.) Short records are displayed in a window that is identical to the Full Record window except for the name at the top of the window.

## Displaying Documents in Page-Image Format

*Motif.* By fall semester 1992, LIS II will deliver full-text documents in page-image format to personal computers capable of

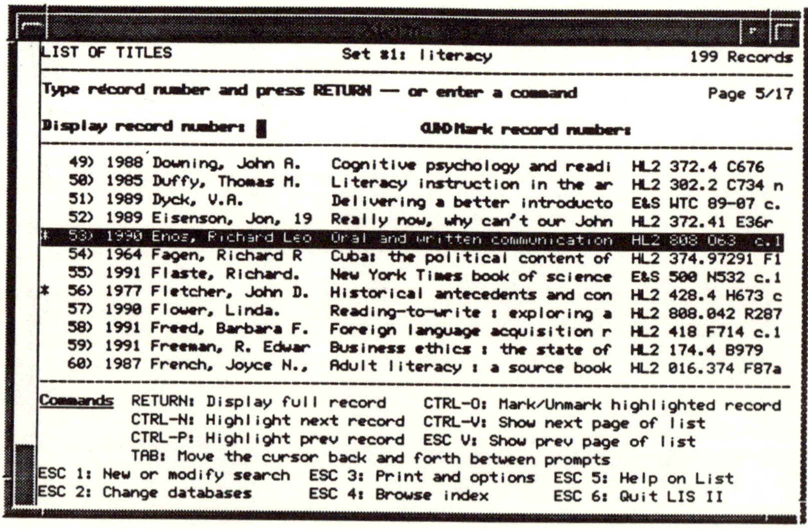


*Figure 11.*   The VT100 List of Titles Window

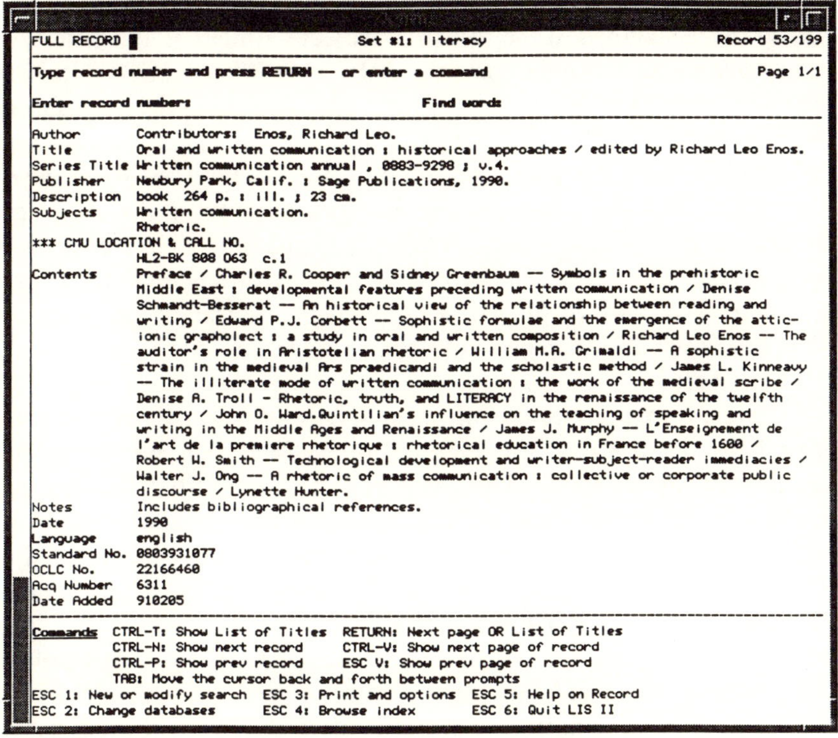


*Figure 12.* The VT100 Full Record Window Enlarged to
View a Full Bibliographic Record

displaying bitmapped images. The images will be linked to
bibliographic records in INSPEC, and they will also be available
using an Image Browser. Both access points will display the pages
in what is currently called the Image window. The names "Image
window" and "Image Browser" may be changed before their release
to campus based on user interface tests that are currently underway.
Images are not displayed in the Records window, where ASCII
documents are displayed, because the retrieval and presentation
protocols for images are different from those for ASCII. Also, what
users can do with image and ASCII documents is different. For
example, users can copy and paste passages in ASCII text; they
cannot copy and paste passages in bitmapped page images. Providing
images in a different window changes user expectations and facilitates
learning.

The images that will be available for online viewing by fall 1992 will be those scanned in the research project with IEEE and Elsevier. Pages are being scanned using a DEC MD400 (RICOH IS 50) scanner that averages four pages per minute at 400 DPI. Uncompressed, each page image is approximately 1.7 megabytes. Using TIFF Group 4 Fax compression, the compressed size ranges from 45 to 70 KB for normal text and graphics (100 KB if the page includes halftone pictures or graytone backgrounds). The images are sent across the network at the user's request, and they are decompressed and displayed at the client as the image arrives. Approximately 27,000 pages have been scanned to date. They require 3 GB of storage.

Two test implementations of page images linked to INSPEC have been built. In the first implementation, a field that indicated the location of the scanned images was added to the INSPEC records. When users displayed a full bibliographic record containing this field, the user interface displayed an Image button at the bottom of the Records window. If users clicked the Image button, the Image window opened and displayed the first page of the article. This implementation was demonstrated at EDUCOM '91. To simplify maintenance, a second test implementation was built that did not require adding information to INSPEC records. Instead, when users display a full bibliographic record, LIS II uses source information from several fields in the record and does a quick lookup in a table of journal titles, volumes, and issues that have been scanned. If the source information has a match in the table, then the user interface displays the Image button at the bottom of the Records window. If users click the Image button, the Image window opens and displays the first page of the article. Since the lookup is very fast, the development group decided to do it automatically rather than force users to request it. The second implementation is the one that will be released to campus. It was demonstrated at DECWorld in May 1992.

Figure 13 shows a full-text page image displayed in the Image window. The initial version of the window, being tested now, provides keyboard and mouse commands to zoom and navigate the images. No buttons, menus, or scroll bars are provided. Two levels of zoom facilitate reading; see Figure 14. Users can request the next, previous, first, or last pages of the article, or specify a number of pages to move forward or backward through the article. The "concept" of an article

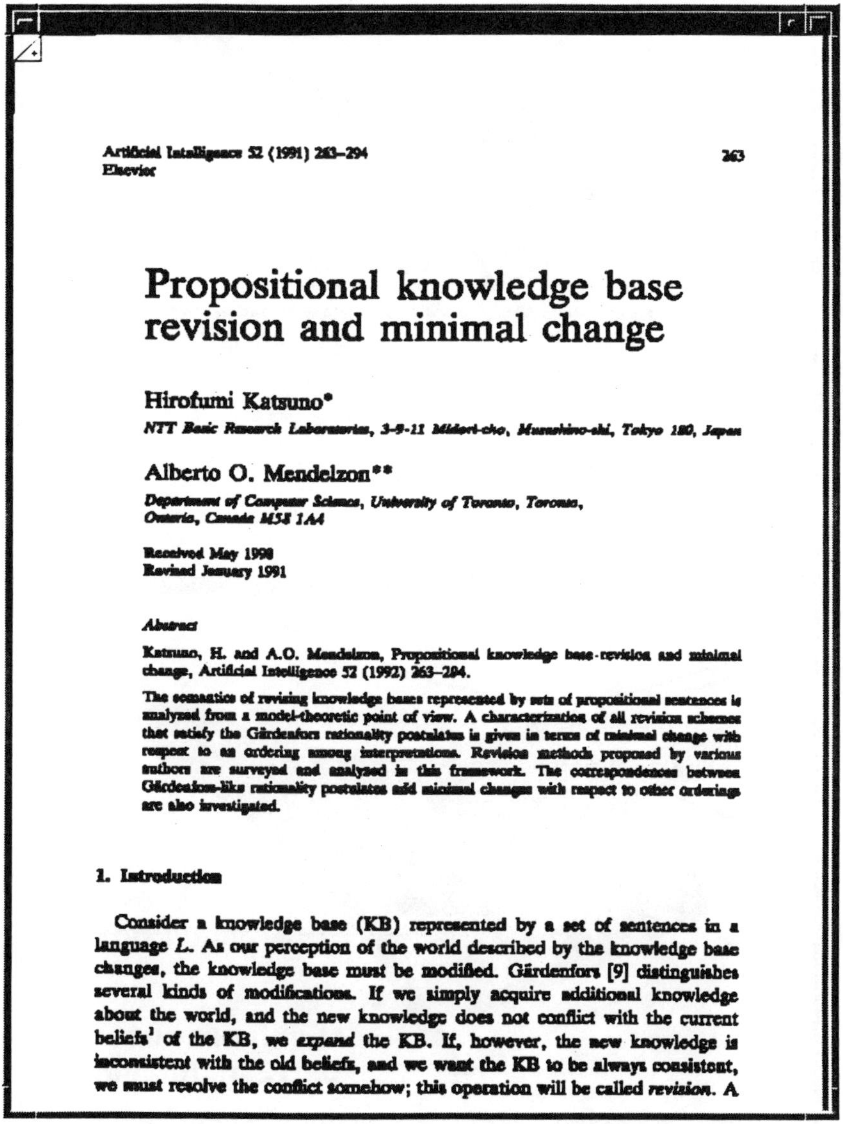

Artificial Intelligence 52 (1991) 263–294
Elsevier

263

# Propositional knowledge base revision and minimal change

Hirofumi Katsuno*
*NTT Basic Research Laboratories, 3-9-11 Midori-cho, Musashino-shi, Tokyo 180, Japan*

Alberto O. Mendelzon**
*Department of Computer Science, University of Toronto, Toronto,
Ontario, Canada M5S 1A4*

Received May 1990
Revised January 1991

*Abstract*

Katsuno, H. and A.O. Mendelzon, Propositional knowledge base-revision and minimal change, Artificial Intelligence 52 (1992) 263–294.

The semantics of revising knowledge bases represented by sets of propositional sentences is analyzed from a model-theoretic point of view. A characterization of all revision schemes that satisfy the Gärdenfors rationality postulates is given in terms of minimal change with respect to an ordering among interpretations. Revision methods proposed by various authors are surveyed and analyzed in this framework. The correspondences between Gärdenfors-like rationality postulates and minimal change with respect to other orderings are also investigated.

## 1. Introduction

Consider a knowledge base (KB) represented by a set of sentences in a language $L$. As our perception of the world described by the knowledge base changes, the knowledge base must be modified. Gärdenfors [9] distinguishes several kinds of modifications. If we simply acquire additional knowledge about the world, and the new knowledge does not conflict with the current beliefs[1] of the KB, we *expand* the KB. If, however, the new knowledge is inconsistent with the old beliefs, and we want the KB to be always consistent, we must resolve the conflict somehow; this operation will be called *revision*. A

*Figure 13.*  The Motif Image Window Displaying a
Page Image of a Journal Article

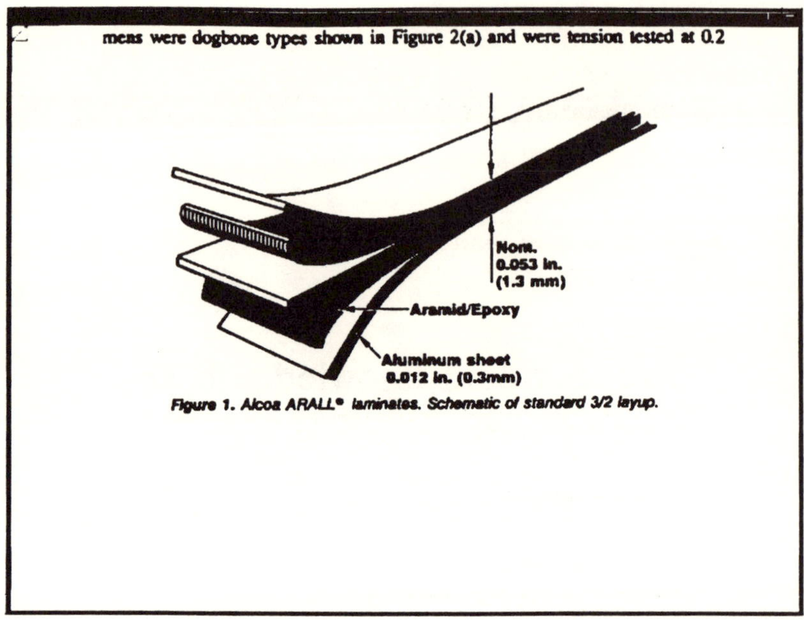


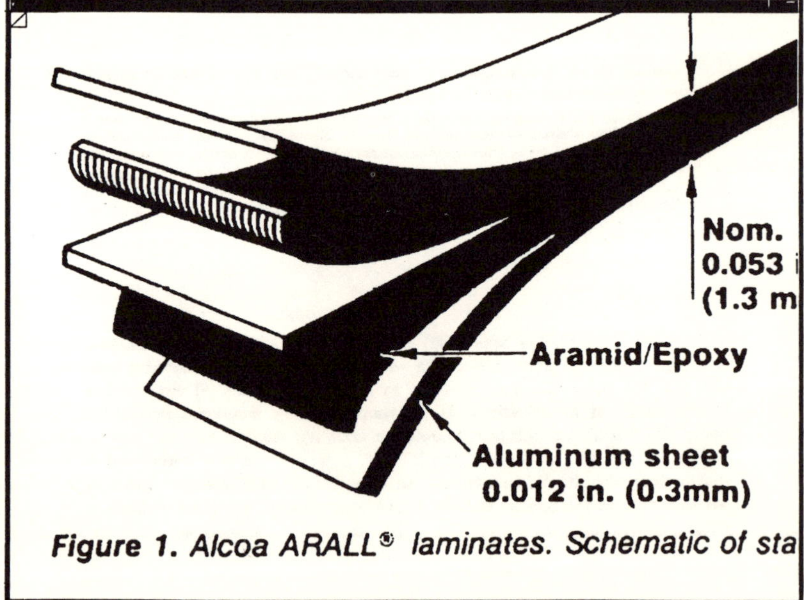


*Figure 14.* The Motif Image Window "Zoomed In"
for Easy Reading

derives from the source information in the bibliographic record and the lookup table. Instructions are displayed by typing the letter "H" for Help; typing "H" again hides the Help.

Though the data has not yet been thoroughly analyzed, image protocol studies indicate that users have many problems with the Image window. First, they do not notice when the Image button is displayed at the bottom of the Records window. A different, more eye-catching way to indicate the availability of page images will have to be devised or users will overlook the feature. Users also have problems navigating the images because they do not understand the vocabulary of the help text or know how to use a three-button mouse. When they zoom in and pan around, they quickly lose track of where they are. Based on the results of the user interface tests, the help text will be significantly revised, many of the commands will be moved to menus or buttons, and a context will be provided by graphically indicating what piece of the image is current visible in the window.

The second access point for the scanned images (other than the link with INSPEC) is the Image Browser. Using this feature, users can select an issue of a journal and view and navigate it the way they would naturally move through a printed journal. The feature will facilitate current awareness, serendipitous searching, and known item retrieval. In the test implementation available now, the Image Browser can be opened from within the Image window in LIS II or run as an independent program outside of LIS II. In the near future, a feature will be added that enables users to open the Image Browser in LIS II without having opened the Image window first using links in INSPEC. When the Browser is released to campus, people will be able to use it inside or outside of LIS II.

Using the Image Browser, users first choose a document type. By fall 1992, the Browser will deliver page images of selected journals and technical reports. When users specify a document type, the browser displays a list of what is available. If they select "journal," the browser displays an alphabetical list of available journal titles. If they select "technical report," it displays a list of institutions whose technical report series are available; when users select an institution, the browser displays a list of the available technical report series from that institution. When users choose a title or series, the browser displays a list of the available documents (e.g., the list of journal issues available for the selected title or the list of technical reports available from the selected series). When users choose a specific document from the list, the browser prompts them to select a page. When they select a page, it is displayed in the Image window. Users can navigate and zoom in the ways described above. The Image Browser has a concept of the article and of the entire document.

Two versions of the table of contents for journals are available. One version is the scanned image of the table of contents. The image can be viewed, but it is not interactive. The other version of the table of contents is an interactive ASCII version. The ASCII text is created by running OCR (Optical Character Recognition) software on the scanned images and manually fixing errors. Users can click on a title in the ASCII table of contents and retrieve the first page (image) of the article. The page images are displayed in the Image window.

Protocol studies indicate that the current implementation of the Image Browser is very difficult to use. The user interface does not indicate clearly what is an on-screen instruction and what is interactive text, so users often click the wrong place. Frustration increases as they try to navigate the lists of titles, volumes, issues, and pages. When they pop up and down in the hierarchy, they quickly lose track of where they are and what they have seen. The problems are compounded by the vocabulary and dense presentation of the help text. Based on the results of the protocols, the help text will be significantly revised, clickable text will be clearly distinguished from on-screen instructions, and a context may be provided by graphically marking the items that have been seen.

Prior to the campus release, a second set of image protocols will be done after the user interface has been redesigned and implemented.


*VT100.* The VT100 user interface cannot display images. However, users can submit requests to print images, and, if they run VT100 LIS II on a workstation running X.11 windows, they can indeed open the Image window and Image Browser from within the VT100 user interface. Features are provided in the VT100 user interface to do this, and the software is smart enough to know whether the user's equipment can display images. In the test implementation, the feature to "Display Images" is provided in the Options dialog box displayed when users press ESC 3 in the Full Record window.

## Saving, Mailing, and Printing

Integrating LIS II with other network services on campus was a high priority. The first release enables users to save, mail, or print any of the basic (ASCII) information displays. With one command, users can save, mail, or print the list of result sets, a list of up to 500 titles or index terms, up to 100 short records, or one full bibliographic record or full-text document. The details are as follows:

- Authenticated users can save information in the Andrew File System (AFS) or the file system operated by SCS. The default pathname is the user's home directory. Unauthenticated users cannot save information.

- Authenticated users can mail information to an electronic mail address on campus or the Internet. The default e-mail address is the user's user ID and computing domain (e.g., aristotle@andrew.cmu.edu or socrates@.cmu.edu). Unauthenticated users cannot mail information.

- Printing is handled somewhat differently, depending on whether the user is in the University Libraries or outside of the University Libraries. People who use the dedicated LIS II workstations located in the libraries can only print on printers in the libraries. Authenticated users running LIS II outside of the libraries can print on any accessible networked printer on campus. Internet guests cannot print information unless they have a print screen function on their machine.

*Motif.*  Access to the Save, Mail, and Print functions is provided on the File menu in the Motif Search, Browse, and Records windows. When users choose one of these options, a dialog box opens and displays a list of the information that they can save, mail, or print. It also displays a prompt for specifying the pathname, e-mail address, or printer name. Since the monitor of a UNIX workstation has sufficient space for all of the LIS II windows to be open at once, Motif LIS II prompts users to specify which information they want. The default selection is determined by the window in which users request the service. For example, if they choose Print from the Search window, the default selection is to print the list of result sets; if they choose Save from the Records window, the default is to save the full

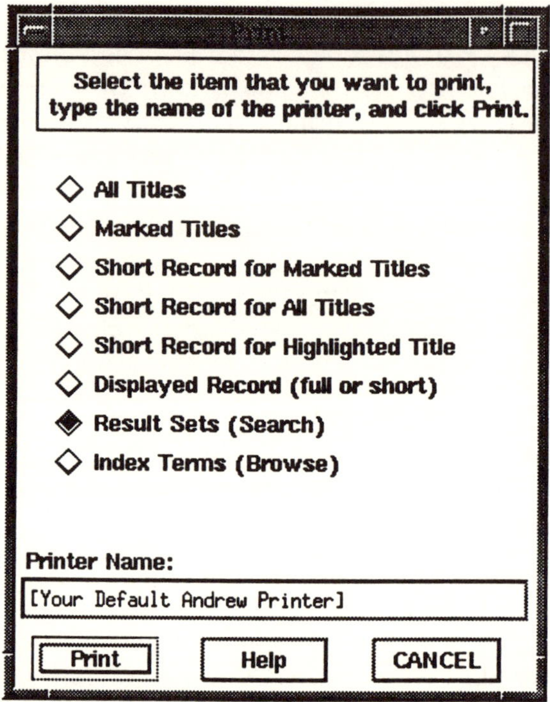



*Figure 15.*    The Motif Print Dialog Box

record. In the initial implementation, the default for the Records window was the list of titles, but user feedback warranted changing the default to the full record. Users also wanted a more conspicuous way to print full records, so a Print button was added to the Records window prior to the campus release. Users select the information they want by clicking a button, change the text at the prompt if the default is not what they want, and then click OK. Protocols indicated that the list of information in the initial dialog box was ambiguous, so the list was revised. The revised list is shown in Figure 15. Protocols also revealed that users were annoyed because the initial implementation of LIS II did not display a message saying that their information was saved, mailed, or printed. These status messages were added prior to the campus release; they appear in the window where the user submitted the request.

In addition to enabling users to mail ASCII information to campus and Internet electronic mail addresses, Motif LIS II also enables users to mail questions, comments, and bug reports to a private electronic bulletin board. Users choose "Send Comment/Bug Report" from the Options menu in the Search window, and a mail window appears on their screen. The bulletin board where messages are posted is read by the LIS II development group. All messages receive a response from the Systems Librarian within 48 hours; the Systems Librarian is a member of the development group. Users receive responses privately in electronic mail, and anonymous question-answer pairs are posted publicly on an electronic bulletin board created for this purpose.

*VT100.*   The VT100 user interface cannot display multiple views of information at once, so requests to save, mail, or print act on the information currently displayed (e.g., the list of result sets in the Search window and the bibliographic record in the Full Record window). The Save, Mail, and Print commands are provided in the Options dialog box displayed when users press ESC 3. In the initial implementation of the ESC commands, the on-screen instructions for ESC 3 said "Show other options." However, users accustomed to a print screen function were confused when they did not see a Print command displayed in the user interface. To make printing conspicuous, the text describing the ESC 3 command at the bottom of each window was changed from "Show other options" to "Print and options." The VT100 user interface does not yet have a Send Comment/Bug Report feature.

By fall 1992, LIS II will also enable users to print—but not save or mail—full-text documents in page-image format. The images will be from General Periodicals Ondisc, Business Periodicals Ondisc, and Social Sciences Ondisc (UMI databases stored on CD-ROM). The CD-ROM products are mounted in jukeboxes in a private room in the main library. Users will search Periodical Abstracts, ABI/ Inform, or Social Sciences Index (ASCII bibliographic databases linked to the image databases) and submit electronic requests to print the full text of the articles on a designated printer in the library. There will be a small fee for print service, comparable to the fee for the University Libraries' Journal Article Delivery Service (JADS), which delivers copies of journal articles to users with campus (hardcopy) mail addresses. Usage of the bibliographic databases will be monitored at the retrieval servers; usage of the CD-ROM products will be monitored at the UMI print server. In the second phase of the UMI project, users will be able to view the full text of the articles on personal computers with the ability to display bitmapped page images. Sometime later, an option may be provided to enable users to print the page images on networked printers located outside of the library. The UMI print service request form for both the Motif and VT100 user interfaces will be tested in the summer. By the end of 1992, users will also be able to print the images scanned in the project with Elsevier and IEEE. Usage monitoring of the Elsevier and IEEE image collection was discussed earlier in this paper.

### Requesting Non-Electronic Services

In addition to enabling users to save, mail, or print information in different formats, by the end of 1992 LIS II will facilitate the delivery of documents currently unavailable in machine-readable form. Users will be able to submit electronic requests for the following services:

- *Journal Article Delivery Service* (*JADS*). "Copy this article in the local collection and send it to me in campus mail."

- *Interlibrary Loan*. "Find this article in a collection not in the University Libraries, request a copy, and deliver it to my branch library."

- *Book Check Out*. "Get this book from the local collection, check it out to me, and hold it at the circulation desk for me to pick up."

- *Book Reserve*. "Get this book from the local collection and put it on reserve for my class to use."

Requests for these services will automatically include the full bibliographic record that the user was viewing at the time of the request. The various electronic requests forms will be tested in the fall. Electronic requests for JADS, interlibrary loan, and so forth will be monitored when this feature is released to campus.

### Getting the Vocabulary Right

*Motif.*   Vocabulary was a significant problem that surfaced in all of the LIS II usability tests. Changes in button labels and menu options have already been discussed. Getting the vocabulary right in the error messages and dialog boxes was more difficult. Protocols indicated clearly that LIS II error messages were cryptic, used vocabulary inconsistently, and, in many cases, used computer jargon that was unintelligible to library users. In May 1991, a study was undertaken of the error messages displayed in Motif LIS II. Nine subjects, all librarians, evaluated 20 problematic messages and suggested revisions, and then engaged in an open discussion of the appropriate vocabulary for LIS II. The error messages tested were those that consistently caused problems during the protocol studies. The suggested revisions described what was wrong and what the user could do to fix it. The goal of the study was to identify and solve vocabulary problems. The agreed upon user-friendly vocabulary would then be proliferated throughout the information displays, user interfaces, and documentation.

The error message study was potentially the most productive usability test of 1991. Results showed that, while the suggested revisions for the problematic messages were far superior to the original text, the vocabulary was still wrong in several cases. Furthermore, the study revealed that users expect error messages to provide not only information about what is wrong and what they can do to fix it, but, in many cases, interactive choices. They wanted buttons that they could click to have the system do something other than just get rid of the error message or cancel what they were doing.

Two error messages warrant special note because of the system functionality that prompts them. The Newton retrieval software provides a two level "resource control service" to prohibit users from making poor searches and wasting both their time and system resources.[34] Generally, resource control is applied to searches involving truncated terms, which are expanded into logical "ORs" of terms in the index that meet the truncation criterion. When a search expands to 300 terms, LIS II warns the user that it may take a long time to run and provides an option to cancel the search. When a search expands to 1,000 terms, LIS II will not do the search, but it provides an option to browse the database indexes to select more specific terms.

In the original implementation, when the first level of resource control was triggered, the system stopped searching, displayed a message saying that the search expanded into hundreds of terms, and told the user to click a Continue button to proceed with the search or a Cancel button to cancel the search. Users were confused by the text of the message and annoyed that the search had been stopped. They complained that it took them longer to read and try to decipher the message than it would to run the search. Based on this information, the text of the error message was revised and the software was changed to not interrupt the search. Now, the error message contains only a Cancel button.

The original error message for the second level of resource control informed the user that the search expanded into hundreds of terms and suggested that the user browse the database indexes to select more specific terms. The error message dialog box included a Browse button, which would open the Browse window, and a Cancel button, which was unexplained. Users were confused by the text of the message and annoyed that they were not allowed to do the search. The revised error message says simply that the search is too general to do, and it explains both the Browse and the Cancel buttons. In addition to these changes, the software itself was changed so that the second level of resource control is not triggered until the expansion exceeds the maximum number of terms that Newton will allow.

The open discussion that followed the evaluation of the error messages revealed that the overall vocabulary of the development group was different from the vocabulary of the users. The differences confused users and promoted an inadequate conceptual model of the system. Based on the results of this discussion, several significant changes were made to the vocabulary used in the error messages. The changes were then promulgated throughout the user interface and the documentation. For example, the term "query" was replaced with "search." "Results," "search sets," and so forth. were replaced with "result sets." "List of records" was replaced with "list of titles." "Marking records" was replaced with "marking titles." Users limit searching to a particular "field," but they limit browsing to a particular "index." In addition, all OK buttons were changed to close the error message dialog box without doing anything (e.g., without deleting text at the search prompt). All Cancel buttons were made to undo what the user had been doing when the error message was displayed (e.g., to delete text at the search prompt). To improve readability, all error messages were changed to display text flush left, rather than centered. A blank line is provided between the statement of the problem and the instructions for how to fix it.

*VT100.* The user-friendly vocabulary derived from the Motif error messages study was incorporated into the VT100 user interface and documentation, but VT100 protocols pinpointed additional problems that required changing the user interface. Ironically, the first implementation of the interface was less cluttered than the released version. For example, in the initial version, the text of the commands displayed at the bottom of the windows was cryptic (e.g., "CTRL-N: Next set" and "CTRL-V: Next page"). The meaning of these commands eluded users, so the descriptions were expanded to provide more information. For example, in the Search window "Next set" was changed to "Highlight next set"; "Next page" was changed to "Show next page of sets."

The initial vocabulary of the VT100 user interface also caused problems when users tried to navigate the windows and information displays. The term "screen" was ambiguous. Did it refer to a particular kind of information display (e.g., result sets, list of titles, or full bibliographic record); or did it refer to a piece of an information display (e.g., the beginning of a list of titles or a subsequent piece of the list)? Because of this ambiguity, the next iteration of the VT100 interface used the word "window" to indicate a particular kind of information display, and the word "page" for a piece of a particular display. Admittedly, "window" and "page" are metaphors in this context, but they are intelligible and unambiguous to users. The name of each window appears in the top left corner of the window; the page number appears in the top right corner. The metaphor of the page is also used in dialog boxes. (See Figures 5 and 7.)

Error messages in the VT100 user interface are particularly problematic because of the space constraints. To date, only one line has been allocated in the user interface for error messages—the single line above the prompt. The Motif error messages study made it clear that users want error messages that not only tell them what the problem is, but provide suggestions—even interactive options—for solving the problem. One line is not enough space to do this. In the future, VT100 error and status messages will be revised and implemented differently. Status messages, like those indicating that information has been saved, mailed, or printed, will continue to be displayed on one line above the prompt. Error messages will be revised following the model used in the Motif study and displayed at the bottom of the VT100 windows. The error messages will overwrite the ESC and CTRL commands displayed at the bottom of each window. Protocol subjects and librarians in the error messages study recommended this strategy. They did not want status messages to appear at the bottom of the windows because of the time it will take to overwrite the command lines. However, in the case of an error, which stops activity and disables the commands at the bottom of the window until the problem is resolved, the advantage of having more descriptive (six-line) error messages will compensate for the time it will take to overwrite the command lines.

## Documentation

Though the University Libraries endeavored to produce a retrieval system that was easy and convenient to use, there is no such thing as an "intuitive" user interface. What's "intuitive" to a system designer may not be intuitive to a user. Users are able to do searches and display records in LIS II without assistance, but, to take advantage of the full power of LIS II, they need help. Online help is provided in the Motif and VT100 user interfaces. The text is produced and maintained by the development group and approved by the University Libraries' Editorial Board, which offers another vocabulary check. The first implementation of online help is a minimal system that provides information about what can be done in each LIS II window. The help is not hierarchical or interactive, though it is comprehensive and up to date. Feedback from users indicates that the current implementation is inadequate. Improving the help system is a high priority for development in the spring. Plans include providing an interactive table of contents. The Motif user interface released to campus uses Motif version 1.0.A. Upgrading to Motif version 1.1.2 (currently underway) provides access to a Motif help system that will improve service.

In addition to online help provided within LIS II, printed manuals are available for the Motif and VT100 user interfaces. The manuals are written in "stand-alone" modules that users can remove and carry with them. Task-oriented modules contain details about every feature in the system and provide multiple examples. Quick-reference modules contain overviews of every menu, button, or option. Labeled pictures are included. The manuals were produced by members of the development group and approved by the University Libraries' Editorial Board. They will be maintained and revised by the Editorial

Board. The manuals can be purchased in the Carnegie Mellon Computer Store. Selected modules from the manuals have been freely distributed in the University Libraries since fall 1991, when Motif LIS II became available in the libraries. In addition to the LIS II user manuals for the Motif and VT100 user interfaces, two additional manuals will be prepared. The Macintosh user interface will be documented, and a technical manual is being prepared for the programmers who build and maintain the databases and install the server software. The technical manual is underway and scheduled to be available this summer.

In addition to online help and printed documentation, other documents are required to position LIS II effectively in the Carnegie Mellon computing environment. Several of these documents are mentioned here to indicate the collaboration required between the development group and computing groups outside of the University Libraries.

- The Andrew Help System provides information about all of the software accessible in the Andrew File System. The LIS II development group maintains the "library" and library "changes" files in the Andrew Help System.

- The "Computing Skills Workshop" (CSW), a required course for undergraduates at Carnegie Mellon, teaches a unit on Motif LIS II. The development group contributes significantly to the preparation of the LIS II documentation for CSW.

- Academic Computing and Media produces and maintains several documents in conjunction with Special Projects, a software development group within Computing and Communications at Carnegie Mellon, that detail "how to get there from here" (for example, how to get to LIS II from a Macintosh or an IBM PC). The development group helps to revise these documents to ensure accuracy.

When significant changes or additions are made to the Library Information System, the development group also prepares articles for *Cursor*, the computing newsletter edited by Academic Computing and Media; *Resources*, a newsletter for faculty, alumni, and friends of the University Libraries; and the newsletter produced by the

Oakland Library Consortium, which provides the OLC Connection software mentioned earlier in this paper.

Instructions for Internet access to LIS II have been published in the guides to OPACs (Online Public Access Catalogs) on the Internet and made available to PREPnet members. Development group staff prepared and distributed these instructions, but in the future this activity will be done by the EISC (the University Libraries' Electronic Information Services Committee).

## CONCLUSION

As libraries try to maintain or add services amidst budget cuts and increasing demands from users, the lessons learned from designing, implementing, testing, and releasing LIS II have much to offer. Mainframe computing cannot keep pace with user expectations; distributed computing can. The distributed architecture of clients and servers in LIS II improves service while decreasing costs. For example, distributed computing can provide multiple user interfaces and information in multiple formats; mainframe computing cannot. Furthermore, a distributed system can easily be scaled upward to accommodate more databases by adding more disk space or (eventually) more server machines. With appropriate documentation, the system can be maintained (e.g., databases released and updated) by personnel with a minimal understanding of the architecture.

Building a retrieval system with multiple user interfaces is admittedly more work than building a system with one user interface. Similarly, building a system that is machine-independent and uses emerging standards is more work than a system that is grounded in one operating system ideology. However, the rewards are worth the effort. Using the conventions of the operating system with which users are familiar facilitates learning and thus the transition to a new system. Though the varying availability of databases in a distributed system and the many lists created dynamically at run time challenge the user's (mainframe) model of information retrieval, giving the Macintosh user Macintosh menus, buttons, and scroll bars (or the Motif user Motif menus, buttons, and scroll bars) helps the user transfer knowledge from other applications and quickly become comfortable. Machine-independence enables the system to accommodate new clients in the future, as vendors market new personal computers. LIS II can serve these new computers simply by providing another client; the underlying retrieval system does not have to change. Standard retrieval protocols enable the system to send queries to retrieval systems at other sites that use the same protocols. As libraries cease to purchase materials and instead provide access to information, querying other systems becomes cost effective.

With proper design and testing, a distributed system can be made secure and easy to use. Security is important because database vendors want usage restricted to people covered by the site license. Security can be provided by interrelated administrative services that identify users and locate and control access to the databases. Ease of use is important because users want to find information quickly, not spend time learning how to find information. The usability tests done on LIS II prior to its release indicate that the most significant design decisions in the user interface pertain to the arrangement and presentation of information. The goal is to provide a coherent, intelligible set of features without cluttering the user interface. Frequently used features, such as limits, should be foregrounded in the user interface, either on a button or as the name of a menu. Features that are seldom used should be provided as menu options or in dialog boxes. Often the vocabulary used to label buttons and menus and provide on-screen instructions is the critical difference between user satisfaction and user frustration. Testing also locates problems in functionality. What users want and expect a feature to do sometimes surprises even experienced system designers.

## NOTES

1. See Denise A. Troll, "The Mercury Project: Meeting the Needs and Expectations of Electronic Library Patrons," in *Advances in Online Public Access Catalogs* (Westport, CT: Meckler, 1992), 114-135.

2. The Mercury Electronic Library Project is supported by Carnegie Mellon University, Pew Charitable Trusts, Digital Equipment Corporation (DEC), Online Computer Library Center (OCLC), and Apple Computers.

3. There are several other computing systems on campus, including that of the Electrical and Computer Engineering Department (ECE), the Software Engineering Institute (SEI), and a VAX/VMS system. One of the long-term goals of the university is to merge authentication of all of these systems. The LIS II development group contributes significantly to this effort.

4. LIS II monitors user activity and, if nothing is done for a considerable period of time, the system closes connections to the servers, logs the user out, and stops

running the user interface. The timeout period is 20 minutes on workstations located in the University Libraries because these machines run only LIS II and no other software. Timeout for machines outside of the University Libraries is set at 40 minutes. Providing a timeout feature is necessary to maintain performance because idle connections use memory. In the future, the software may be changed so that timeouts disconnect clients from servers, but do not log users out or stop the user interface. When users issue a search or change databases after a timeout, LIS II will reconnect them to the appropriate server.

5. Ideally, LIS II would also log whether the user was an undergraduate student, graduate student, faculty member, or staff member, but this raises an ethical concern about protecting the identity of this individual. Some categories may at times have only one member. For example, a graduate program may have only one student for a semester.

6. The proposed study, "Changing Attitudes and Behaviors in the Library Without Walls," is a collaborative effort of University Libraries and faculty in the Graduate School of Industrial Administration at Carnegie Mellon. Attitudes and behaviors of a stratified sample of users and potential users of electronically provided materials will be monitored from 1992-1994. Data gathered during the first year will be used to build a model of the relationships between attitudes and behaviors concerning electronic library services. Data collected during the second year will be used to validate the model. The model will be used as the basis for later studies of the effectiveness of various marketing strategies and interventions designed to promote use of library services. It will also provide a framework for analyzing survey and other data to help evaluate and forecast usage rates for various services.

7. In 1992, several other retrieval engines will be tested. For example, CBRS (Content Based Retrieval System) from Digital Equipment Corporation (a variant of Topic from Verity), Ful/Text from Fulcrum, or WAIS (Wide Area Information Server) from Thinking Machines. A long-term goal of LIS II is to support different retrieval engines. For example, one engine may be best for large databases, another for small databases, one for full text, one for bibliographic information, etc.

8. ArchPics is a bibliographic database that indexes architectural pictures in books owned by Carnegie Mellon University Libraries. With the publishers' permission, long-term plans include scanning the pictures and making them available in LIS II as page images.

9. Who's Who is a database of faculty, students, and staff at Carnegie Mellon. It is an online version of the *Faculty and Staff Directory* and the student *C Book*, containing information like names, addresses, telephone numbers, and department affiliation.

10. The *Tartan* is the student newspaper at Carnegie Mellon. *Focus* is the faculty newspaper.

11. ICPSR is an annual guide to statistical data tapes published by the Interuniversity Consortium for Political and Social Research.

12. Members of the LIS II development group participate in the Z39.50 working group. When LIS II requires changing or extending the protocol, the development group lobbies to have the change (or something comparable to it) added to the standard.

13. For example, if usage is very heavy, but the work of only three individuals, the market is small and may not warrant gigabytes of space dedicated to page images

at this time. If users look at the page images for an article only once, then a "pay per view" pricing structure is reasonable, but if they look at the page images a half a dozen different times, then a "pay per view" structure is not reasonable. For more information about economic models for the electronic library, see: *Development Plan for an Electronic Library System*, Mercury Technical Report Series, No. 4 (Pittsburgh, PA: Carnegie Mellon University, 1991).

14. Details of the Catalog enhancement project are provided in: Denise A. Troll, *Library Information System II: Progress Report and Technical Plan*, Mercury Technical Report Series, No. 3 (Pittsburgh, PA: Carnegie Mellon University, 1990).

15. The American Library Association Conference in June 1991 offered a session called "Do Patrons Want a Choice? Evaluating Sources in Public Access Catalogs." The speakers reported that searching the *Choice* database enabled library users to find books in the local collection that they did not find by searching the library catalog. Claire Dudley, former editor of *Choice* magazine, stated that *Choice* book reviews contain an average of 170 words, many of which are not included in bibliographic records.

16. CLARIT is supported by Digital Equipment Corporation and the American Association for Artificial Intelligence. CLARIT is in its fourth year. The project to integrate CLARIT and LIS II would span three years.

17. Because research commitments mandate monitoring usage of the INSPEC database, faculty in the School of Computer Science and the Physics and Electrical and Computer Engineering departments were targeted in the focus groups. Two electronic bulletin boards are provided to facilitate communication about LIS II. One of the bulletin boards is for library staff; the other is for library users. Members of the LIS II development group read and respond to messages on both bulletin boards.

18. LIS provided a feature for using the results of one search as the basis for another search, but, in reality, the search was executed again using both the original query and the additional terms or criteria (e.g., a date range or location in the libraries). Though focus group participants did not know this technical point, they suspected as much. They complained that limits were unreasonably slow—if they were indeed limits on previous search results and not comprehensive searches of the database.

19. LIS enabled users to mail bibliographic records to any electronic mail address and to print using a print screen function. Focus group participants wanted LIS II to enable them to save, mail, or print information, and they wanted printing to work for an entire bibliographic record or full-text document, not just what was visible on the computer screen.

20. INSPEC logs were used to build the model because the size and complexity of the database force users to compose queries carefully, otherwise they retrieve too many records or too much irrelevant information. University Libraries wanted to know what users did when they had to think strategically about information retrieval. INSPEC also represents a trend in database construction. All indications are that databases will grow in size and complexity in all subject areas. The search strategies that surface in INSPEC transaction logs may foreshadow what will be seen in other discipline-specific databases of comparable sophistication.

21.   According to the logs, 143 command searches were done in INSPEC in February 1990. These searches used 182 operators, 70% of which were "ADJ" (adjacency), and 14% were "OR." The "NOT" operator was seldom used.

22.   LIS transaction logs stored actual user queries, but they contained no information that could be used to identify the user who submitted a particular query. LIS II stores encrypted user IDs and therefore removes subject information from user queries to maintain the user's privacy.

23.   An experimental Macintosh user interface was developed in 1991 using HyperCard and an intermediate server. Performance tests revealed that this implementation was inadequate. Therefore a native application user interface, written in C, is being developed for release in late 1992. The interface will incorporate many of the lessons learned from experience with the Motif and VT100 user interfaces. The window structure will be much like the existing user interfaces, but navigation will be distinctly Macintosh.

24.   LIS is still available, but the databases are no longer updated; the mainframe will be turned off in May 1992.

25.   The Search and Browse windows were combined because they both present a prompt where users enter queries, and they both display the results of entering these queries. The List of Records and Full Record windows were combined because they both display records retrieved in a search.

26.   People issued commands in LIS using single alphanumeric characters (e.g., "R" to return to the Search screen and start a new search). This behavior could not be replicated in LIS II because Newton, the retrieval software, enables uses to search single characters. Therefore, VT100 LIS II required a different way to issue commands. The decision was made to use the CTRL and ESC keys for VT100 LIS II because all keyboards have CTRL and ESC keys, but they do not necessarily have function keys.

27.   Library.andrew.cmu.edu is an intermediate server in LIS II, meaning that it sits between the clients and the retrieval servers. When users login to library.andrew.cmu.edu, the intermediate server connects them to the LIS II retrieval servers.

28.   What users did with LIS was constrained in part by the design of LIS, but comments from focus group participants did not indicate that database selection was particularly problematic in LIS or that it influenced how frequently they changed databases.

29.   See the version of the Z39.50 standard documented in ISO draft 8777.

30.   Author searching was not a problem in LIS because LIS provided only one index for each database. Author searching was supported by a template that limited a search to fields in database records that contained author information. When records enhanced with table of contents information were added to LIS, author searching did not change and therefore did not retrieve records based on the author information in Contents fields.

31.   The Library Catalog was rebuilt once based on user feedback. The rebuild changed the indexing to solve the author search problems, added the location and call number to the list of titles to enable sort types that users wanted, and fixed a problem in the full record display.

32.   See: Rachael Naismith and Joan Stein, "Library Jargon: Student Comprehension of Technical Language Used by Librarians," *College and Research*

*Libraries* 50 (September 1989): 543-552. The article received the K.G. Saur Award for the best article in *College and Research Libraries* in 1990.

33.   The three versions or sequences of fields tested were: (1) X: the sequence of fields displayed in LIS; (2) Y: a sequence of fields based on research done at other institutions, particularly the University of Bath study of what fields people typically use in bibliographic records; and (3) Z: a slightly revised version of sequence Y, based on comments from librarians and conflicts between research results from other institutions and sequences used in other OPACs.

34.   The notion of resource control is consistent with Z39.50 version one.

# NOTES ON THE CONTRIBUTORS

**CHARLES W. BAILEY, JR.** is the Assistant Director for Systems at the University of Houston Libraries. He is the co-editor of *Advances in Library Automation and Networking*. Mr. Bailey is the founder and former moderator of PACS-L, a large discussion list on the Internet and other networks. He is the Editor-in-Chief of *The Public-Access Computer Systems Review*, a refereed electronic journal, and the former co-editor of *Public-Access Computer Systems News*, an electronic newsletter. For his electronic publishing efforts, Mr. Bailey has received a Network Citizen Award from the Apple Library of Apple Computer, Inc. and a LITA/*Library Hi Tech* Award. He was the Project Manager for the Intelligent Reference Information System (IRIS) Project, which was named as one of the Joe Wyatt Challenge Success Stories by EDUCOM. Mr. Bailey has published papers dealing with artificial intelligence, CD-ROM networking, electronic publishing, multimedia computing, and public-access computer systems that have appeared in *Information Technology and Libraries, Library Hi Tech, Reference Services Review, Serials Review*, and other publications. He holds an M.L.S. from Syracuse University as well as a B.A. and an M.A. from the University of Connecticut.

**GERI BUNKER** is the Head of Computing Services for University Libraries at the University of Washington. Having managed library automation conversion projects at Texas A&M University, Geri moved on to Washington where she has been active in the development of both character-based and graphical interfaces to bibliographic information.

**TRACY CASORSO** was Project Manager for the Digitized Document Transmission Project, a collaborative effort with the National Agricultural Library, North Carolina State University (NCSU) Academic Computing Center and the NCSU Libraries. She received a B.S. in business administration from Aquinas College in Grand Rapids, MI, and her A.M.L.S. from the University of Michigan. Prior to her appointment at North Carolina State, Ms. Casorso was chief architect and manager of INQUIRE, and on-demand, fee-based research and document delivery service at George Washington University in Washington D.C. She has spoken and written on topics related to network-based delivery of information and marketing library services to the private sector.

**MONA COUTS** is Assistant Director for Information Systems and Resources Management at the Health Sciences Library of the University of North Carolina University at Chapel Hill. She received the M.L.S. degree from Emory University. Prior to her appointment at the University of North Carolina, Ms. Couts held positions as Vice President of Blackwell Library Systems, and Vice President of Information Systems for Warner-Eddison Associates. She has spoken widely on topics related to library automation and database design.

**CAROLYN FROST** is Associate Dean and Professor at the School of Information & Library Studies, University of Michigan, where she has been a faculty members since 1977. She has also taught at the University of Chicago, the University of Oregon, and the University of Illinois at Chicago. She received the Ph.D. in library science from the University of Chicago. Her teaching and research interests include citation analysis, collaborative research, and bibliographic organization and access, with specialization in subject access and in nonbook materials.

**CHARLES GILREATH** is Associate Director for Public Services at North Carolina State University Libraries. He received the B.A., M.A., and M.L.S. degrees from the University of Texas at Austin. Prior to his appointment at North Carolina State, Mr. Gilreath held positions as head of the Central Reference Department at the University of Arizona and head of the Automated Information Retrieval Service at Texas A&M. He has spoken widely on topics related to online literature searching, and his major publications include the *Agricola User's Guide and Computer Literature Searching: Research Strategies and Databases*, published by Westview Press in 1984.

**JUDY HALLMAN** is Manager of Information Services, Office of Information Technology, University of North Carolina at Chapel Hill. She has a B.A. and an M.A. both in mathematics from the University of North Carolina at Chapel Hill. She has participated in the planning and development of a wide range of computer systems as well as supervising computer consulting and documentation services during her 25 years with the computer department at the University of North Carolina at Chapel Hill. Prior experience includes computer programming at Western Electric Company and at Bell Telephone Laboratories.

**JOE A. HEWITT** is Associate Provost for University Libraries and Director of the Academic Affairs Library at the University of North Carolina, Chapel Hill, where he previously served as Associate University Librarian for Technical Services for 18 years. He has written on cooperative collection development, the impact of automation and networking on library organizations and operations, and on the role of research in librarianship.

**MARK KIBBEY** is the Associate Director for Library Systems at the University of Washington. Mark came to UW via a westward migration from Columbia University and Carnegie Mellon. He has spent much of the last decade using computers and networks to improve access to library resources. His main focus has been on information retrieval systems and the standards and interfaces that will make them more usable in the 90's. At Carnegie Mellon Mark developed their original online retrieval system in 1986 and later served as project manager for the Mercury Project which is an attempt to create a pilot electronic library. Currently he is active in CNI and is helping to develop both campus and regional information services.

**CAROL TENOPIR** is Professor at the School of Library and Information Science, University of Tennessee at Knoxville. Her "Online Databases" column has appeared monthly in *Library*

*Journal* since 1983. She is the author of many articles about databases and database searching. Full text databases and text retrieval software are her specialties. Her third book, *Full Text Databases* with Jung Soon Po, was published by Greenwood in 1990. Dr. Tenopir holds a Ph.D. degree from the University of Illinois.

**DENISE TROLL** is Senior Researcher, Mercury Electronic Library Project, at Carnegie Mellon University. She received the Ph.D. in Rhetoric from Carnegie Mellon. Since 1984 she has held a variety of positions at Carnegie Mellon including writer for the Robotics Institute, teacher in the English Department, and Documentation Coordinator in Academic Computing. Dr. Troll's research interests include the application of technology to library management and service, retrieval systems architecture, user interface design and testing, usage modeling, and the history of information storage and retrieval.

**JOHN ULMSCHNEIDER** is Assistant Director for Library Systems, North Carolina State University Libraries. In addition to information systems management for the NCSU Libraries, he is project director for a research and development effort undertaken by Duke University, North Carolina State University, and the University of North Carolina at Chapel Hill (comprising TRLN, the Triangle Research Libraries Network) to create a model integrated electronic document delivery service for library constituencies. Mr. Ulmschneider's background includes training and experience in software design, development, and implementation, project management, systems management, network design, and library administration. His writings and talks have focused on the technical aspects of developing information systems to provide better access to image, textual, and compound document data. Prior to his current position, he was Systems Manager at the College of William and Mary and Systems Librarian at the National Library of Medicine. Mr. Ulmschneider received the B.A. from the University of Virginia and the M.S.L.S. from the University of North Carolina at Chapel Hill.

J A I

P R E S S

## Advances in Library Automation and Networking

Edited by **Joe A. Hewitt,** *University of North Carolina, Chapel Hill*

The purpose of this series is to present a broad spectrum of in-depth, analytical articles on the technical, organizational, and policy aspects of library automation and networking. The series will include detailed examinations and evaluations of particular computer applications in libraries, status surveys, and perspective papers on the implications of various computing and networking technologies for library services and management. The emphasis will be on the information and policy frameworks needed for librarians and administrators to make informed decisions related to developing or acquiring automated systems and network services with special attention to maximizing the positive effects of these technologies on library organization.

**REVIEWS:** "Recommended as an important source for students and particularly library directors and library automation personnel who want to increase their knowledge across the broad spectrum of automation issues."

*-- American Reference Books Annual*

"... a promising start to what could turn out to be a landmark of the literature of bibliographic control."

*-- The Library Quarterly*

**Volume 1**, 1987, 232 pp.                    $73.25
ISBN 0-89232-358-X

**CONTENTS:** Introduction, *Joe A. Hewitt.* The Linked Systems Project: Implications for Library Automation and Networking, *Sally H. McCallum.* The Impact of Advances in Telecommunications on Library and Information Systems, *Larry L. Learn.* Classification in the Online Catalog, *Robert P. Holley.* Bibliographic Accessibility of Machine-Readable Data Files-Including Mainframe and Microcomputer Software, *Sue A. Dodd.* Online Systems and the Management of Collections: Use and Implication, *Susan K. Nutter.* The Organization of Academic Libraries in the Light of Automation, *Michael*

*Gorman.* Trends in the Development of State Networks, *Ruth M. Katz.* Cooperative Collection Development Among Research Libraries in the Age of Networking: Report of a Survey of ARL Libraries, *Joe A. Hewitt and John S. Shipman.*

**Volume 2**, 1988, 259 pp.  $73.25
ISBN 0-89232-673-5

**CONTENTS:** Introduction, *Joe A. Hewitt.* Application of Expert Systems to Libraries, *Rao Aluri and Donald E. Riggs.* Information Access Requirements: An Historical and Future Perspective, *Francis Milsa.* The OCLC Users Council: Control and Influence of Dependent Members, *J. Drew Racine.* Performance Evaluation of Computerized Library Systems, *Jerry V. Caswell.* Library Marc Tapes as a Resource for Collection Analysis: The Amigos Service, *Ann Armbrister.* Riding the Technology Express: The Causes and Costs of System Upgrades, *Wilson M. Stahl.* Closing the Card Catalog, *Jaye Bausser.* Microcomputer Data Files in Academic Libraries, *Carson Holloway.* Vision, Focus, and Technology in Academic Research Libraries: 1971 to 2001, *Arnold Hirshon.*

**Volume 3**, 1989, 269 pp.  $73.25
ISBN 0-89232-966-1

**CONTENTS:** Introduction, *Joe A. Hewitt.* Integrated Public-Access Computer Systems: The Heart of the Electronic University, *Charles W. Bailey, Jr.* Opac Transaction Log Analysis: The First Decade, *Charles W. Simpson.* Automation: A Book Vendors Perspective, *Amy Miller.* Collection Assessment in the Pacific Northwest: Building a Foundation for Cooperation, *Peggy J. Forcier and Nancy Powell.* Online Catalog Access to the Titles in Major Microform Sets, *James F. Jones.* An Electronic Odyssey: The Microcomputer and its Applications in a Collection Development Department, 1982-1989, *Peter J. Schledron and John S. Shipman.* Carl: Creating Systems That Inform an Organizational Model, *Rebecca T. Lenzini.* Florida Center for Library Automation: The Organization, *Michele I. Dalehite.* The Florida Center for Library Automation: The System, *Elaine Henjum.* Clemson University: A Case History in Library-Computer Center Cooperation, *George D. Alexander, Joseph F. Boykin, Jr., and Richard W. Meyer.*

JAI PRESS

**Volume 4**, 1991, 242 pp.                                    $73.25
ISBN 1-55938-188-4

**CONTENTS:** Introduction, *Joe A. Hewitt.* Intelligent Library Systems: Artificial Intelligence Technology and Library Automation Systems, *Charles W. Bailey, Jr.* Refereed Electronic Journals and the Future of Scholarly Publishing, *Eyal Amiran, Elaine Orr, and John Unsworth.* The Large Retrieval Phenomenon, *Chandra Prabha.* The Hidden Structures of Research: The Problem of Authority Control in an Online Catalog, *Gregory Lowchy.* Hypertext/Hypermedia for Libraries, *Dan Marmion.* Automation and Bibliographic Instruction, *Sue Stigleman.* Shamans of the Infosphere: Librarians and the Digitalization of Information, *Wilson M. Stahl.* Before and After Automation: Cataloguing Staff, Productivity, and Labor Costs at the University of British Columbia Library, *Erik de Bruijn,.* Notes on Contributors. Index.

FACULTY/PROFESSIONAL discounts are available in the U.S. and Canada at a rate of 40% off the list price when prepaid by personal check or credit card and ordered directly from the publisher.

**JAI PRESS INC.**
55 Old Post Road # 2 - P.O. Box 1678
Greenwich, Connecticut 06836-1678
Tel: (203) 661- 7602    Fax: (203) 661-0792

*New !*

## Advances in Acquisitions, Collection Development and Resource Management

Edited by **Thomas W. Leonhardt,**
*University of Oklahoma*

**Volume 1**, In preparation Fall 1995
ISBN 1-55938-213-9          Approx $73.25

**TENTATIVE CONTENTS:** Introduction, *Thomas W. Leonhardt.* Duplication and Overlap Among Library Collections: A Chronological Review of the Literature, *Sue O. Medina.* Weeding Academic Libraries: Theory Into Practice, *Mary Bushing.* Censorship in Academe: The Necessity for Vigilance, *A. Bruce Strauch.* The Distributed National Collection of Australia, *Margaret Henty.* Computer and Information System Warranties: Caveat Emptor, *J. Michael Alfred* and *A. Bruce Strauch.* Statewide Cooperation To Improve Academic Library Resources: The Alabama Experience, *Sue O. Median* and *William C. Highfill.* Education for Acquisitions, *William Fisher.* Major Microform Sets: The Alabama Experience, *Sue O. Medina, T. Harmon Straiton, Jr. ,* and *Cecilia Schmitz.*

> **FACULTY/PROFESSIONAL** discounts are available in the U.S. and Canada at a rate of 40% off the list price when prepaid by personal check or credit card and ordered directly from the publisher.

## JAI PRESS INC.
55 Old Post Road # 2 - P.O. Box 1678
Greenwich, Connecticut 06836-1678
Tel: (203) 661- 7602     Fax: (203) 661-0792

J A I

P R E S S